THE DIARY OF A NOVICE INVESTOR

THE DIARY OF

A~~N~~ INVESTOR
^NOVICE

THE BULLET TRAIN TO WEALTH LEFT WHEN??

WRITTEN BY
MARK SLAUTER

ILLUSTRATIONS BY
DOUGLAS FUCHS

Lee and Lea
Richmond, VA

Printed in the United States of America
First Edition Printing, 2017

www.leeandleapublishing.com
info@leeandleapublishing.com

ISBN-13: 978-0-9974297-0-1
Library of Congress Control Number: 2016915501

Cover Art & Illustrations by Douglas Fuchs
Cover Design & Layout by Inkwell Book Co.
www.InkwellBookCompany.com

TABLE OF CONTENTS

ACKNOWLEDGMENTS

My editors, Meghan Codd-Walker and Deanna Lorianni of Zuula Consulting, Inc., provided inestimable value through their guidance and insights that helped to shape this book.

The illustrator, Doug Fuchs, did a great job interpreting my intentions for the covers and one-line phrases that enliven the story.

Completion of this project would not have been possible without the patience and support of my family. Though Dad is no longer with us, and Mom is unable to provide any cognitive response to this, I have no doubt that they would have been thrilled, if for no other reason than the fact that I completed this project. And, particularly my wife Margaret, who has patiently waited for me to get back to doing things around the house.

To my late father, Charles, and my mother, Nancy,
without whom I may never have had
a good home and a loving family.

PREFACE

I wrote this book to provide insight to readers who are interested in investing, but have no previous exposure to the emotional roller coaster investing can create. I am not an analyst nor certified in any way as an investment advisor or financial planner, and I do not intend for anyone to use the information provided in this book as professional investment advice. Rather, my goal is to express my first-person experience learning about investing, and offer the reader insight into the angst, frustration, elation, and thought-processes I experienced as a novice investor—and continue working through today.

A portrait of my friend Ira Noveece

THE SET UP

We can't solve problems by using the same kind of
thinking we used when we created them.

—Albert Einstein

You know you're a novice investor when...

You think DOW is a kind of boat.

Problems can be elusive creatures. Even though you may recognize a problem as it's happening, its genesis and evolution become clearer when you stare backward through the looking glass of time.

In 2008, my sister, Mary, and I knew Mom and Dad were in real trouble when we planned a family vacation on the Outer Banks of North Carolina, which was about a three-hour drive from their house. This was a special trip to celebrate Mom's 80th birthday. However, the first two days were nightmarish as our parents made three attempts to drive to the vacation rental and never made it. Despite their age, Mom and Dad used to drive everywhere, and it was never an issue…until this. We finally drove to their house, picked them up, brought them to the rental unit, enjoyed our vacation, and then drove them home.

Surprisingly, we never got the full story as to what happened. Mom wasn't sure, and Dad refused to discuss it. The sudden apparent loss of being able to make this trip is similar to someone commuting from point A to point B for 20 years, and then one day they don't show up and can't (or won't) explain why. This was the first major low point and true reflection of our parent's diminishing capability.

But, despite vocalizing our concern, we couldn't convince Dad to move out of the house. Even by 2008, Mom had wanted to get out of the house for a few years, but Dad wasn't budging. As the years passed, their ability to be independent only declined. No matter our concern or how frequently we tried to convince Dad that relocating was the right decision, he refused. He would not acknowledge the fact that they both had issues, and since everything was good (in his mind) and they were getting along just fine, they had no reason to move. Fast forward to the summer of 2011: Hurricane Irene roared up the coast and just about ran right over their house. I live in Virginia, and Mary is in Texas. My job requires me to work on response and recovery issues. With Irene crashing over Virginia, as well, I wasn't going anywhere. We both knew we had to help Mom and Dad before the hurricane made landfall near their home.

To get our parents to safety, Mary booked them a room at a hotel in New Bern, which is about 45 minutes west of their house, and out of the projected path of the hurricane. Separately, we both called the house and talked with Dad. My conversation focused on the danger of the storm. I told him it was going to be really bad, that they should leave, and that Mary was booking them a hotel room. She called and talked to Dad, telling him which hotel she had booked a room at. Dad agreed that they would go. As night fell and Irene was about to land in N.C., my sister called the house. No answer. *Good. They've left, she thought and called the hotel to double check. But, they weren't there. Shit, not good. Where the hell are they?*

She called the house multiple times until Dad finally answered.

"We're not supposed to go to a hotel," he explained.

"Yes, Dad, you were," she pleaded. "I already booked a room."

In his typically nonchalant manner, Dad said, "Oh. Well, we changed our minds."

The bottom line is that he didn't remember the previous phone calls.

So, we called the next day to check in on them, and the next and the next and the next.

"How's it going?"

"Okay. No real problems," he reported. "The water came up into the yard, but every thing's okay."

In previous storms, they had experienced water on the street or into the yard. Dad was acting like it was a "typical" storm and leading us to believe things weren't so bad. At this point, I was focused on what happened in Virginia and hadn't seen any full reports out of North Carolina. I knew there were hard-hit areas, I just didn't know that Mom and Dad were in one.

Maybe four or five days after the storm hit, Mary answered a call from one of our parent's neighbors who wanted to know where the hell we were and why we had abandoned our parents. "They're without power and have no food, no water and no toilet," she complained about our apparent carelessness.

So, Mary called me, and I then called emergency services personnel in North Carolina to get some facts about the situation. Their response was to the point. "The eye of the hurricane came over the County. We got hammered and have nothing." In disaster parlance, I knew what this meant: Mom and Dad were screwed and lied to us, because they didn't fully recognize their situation.

Once we knew the truth of our parent's situation, we were both down in North Carolina within 48 hours. Before I even got to Pamlico County (I was still about an hour away), I was driving past downed trees and power lines, houses with tarps on the roof, and debris piled up along the road. The closer I got to Oriental, the more debris there was along the road: trees, furniture, duct work, insulation, clothes, etc. At certain points, there was so much crap piled up it created a roadside berm.

When I pulled into their driveway, Mom was in the yard picking up tree limbs and stuff that washed in from the small creek behind the house. Dad, on the other hand, had pulled out the back seat of one of the cars and placed it in the breezeway to dry it out. After some hugs and chit chat, I started to take a closer look around.

My first place to check was the garage to look at the car. Dad had the battery charger hooked up. I looked in the car and saw water still sitting in the cup holders of the console. *It's totaled, and he doesn't even know it,* I thought. I got that straightened out with the insurance company later. While inspecting, I'd noticed a small pile of insulation in front of the house, and Dad told me a few guys came over and took out the bad stuff and put in new insulation. So, I crawled under the house and saw that the air ducts were sagging, because they were full of water. On top of that, the guys only replaced about 20% of the insulation. I immediately realized my parents had been ripped off by schmucks. As some would say, "There's a special place in Hell for people like that."

Meanwhile, my sister Mary had flown into New Bern, N.C.,

rented a car, and arrived a few hours after I did. Without power, water, or toilets, the house was untenable. We dragged Mom and Dad to a nearby operational hotel, so we could have some semblance of normalcy.

During this time, my sister and I hired a law firm to pursue guardianship so that we could legally remove our parents from their home if it came to that. We had to plan these details in secret, so our parent's wouldn't know. If Dad knew, he would have been immeasurably pissed off and probably disowned us.

By the fall of 2011, just months after the hurricane hit, Mom's downward spiral into the hell of dementia began to exceed Dad's capabilities. Growing increasingly concerned, Mary and I convinced Dad to hire outside help during the day to assist him in keeping Mom entertained, because that was the only way to acquire Dad's agreement. He had to think it was really his idea and that it was because Mom had issues, not him. However, he would go nuts every time an invoice for services came in the mail. He couldn't understand why it cost so much and why Mom needed help anyway.

Though we knew that in-home assistance wasn't the type of help Mom really needed, it was a start. That fall, Dad made several calls to 911, because he "couldn't handle" Mom. Sadly, he'd forget that he'd even called emergency services. Trying the tough-love approach, I played the tapes for him, because he didn't believe what I was telling him. I think if he had the energy or was alone, he may have cried while listening to them. I was at the point of needing to force Dad into accepting and understanding the situation. An hour later, he didn't remember, and I sadly played the tapes again.

While my sister and I looked out for our parents' physical safety, we also started to question another hugely important detail: their financial safety. Over the years, Dad was always interested in knowing our financials but not so keen on sharing his. So, we started to sneak peeks at their financials. In hindsight, there are very few things I've ever felt guilty about, but sneaking around behind their backs is still distasteful, regardless of my intentions. It's not like finding the bank or mutual fund statements was hard; we knew where those were filed. The problem was that they didn't really leave the house much, so we had to resort to creating excuses to get Dad out of the house, like a bogus reason to run to the grocery store. We weren't worried about Mom seeing us looking through the files, because she wouldn't remember it. It wasn't until early 2013, that we were able to create a complete picture of their financials. Fortunately, they were in good shape.

In April 2012, Mom was having stomach pains and Dad took her the hospital, which he didn't recall doing. Since she had dementia, the hospital would only keep her for five days because they aren't structured to take care of patients with dementia. As I forced Dad into accepting that Mom had dementia, with the doctors telling him the same thing, we finally moved her to the dementia unit at a nearby healthcare facility. Meanwhile, Dad had his own short-term memory issues, not that he would ever admit it. As a result, having Mom out of the house created a severe level of stress for Dad, because it disrupted his version of normal.

Unequivocally, Dad was a trooper this whole time. His love and strength of commitment to Mom forced him to learn how to drive from the house to where she was, 45 minutes away. The man couldn't remember to pay a bill, but he could find his wife. We were amazed, at least up to the point when a County Sheriff's Deputy called me.

For me, the Deputy's call was both sad and funny, because it was part of a string of events that left me shaking my head concurrently in amazement and amusement. The Deputy called on an early afternoon and shared with me that he'd found my business card in Dad's wallet. He informed me that Dad was at a grocery store claiming Mom had been kidnapped. While talking with the Deputy, I could tell that he was pissed off.

The Deputy told me that Dad shouldn't be driving. He stated

he was taking Dad home—a 90-minute round trip for him—and, "You can find his car in the parking lot, and I'm going to file a report with the state Department of Motor Vehicles." In my mind I was thinking that this was the final straw I needed to get my parents out of the house. *The moving ticket has been PUNCHED... Elvis has left the building!*

So, I told the Deputy the name of the healthcare facility where we had recently moved Mom. Since it was in his County, he knew the place. I then encouraged him to please file the report with DMV, as we've been trying to get Dad to stop driving.

And so, this became another trip for me to North Carolina. I arrived at the house and spoke with Dad about what happened (he didn't quite remember it). I then gave him two choices: 1) stay at home and not see Mom, or 2) take a room at the same place and be near her. Surprisingly (and fortunately), he opted for taking a room. A funny thing about elderly people who are used to having a car, once you take it away, it's the only thing they can focus on. Once he moved into the facility, Dad would walk outside the building at least once every hour to look for the car.

The kicker in all of this was that I had to get Dad to DMV so he could take a driving test. I even told the DMV staff that they needed to find a way to fail him if he passed. Of course, they understood my situation, but they can't just make something up to fail him. I knew what would happen.

As a related side note, if you haven't dealt with alcoholics and people suffering from senility or dementia, let me pass along an observation I have from dealing with both forms of the human condition: They are eerily similar. In both cases, the individual can appear to be fully functional in situations or environments that are familiar to them. However, once you change the playing field, all of the shortcomings and problems become readily apparent.

So, what happened to Dad when he took the driving test? He and a DMV person got in his car for an actual driving test in downtown New Bern, an urban location with lots of traffic lights and cars. The test consisted of the DMV person telling Dad where to make several right and left turns, creating an extended around-the-block drive. Sure as shit, Dad passed his test. The man was 88 years old and had been driving since he was fourteen, what other outcome could there possibly be?

Fortunately, with Dad out of the house, I was responsible for getting the mail—which meant I could keep better tabs on the bills, and everyone asking for their money. When DMV mailed his test results to their house, I was able to snatch the mail. I never showed him the results. Knowing that his driving status was our only chance to get them permanently out of the house and with the care they needed, I lied. I told him a bold-faced, straight-up lie. Even on those days when he would ask me 20 times about the test, my answer was always the same: "Sorry Dad, you didn't pass the test."

With all of these pieces of the puzzle in place, we were able to convince Dad that moving to Virginia was better for them and the family. So, in June 2012, we moved him first and then brought Mom up a week later. As stressful as this was for us, the greatest impact hit Dad, because he was now out of his element, not in his house, and it was all very confusing to him. He used to leave voicemail messages on their house phone for Mom saying he was in a hotel somewhere and that he swore this was his last business trip. I can still hear the quivering voice telling Mom that he loved her, "… so let me pat your hand and give you a kiss goodnight. I'll be home soon." Sadly, he couldn't remember that he had already spent part of the day with her and that she was only 100-feet away in another part of the building.

When Dad unexpectedly died two months later in August, I went to his room to begin the task of deciding what to do with his things. We had moved his piano from the house to the new place so he could have it. We moved several items from the house to make it feel like home for him. As I somewhat aimlessly roamed through the two-room apartment, I found myself standing at the piano reminiscing. As usual, I found a book of sheet music open, this time to the "Widow's Waltz." I'll never know what to make of this.

With Dad's passing behind us, we now had to focus solely on Mom.

Our next goal? Truly understand her financial health.

We started learning about all the investments our parents held, and at the same time, had to evaluate how to maintain income against a huge increase in expenses due to Mom's declining health. Healthcare costs for someone with dementia are unbelievably expensive. You have room rent, food, doctors' visits, prescriptions, clothes that get lost and stolen, insurance payments, forms, and reimbursements, etc. The swirling details are enough to drive a sane person crazy. *Side note: If you've not had the pleasure of dealing with healthcare for the elderly, I highly suggest that, when looking to your own future, you make sure that whoever is designated to take care of you in your old age can actually do so. It's FUBAR!*

Discussions with loved ones about money are not always easy. Fortunately, my sister and I get along quite well, and our conversations have always revolved around what we could or should do to make our parents comfortable. Now, with only Mom to look after, we really had to dig into the financials and determine what was in her best interest. Fortunately, we knew their investment philosophy from conversations over the years: Protect capital while generating some income, and primarily focus on utilities and energy investments. What we didn't know is how all of it was structured. We had to ensure that the investments would generate enough income to cover Mom's rising medical expenses. And in the back of my mind I was thinking, How are we going to compete or compare with two people that had 100+ years of collective investing experience between them?

Now, let me digress a bit...

I grew up in a household that, through the years, contained

any number of business publications: Forbes, Business Week, the Wall Street Journal, Kiplinger, Fortune, etc. We also always had innumerable mailings and newsletters from anyone that got hold of our address. We were receiving junk mail before the term was even created. Of course, as a curious child who liked to read, I had to check out Dad's magazines. Even if I didn't understand anything, I at least had to look.

Though I would thumb through these publications without really understanding what I was looking at, my first real experience with investing came about as an 8th-grade class project, when we had to choose a stock and track it. For no particular reason, I chose Exxon, maybe because that was the gas station we always went to. After conducting my school project, I understood how investing money could make me more money, and I decided that I wanted to invest some money I'd earned from mowing lawns and shoveling snow. I sat with Dad to explore my options and decided to buy some Exxon stock with real money. When I was in my late teens, I also bought the real estate investment trust (REIT) Trammel Crow. Until being responsible for Mom's financial situation, those investments were my only proactive investment experience. Since then, I haven't really done anything but rely on employer retirement plans like most people I know.

With Dad's passing, I began reintroducing myself to the world of investing. While the concept of the markets wasn't new to me, the scale of the financial insight and responsibility was on a level I hadn't experienced. I realized that the investing world has a ton of puzzle pieces to understand and fit together—and these pieces were much different than other areas of expertise I have. So, with the pressure of ensuring we met Mom's health needs, I urgently began pursuing a coherent grasp of the big financial picture and what it meant for everyone involved.

My parents were both born during the 1920s, lived through the Great Depression and World War II, and were college graduates.

They were conservative and smart with their money—a common trait among the "Greatest Generation." My childhood homes had air conditioning that we never used, and I don't recall ever seeing the thermostat above 62 degrees during winter (which was especially tough growing up in Buffalo, New York; and Cleveland, Ohio!). To further save money, Mom tore paper napkins in half to make the pack last longer and bought generic brand food items. Crazy? Maybe. But her money-saving habits kept food on our table, a roof over our heads, provided for our needs—and was now providing for her when she needed her savings the most.

I felt I had no choice but to respect their success. The question became: Can I match it?

Between August and December of 2012, my sister and I focused on getting a handle on Mom's finances. With Dad's death, untangling the details became a drawn-out process, because we now had to deal with legally establishing who had access to the accounts. Fortunately, our parents were smart enough to establish a living trust; my sister and I became co-trustees of the Trust and Co-Powers-of-Attorney (POA) for the estate.

We quickly learned that updating account information is a pain in the ass. Everyone wants a copy of the death certificate, copies of the Power of Attorney, copies of the Living Trust, letters of testament from the doctor regarding Mom being incapacitated, etc. And, to boot, you have to provide most of the forms with original notarized signatures. Certain forms require submission with original signatures and a special stamp of authorization from a financial institution. Then to top it all off, after you submit the forms, you receive a letter stating the changes can't be made, because you submitted the wrong form, which is the one they emailed to you in the first place!

The most frustrating interaction came when I had to change the mailing address for one account: The company required submission of another notarized copy of the Power-Of-Attorney. Since Mary and I live in different states, we had to literally mail materials back and forth. We were dumbfounded at the antiquated process, which we later found out was supposedly to reduce the use of fake POA documents.

Hoping to streamline the process, I asked a company representative, "How would you know whether or not my notarized POA was fake, regardless of how many times I submit one?"

"We wouldn't," the rep casually responded.

"Then, what's the point?" I countered.

"It's our policy," he stated.

Well, that's fucking helpful!! I thought. I wanted to reach through the phone and slap him.

Now, while I appreciate a firm taking steps to protect client assets (and their own ass), I absolutely can't think of a valid reason to request new copies of documentation when you already have everything on file. Especially, when you know I have the legal right to make changes to an account. *Just un-fucking-believable.* I didn't bother following through on the address change (another reason to ensure your caretaker has the right information).

Since Dad never wanted to discuss their finances, his response was always, "Everything you need to know is in the safe or the safety deposit box." The safe was in the house...unlocked. So, we believed him and didn't press the issue. Well, our assumption came back to bite us. We quickly found out there's a difference between storing everything and storing the right documents. While he *had* stored some files for safekeeping, a bunch of important information wasn't there. For example, when figuring out their insurance details, we had to navigate a maze of policies from companies that had been sold over the years. The oldest one was from the 1930s! It took us three days to determine that the policy wasn't valid. I found tax returns from the 1950s (that had even been flooded at least twice). *Who keeps their tax returns for 60 years?* You guessed it, my parents did.

Our efforts took about a year to get everything straightened out, weeks of time off from work, and about $10,000 in legal fees. Over the course of all the endless paperwork, the concerned conversations, the exasperated head-scratches, I emerged from the experience with three key lessons:

o   If you have children, at some point, they become mature enough to know your finances. Don't wait. They may not be as smart about them as you are or understand what you want, but they can still start understanding what will need to be done. Plus, if you don't explain details to them, you leave them in the dark once you're no longer around or capable to give them your insight.

o   Take the appropriate measures in advance to ensure someone can manage your affairs and determine how you want your assets distributed.

o   Don't keep useless pieces of financial paperwork. If it's important and has utility, make sure you explain why. Otherwise, ditch the clutter.

As I began to put all of Mom's details into place, in 2013, I started to write in a journal as a personal guide to track my experience and decisions. Seeing the insight I was gaining from the experience, the diary subsequently bloomed into the idea of writing a book so that I could help others. A reality-based description that could be provided in the context of real time.

Time is a key component of an investing approach. Since the majority of advisors suggest taking a long-term view of investing, my initial target was to conduct my project for one year. I had no way of knowing whether or not Mom would still be alive when I finished this investing journey, which is now sort of a moot point, since I realized I should be doing this anyway for my own family. So, here I am in 2015. I'm still following the markets, Mom is still with us, and I'm still learning about investing.

The *Diary of a Novice Investor (The Bullet Train to Wealth Left When?)* tells the tale of my experiences in coming to terms with Mom's declining health and my need to learn a higher degree of financial responsibility. I wanted to develop something to express a real-time experience and the emotions it encompasses so that you, the reader, will be more prepared for your own efforts.

Investing should not be a scary unknown that prevents you from creating a more secure future. It's never too late to start. Consider this, if you won a lottery jackpot of $250,000 would you prefer to have some idea of how to invest it, or no idea at all? Could you, in blind faith, give it to a broker and believe they will do what's in your best interest without having some understanding of what they're doing?

Me neither. Arm yourself with some knowledge and awareness so that when you decide to begin investing you can begin from a better starting point.

INTRODUCTION

I put a dollar in one of those change machines. Nothing changed.
—George Carlin

You know you're a novice investor when...

You thought buying into SENSEX was investing in the porn industry.

Before I bring you too far along on my journey, I want to make abundantly clear that this book is not about economic, financial, or investing theory. I don't do theory, and this is not a textbook. *The Diary of a Novice Investor* emerged from a need to determine what my skill level was with investing and understand how well I could support Mom's needs. I only knew one way how to figure these details out for her and avoid costly mistakes: I created a fantasy investment portfolio. Think of this approach as a variation on playing Monopoly where I can buy and sell Boardwalk or Park Place without using real money. Only in this instance, my game board is Wall Street.

Basically, I created my own game with two initial players, just Mom and myself. To test myself I had to create a level playing field in terms of how much money or how many stocks to start with. Since my Mom owns quite a few individual stocks and funds, I decided that I would just buy 100 shares of everything she owned to create a baseline.

Why did I do this? Simply because I knew what she has, and it hasn't changed much over the years. Furthermore, I wasn't going to alter her portfolio, which meant her portfolio was stable. Also, her portfolio represented a particular style or focus of investing, with about 55% of it invested within the utilities and energy sectors. The fact that her portfolio was static and unchanging translated into being able to better understand that approach and evaluate how effective it is, and how effective I am (or not) in my selections and approach, which is much more aggressive and accepting of a higher risk level.

In total, Mom spent about $175k of play money to compete in my game. Yes, this is a competition. I love Mom, but I still want to win.

Now I had to figure out what I was going to buy. Based on my limited experience, I already had some ideas of what I wanted. Also, I was already looking at online resources like *The Wall Street Journal, Morningstar, The Street, Yahoo Finance, Investor's Business*

Daily, and others. I had two primary objectives for differentiating my portfolio from Mom's: 1) Have a greater diversity in the types of stocks and 2) don't buy the same ones she owned. I really wanted to develop my portfolio from scratch, so this experiment became a valid test of my skills.

And, just to make testing myself even more entertaining, I decided that my portfolio would be a mix of selections made by professional suggestions that I concurred with and my own personal selections. Though unintentional, my portfolio initially ended up being about a 50/50 split between my choices and what I accepted from the Pros. After making my initial selections, the cost of acquisition was about $288k.

At one point later in the year, I decided to bring a third player into the game and created a new and separate portfolio based solely on selections by the Pros. This created an additional evaluation tool for me. Yeah, that'll teach me to mess with me.

Upon starting my fantasy portfolio, the initial investing process exploded with questions:

o   When will I be fluent in the market's language?

o   How can I manage the information?

o   The market is in an upward trend. Am I buying at the right time?

o   Will the market top out and make a significant correction?

o   How do I balance the goal for income against the selection of riskier investments without a dividend yield?

o   What are the key indicators I should pay attention to?

o   Whose recommendations are better?

Remember that investing is a complex world filled with many intricate, interconnected puzzle pieces. Making sense of them all takes time, attention to detail, and experience. There are a few other items to expand upon here such as, exchanges, indexes, commodities, and index funds. Simply stated, an exchange is a recognized marketplace where stocks can be traded. In the U.S. a few of the major exchanges are the New York Stock Exchange (NYSE), National Association of Securities Dealers Automated Quotations Systems (NASDAQ), or the Chicago Mercantile Exchange (CME).

Exchanges exist all over the world, such as the Toronto Stock Exchange (TSX) in Canada and the Tokyo Stock Exchange (TSE) in Japan. Investors can acquire stocks in any of these exchanges, but there may be additional fees and tax implications. Some companies are listed on multiple exchanges.

While all of this may already sound daunting or confusing, think of the word "marketplace" replacing the word "exchange." An exchange is no different than going to the local market or grocery store. Granted, the transactions are a lot more expensive, but it's the same concept. I can go to a store and buy potato chips, soda, bread, etc. The only difference is that when I buy something listed on the NYSE versus the grocery store, I'm buying stock in the companies that make what I buy in a grocery store. I can even buy stock in the grocery store company itself.

For my fantasy portfolio, I decided to primarily focus on the Dow Jones Industrial Average (DJIA), which is a weighted index of the largest and best known industrial stocks listed on the NYSE. When the news media states that the current market value is up to 15566 (the number typically changes daily), they're referring to the DJIA. Usually referred to as "blue chip" stocks, these are well-established stocks with a proven ability to pay dividends in both good and bad markets, such as Exxon Mobile, General Electric, and Verizon.

To jump-start my portfolio, I started with four general objectives:

○ **Diversity:** I wanted diversity across the economy and not heavily weight my portfolio within one or two sectors. In other words, I didn't want to have too much money in utilities or healthcare. I wanted to focus on stocks from multiple sectors.

○ **Income:** I wanted to position myself with a reasonable expectation of generating income. I wanted to have some stocks that are relatively stable and would provide me with payments on a regular schedule (these payments are called "dividends").

○ **Reasonable Risk:** In determining risk tolerance, people have different positions. Think of this like being on a highway with no speed limit. Some people won't drive over 60, while others will gladly zip along at 130 mph. When it comes to investing, I'm at the age of being able to take some risk and look for other opportunities that provide a potential higher return but are also higher in risk. In many instances, the higher risk investments don't provide a scheduled payment. The intent is to take advantage of the potential for rapidly increasing share value and capture that growth. Some of these high fliers do well enough to start making payments in the future. I decided that making a few speculative investments was an acceptable risk for me.

○ **Mutual Funds:** The last objective of my strategy was to include some funds. My primary reason for this is that a mutual fund provides a certain stability by holding a mix of stocks within a given sector or across sectors. In other words, a fund can reduce the volatility associated with owning an individual stock because that stock is pooled with a bunch of other stocks. My analogy is to think of the insurance industry. As an individual, I pay a certain (usually lower) amount for insurance because the company insures thousands of people and is therefore spreading the risk among all rather than just one. Because of this pooling of stocks, funds are typically less susceptible to wide price swings. Although, I have to admit, the safety of owning a fund translated into me jumping on a few highly volatile, high-risk stocks. Smart or stupid? Only time tells.

With regard to stock types, here's where I wanted to start:

o **Consumer stocks.** I was really thinking about retail, such as Macy's.

o **Energy stocks.** Could be oil, gas, mining, etc.

o **Healthcare/Pharmaceuticals/Biotech stocks.** With ever-increasing healthcare costs and the recently enacted federal healthcare law, I thought this was an opportunity for investing.

o **Technology stocks.** Could be communications, computers, or the Internet.

o **Utility stocks.** These are generally income earners because their dividends (payments) tend to be above the market average.

Once I selected my investments for my fantasy portfolio, I was ready to play my game. Here's how Mom and I compared with regard to stocks and sectors. Not shown in the table is that we both had five mutual funds.

Market Sectors	My Portfolio		Mom's Portfolio	
	# of Items	Percentages	# of Items	Percentages
Basic Materials	3	13%	0	0%
Communications	1	4%	3	8%
Consumer Cyclical	2	9%	0	0%
Consumer Defensive	1	4%	3	8%
Energy	5	22%	10	25%
Financial Services	3	13%	5	13%
Healthcare	1	4%	0	0%
Industrials	2	9%	4	10%
Real Estate	0	0%	1	3%
Technology	3	13%	1	3%
Utilities	2	9%	13	33%
	23	100%	40	100%

Percentages do equal 100% due to rounding.

Unless you inherit a ton of money from a long-lost relative, or are the one-in-one-hundred-seventy-million that wins the big lottery jackpot, there is no bullet train to wealth.

Is investing hard?

Yes.

Is investing confusing?

Yes.

Is investing emotional?

Yes.

Is investing impossible.

No. It's not time travel.

Investing in the markets can be hard, confusing, and emotional but not because it can't be done—rather, when you're a novice, you lack market familiarity, understanding, and experience. In fact, I liken the experience to the first time you ride a bike, have sex, or drive a car. Each time you try something new you're taking a risk. Fully knowing what you're doing the first time you do anything is nearly impossible, because there are so many variables. However, with more exposure to the new experience, the more understanding you gain. While you may have first stopped your bike by skidding your feet on the pavement, you eventually learned how to use the brakes. Your experience showed you another, better way. The same thinking applies to investing.

"Mark!"

"What, Mom?"

"Don't put your hand near the flame, you'll get burned."

"Yeah, okay."

Mom left the room. I was six or seven or years old and determined to find out for myself, I stuck my hand over the candle flame and felt the heat sizzling my palm. *Mom's right.* I acknowledged. *The flame will hurt me if I leave my hand here too long.*

Sound familiar? Nearly every adult I know challenged the flame growing up. And I'm thankful my mom told me it would hurt. Had she not given me that expectation and information ahead of time, I probably wouldn't have been so cautious with my test. Her context gave me my own point of view to pull from.

Why am I sharing this story with you? I'm telling you now—the investment candle can burn you. To get you started, here's what I learned.

You Should Expect to Make Money and Lose Money

The professionals do, and so will you. Early in writing this book and taking on my investment project, I had two direct experiences with this fact: Atlantic Power and Line Energy were both touted as strong buys from the Pros, so I took their advice and bought both. Turned out that Atlantic Power ran into some legal issues; investors jumped ship and the stock price tanked. Line Energy also found itself embroiled in a legal issue. Again, investors jumped ship and the stock price dropped significantly. I lost 29% and 28% on these two investments, respectively, and the Pros didn't know this would happen either. On the winning side of the money coin, one of my better sales was for a gain of about 24%. If you must know the answer immediately as to how well I did or didn't do, you can always skip to the last chapter. Also, there are tables at the end of each chapter showing monthly results.

You Should Expect to Feel Lost and Frustrated By Investment Language and Vocabulary

Throughout the investment world and all its communications, you'll read abbreviations and words like EPS, dividend, EBITDA, asset allocation, moat, ROI, etc. And you won't know what they all mean. That's okay! Don't freak out. No one knows everything when they first start something new. Plus, today's digital era makes looking up terms a cinch; you'll have no issues looking up additional terms online, as plenty of resources exist.

You Will experience Information Overload

Junk email or "spam" is just part of modern life. So, be forewarned: If you sign up for free investing related e-newsletters, you'll also receive a bunch of crap. I include several junk emails as examples throughout the book, so you know beforehand what to expect. The advantage of the freebies is that you become more familiar with the topics and processes of investing. And in many instances, the articles contain useful information about items you already own or should consider owning. With careful reading and scrutinizing, you'll learn the resources most useful to you.

I can easily understand why people are hesitant to enter into the stock market, particularly when advertisements are asking you if you have a $500k portfolio, or saying if only you'd invested $10k with them it'd be worth $135k today. Add to this the ever present influx of folks asking you to invest in their guaranteed one-of-a-kind whack-a-mole method. This is just noise. It's no different than the junk mail you get in the mailbox. Just ignore it.

The bottom line is, saying "I don't have the money" or "investing is too expensive" are not really viable reasons for not investing. I smoke, drink wine, and pay a monthly fee for my electronic toys, but I could stop or reduce any one of these to set aside money for investing. Money availability is a relative concept. What I actually need and what I want are mutually exclusive.

When my co-workers ask me why I bring my lunch every day, I say it saves me money so I can buy more wine. This is only a partial truth, so I'll describe it another way. Let's say it costs me $1 dollar per day to make my own lunch, which means I spend about $20 per month for lunch. Now, if I went out to lunch and spent $5 every day, that equals $80 per month, meaning I save $60 in expenses by bringing my own lunch! This means that I could now use this money to invest $720 a year—or buy several cases of wine. The cheapest 100 shares I bought with fantasy money was only $636, and at one point, the stock was up 116%!

LIFE, AND INVESTING, IS A TRADE-OFF: I CAN DO (A) TO GET (B), OR DO (C) AND NOT GET (B)

So, it doesn't matter if you're not an investment whiz. Just start by investing in something that interests you: favorite clothing store, fast food joint, pet store, etc. Do you have a favorite gas station or brand? Sometimes, it's just about paying attention to everyday details. If you shop at two different clothing stores and one usually has only a few shoppers and the other always has many, which one might be the better investment?

Remember, the Warren Buffets and Bill Gates of the world had to start somewhere, and it wasn't at the top. The only way to ensure you won't be successful is to not try in the first place.

So, start your own fantasy portfolio to explore the markets and learn how to make play money without losing any real money. This will allow you to try different ideas and approaches, and create a better foundation for investing with real money.

MARCH

LOOKING AT PUZZLE PIECES

*Calling someone who trades actively in the
market an investor is like calling someone who repeatedly
engages in one-night stands a romantic.*

—Warren Buffett

You know you're a novice investor when...

You realize that intelligence is fleeting.

March 4, 2013

Here we go, and I'm ready to roll. Now that I've made my picks, I know I'm going to get rich. Think I'll just sit back and greedily rub my hands together as I bask in the warmth of my genius.

Quick, check how I'm doing. No. Be patient. I said I wouldn't look. Yeah, so what. I need to see how much I've made…it's been two days. Damn! It's like having a new toy or something. I crave to look at my portfolio even though it's only fantasy money.

March 11, 2013

As I roll into the second week of my project, I'm still craving a daily look, but it's not as bad as last week. I've redirected my excitability toward reading the headlines and getting caught up on emails. Ooo-hhh, so many offers - so little time. All these nationally known investors must be aware of my financial savvy, because they want to know me. No, wait. They just want my money. Still, I go down a few rabbit holes.

Take a peek at LinkedIn (LNKD). Hmmm, down a little. Bummer.

March 18, 2013

Get online and check the status of LNKD. I'm not sure why this one sticks out in my mind.

Am I hoping for another huge jump in price? Is it because this is a speculative investment and the only benefit would be a higher share price, since there's no dividend?

Owning this stock makes me nervously excited. This week, I made it to Day 3 before I checked the share price (Woo hoo! It's up!). Well, at least it was only one item, so maybe I have some measure of self-control.

As I started this effort, I was really excited to be back in the market, learning the ropes, and pushing myself to make a lot of money. I was confident in my ability to do this. Looking back, I think creating a fantasy portfolio created a looser approach to spending money. In other words, the money wasn't real, so I could take extra chances without consequence. I also realized that in order to make the transition from a diary to a book format, I needed to change my analysis process from weekly to daily.

The daily perspective was useful to get me into a deeper level of knowing what was taking place in the markets and the economy. The additional detail was both useful and confusing. Useful in the sense that I could see how economic issues were being perceived by investors. Confusing in the sense that I sometimes couldn't understand the reasons why investors were doing what they were doing. I would come to learn that the markets can be solely affected by what investors perceive.

Before jumping too far into my fantasy portfolio journey—and starting one of your own—I recommend that you consult with your tax advisor before you use real money. Investing can include a variety of fees and taxes you may be subject to. Here are some key points to keep in mind:

○ **Learn how taxes affect your portfolio and decisions.** What you owe will depend on the length of ownership and the type of investment. You may also be affected by an international tax rate.

○ **Know what fees you'll be hit with if trading independently.** Be aware of broker fees, mutual fund management fees, or other fees if you trade independently.

○ **Identify how your dividends are taxed.** Dividends (or distributions) can be taxed at different rates depending on being a short- or long-term gain versus a return of capital.

DISCOVERING PATIENCE

"Set it, and forget it" is a common saying and perspective in the investment world.

Translated, that means you buy a stock or bond and let it grow over the long term without worrying about short-term performance. I understand that looking at investing as a long-term activity holds merit. But, there's no way I can subscribe to the "forget it" mentality. When starting my fantasy portfolio, I intended to not look at my portfolio every day; I know that obsessing over the numbers can lead to over-reacting and bad decisions. But, with my investments in place, the sense of desire to see my success easily became overwhelming.

Somehow, I knew I had to find balance.

Over time, tracking daily changes provided me with additional insight into how an array of factors affect my stocks: international affairs; cost of goods, such as oil; company quarterly reports; federal agency reports; etc. The most problematic detail was the number of items I was tracking—more than 70. This was a lot to start with. It would have been less stressful to have started with fewer items, maybe five or ten.

In getting into the groove of managing my investments, part of my daily routine became rummaging through information from e-zines and emails. One day, I came across a report on Coca-Cola (KO), a one-pager chock-full of historical data and analysis of their future earning potential. I felt this report would be good for future reference, yet, I also felt the lure of wanting to know more. *Dang. Now I want to go look at my entire portfolio…which I did.*

Patience is a virtue? I'm not quite convinced.

WEED-EATING MY WAY THROUGH THE WOODS

Access to information in today's world is unprecedented. To manage my portfolio, I needed information, and the best way to begin was by signing up for free emails and digital newsletters. Though I was inundated by emails from multiple sources, I learned that many of those were spam solicitations offering instant wealth if I just give them money. However, some communications are worth scanning over and may contain a useful piece of information for me to research further.

Receiving information and actually understanding it are different beasts. But, since information was a necessary part of my journey and learning process, I dove right in. No toe dipping for me. Apparently, I'm really well liked by entities I know nothing about, because I became inundated with email.

Here, the "expert" wanted me to sell various stocks. Liking a good game of chase-the-rabbit, my ears perked up. The first thing I noticed was that the email author didn't include any dates, so I didn't know what time period to even look for (RED FLAG!!).

From: Dewey Cheatham
Sent: Saturday, March 2, 2013 7:47 PM
To: Mark Slauter <markslauter@novice.investor
Subject: Just $99 gets you the keys to the kingdom

INVESTOR ALERT:
Sell These Stocks Now!

Don't get caught holding yesterday's winners! You can lose a fortune FAST by sticking with a one-time game-changing company for too long. Just ask folks who owned stocks like

Green Mountain Coffee plummeted from $111 to $42—DOWN 62%

Netflix from $295 to just $93—DOWN 68%

First Solar from $311 to $30—DOWN 90%

Apple from $705 to $419—DOWN 40% in just 4 months

Research in Motion from $144 to $11—DOWN 92%

You rarely hear the word SELL from Wall Street or your broker, but I promise you'll hear it from me. And it starts with the dozens of former growth darlings I expose in this new report, "2013 Blacklist—65 Stocks to Sell Now." Get immediate access to the complete list of these toxic stocks and get out now. All I need is your permission to send you your free copy now—**click here.**

Since the "expert" listed Apple with a time interval, I thought that with a little sleuthing, maybe I could figure it out. I checked Yahoo Finance and found the $700 peak close in September 2012, which meant I should find the $419 mark in December /January. *Hmmm...*I found the lowest close at about $432 in March 2013. Maybe I'm mathematically challenged, but this looked like six months to me. This became all the more interesting when I read elsewhere in the email that they touted Apple as one of the 39 winners they bagged in 2012, making them 68.5%!

The point?

When you receive junk mail like this, with the goal to hit you emotionally and get you to spend money, you really have no way to figure out the truth behind their numbers.

When looking at a stock's price each day, there are four primary data points:

- **Open Price.** The value of an investment when an exchange (market) opens.

- **Close Price.** The value of an investment when an exchange closes.

- **Intraday High Value.** The highest value during the time an exchange is open due to the fluctuation of prices throughout day.

○ **Intraday Low Value.** The lowest value of an investment during the time an exchange is open due to the fluctuation of prices throughout day.

Sometimes, the solicitation or marketing products will use the intraday values to make their outcomes appear more valuable. This is neither right nor wrong, but you should be aware of this sales technique.

PAYING ATTENTION TO THE EVERYDAY

Investing is not a static activity. Informed action requires a certain level of engagement, and opportunities can crop up anywhere. For example, one day as I was at work and booking travel arrangements for a business trip, I noticed that InterContinental Hotels Group was the mother ship for one of my credit cards. I mentally noted this detail, deciding I should check into this entity at a later time.

And what happened when I looked more deeply into the details?

When I returned home that very same day, I serendipitously had received an email from Morningstar about lodging operators. Specifically, it focused on those that both manage and franchise hotels, because they have stronger growth prospects. And guess who was on the list: InterContinental Hotels Group (IHG). Some days, life is very coincidental and the world gets just a wee bit smaller. (Karl Jung referred to these types of coincidences as "*synchronicity.*")

Amazed at the timing, I immediately read the article and looked up information on the hotels discussed, which jump-started me wondering if hotel mutual funds exist. Though I didn't find one, the lack of immediate information didn't mean it wasn't out there. I decided to look into this option at another time.

Another similar experience of finding opportunities in everyday details arrived when I was thumbing through a magazine. I realized that I should pay attention to the ads. When I did, one immediately stood out: Domtar Corporation. I looked the company up online and learned it designs, manufactures, markets, and distributes various fiber-based products from communication papers to specialty and packaging papers to adult incontinence products. I wasn't sure about the specialty paper products' market strength, but I knew that adult incontinence was definitely an upward market due to our aging population. Coincidentally, a few weeks later, I was placing paper into the copier at work. I decided to check out the brand, and sure enough, it was Domtar paper...*synchronicity.*

HUNTING FOR RESOURCES

No one can perform a job competently without the right tools, and the deeper I went into my fantasy portfolio, the more quickly I realized that I needed resources to provide me with a sufficient level of awareness. I needed insight into what I owned, what was going on around me, and where the opportunities were (if any). And, I soon saw that as I found various resources, my level of awareness increased. As my awareness level increased, so did my level of understanding and decision-making. And hunting for resources still rings true today.

In my search for resources, I immediately found two items: Investor's Business Daily (IBD) and Morningstar. While IBD uses its own trademarked system for comparing stocks, Morningstar also provides some comparative information. Both of these websites continue to provide a quick perspective on the details I'm seeking. In turn, digging for information can lead me to looking at more detail on a specific item, or lead me to new stocks to review. I found that Morningstar was easier for me to use and provided more detailed information.

Of course, as I was jumping around on websites, I was also checking emails and read one stating how analysts estimated that one out of every two people on the planet use Unilever's (UL) consumer products. That's an awful lot of people. Unilever is a global business that has hundreds of products. Now my interest was piqued.

With such strong demand for its products, this email lead me to believe that Unilever could be a good long-term, stable investment. Since I was learning to check my resources in this initial investment phase, I looked Unilever up on IBD and found it had a dividend of 3% (They'll pay me $3 annually for every $100 I invest) and their debt was at 55%, but not an IBD recommended buy. Meanwhile, Morningstar had a moderate buy on it. UL was about $33/share a year ago and now was at about $42/share. Another resource I found (and continue to use), The Street, showed the share value (stock price) was up about 8% year-to-date (YTD) and showed a mix of analyst buys and sells. If I had a losing or lower yielding stock, I'd consider moving the funds to reposition myself for another potential economic downturn with a buy-and-hold approach on UL.

Meanwhile, as I read the latest email from Investing Daily I came across this:

> Atlantic Power Corp's (TSX: ATP, NYSE: AT) crack-up this month has triggered a wave of shareholder lawsuits against it. But even as management has a long way to restore credibility with investors, it too appears to have turned itself into a hard target, at least for the time being.

I decided I needed to find out what's going on—here's where having research skills matters. You'll get tons of information, all the time. Plus, you'll get countering points, adding to the confusion of knowing what's really going on. Becoming a savvy researcher will help you in the long run. The better you can dig up real facts and not just land on opinions, the stronger your decisions will be across your portfolio.

Near the end of my first month investing, Morningstar released a report on their view of the current market and its valuation. One interesting takeaway for me was this statement:

> A fairly valued market is a challenge from an investing perspective because it doesn't send a clear signal either way. There are a couple of key takeaways for investors, but it boils down to one idea: Be selective with your investment decisions. Just because the overall market is fairly valued doesn't mean that every stock is fairly valued.

Amen to that.

Having a fairly valued market makes it very difficult to know what to do. The setup is like trying to determine whether or not you should kiss each other good night after a really good first date. Signal clarity and perception will make or break the evening.

FINDING MY INNER INVESTOR

In the beginning of my fantasy portfolio, while I was deciding which stocks to buy with fantasy money, I decided that I wouldn't invest in companies with huge debt ratios, because I'm not comfortable with too much debt. Some stocks identified as buys by the Pros were at 500% debt levels. Think of this detail as having a house worth $100k but you borrowed $500k from a bank to buy it. I decided to play it safe; these investments weren't for me, because I'm uncomfortable with a lot of debt.

Knowing your level of risk and comfort is huge in the investment world.

March 20, 2013

Today's market activity seems to have been widespread and touched each of the 10 sectors, finishing the day to the positive side.

Leadership came from the Consumer and Healthcare sectors, which hopefully helped my portfolio

March 25, 2013

Ok, so the market is down 64 points. It's interesting how the lack of the Cypriot Government to neatly address their bad economy affects Wall Street. It's such a tiny country. Apparently, analysts say that it's a template of failure for other countries within the European Union. Of course, having a country next door that can't even elect a government (Italy) doesn't help.

So, when I see this type of information, I ask myself what to do with these details. Does it really matter? I'm immediately reminded that, like it or not, the daily news will drive investing and create changes in the share price of a stock; cultural and societal events matter to the markets. However, the share price doesn't necessarily change the fundamental value of the company. The company can be well managed and profitable, but if investors think some activity might impact profits, they'll sell the stock. If enough investors sell the stock, they'll drive the share price down. Remember, many investors (individual and institutional) are doing this to make money first and foremost, not to support a company. So prioritizing decisions around making money is often the name of the game.

MONTH IN REVIEW

Between March 1 and March 29, 2013, the Dow gained 489 points. Though I was primarily focusing on where things stood at month's end, I could see value in viewing the weekly changes on unrealized gains. By month's end, Mom was about equal with the Dow Jones Industrial Average (DJIA). I was about 5.5 points behind her. Overall, I was off to a lousy start.

Weekly Return on Investment Stats			
	Dow Jones Industrial Average	**Me**	**Mom**
Week 1	2.18%	0.62%	1.40%
Week 2	3.01%	-1.70%	1.76%
Week 3	3.00%	-4.58%	1.88%
Week 4	3.48%	-2.32%	3.19%

Overall in March, I had an unrealized loss of $6,671. While losses were primarily in the Basic Materials, Technology, and Utilities (because of Atlantic Power) sectors, other sectors experienced slight gains.

I must also address another issue in my portfolio: The decreased values in Terra Nitrogen Company and Samsung were killing me. These two companies made up over half of my portfolio (58%). In this scenario, I felt I should be evaluating what to do with these two items due to the potential impact on my portfolio value. A more balanced portfolio would not be subject to this heavy weighting. I knew I needed to reassess where I stood.

But I focused my efforts on first things first: Assessing where my portfolio was compared to Mom's. She had an unrealized gain of $5,581 this month. Mom experienced the same losses in the Energy and Utilities sectors.

COMPARISON

For the month of March, Mom won the round. She made more money and experienced fewer losses on a percentage basis than I did. Plus, her losses were contained to a maximum of about -5%. Me? I got my butt whipped.

I also became interested in how my picks compared to the Pros' portion of my portfolio. In March, my portfolio had 15 items that I invested in based on recommendations from the Pros, which was about 52% (14 items were my picks). At month's end, I did slightly better than the Pros in percentage terms. For value increases, 78.6% of my choices increased while the Pros had a 73.3% increase.

DIVIDENDS FOR MARCH

I received 7 payments totaling $374.83, which equated to $53.55 per payment. Mom received 18 payments for $469.25, which equated to $26.07 per payment. I made about 75% as much as Mom, but with fewer payments and a greater average payment return; the advantage of chasing yield. However, chasing yield can come at a cost. If I was able to invest in equities with better prospects for increasing share value, I could have increased my total returns.

LESSONS LEARNED

There's always something to learn when considering how to invest money. The trick for me was to recognize the lesson(s) being taught.

○ **Patience sucks.** Not checking my portfolio was like having a poison ivy rash and not scratching it.

○ **Always question the numbers.** This is particularly true for any solicitation. In my example of trying to determine whether or not the sales and profit numbers were true for Apple, as presented in an email, I couldn't. I couldn't validate any other figures in the email either. Another thing to consider when reviewing solicitations is whether or not someone is willing to show you how many losses they've had, which they probably won't.

○ **Everyday life can provide great fodder for investing research.** My takeaway from this experience was that when you buy stocks, you're investing in a company. To really start seeing opportunities, look at the everyday items that fill your lives and assess their shelf life or long-term value (think: aging baby boomers = increased need for adult diapers).

Regardless of what any investment advisor says, I only see two sure things in the market: 1) Someone is always willing to take your money, and 2) Identifying an investment that actually provides a decent return on your money is not easy.

The following portfolio tables show what the current value (March 29) is compared to the purchase value. Value is presented in both dollar and percentage terms. The last column has the month-to-month (February to March) change as a percentage to show how items fluctuate monthly compared to the ever lengthening time between the start date and current values.

MY PORTFOLIO FOR MARCH 2013

Note: '0' in last column reflects ownership of less than a month.

Name (Pros in italics)	Purchase $ Value	3-29-13 $ Value	Total Net $ Gain/ Loss	Total Net % Gain/ Loss	Mth to Mth % Change
The AES Corporation	$1,193.00	$1,257.00	$64.00	5.36%	1.95%
Aruba Networks	$2,500.00	$2,474.00	$(26.00)	-1.04%	-3.77%
Atlantic Power Co	$712.00	$493.00	$(219.00)	-30.76%	-9.21%
Coca-Cola	$3,870.00	$4,044.00	$174.00	4.50%	3.11%
Consolidated Communications	$1,637.00	$1,755.00	$118.00	7.21%	2.93%
El Paso Pipeline Partners LP	$4,140.00	$4,386.00	$246.00	5.94%	4.73%
The GEO Group Inc.	$3,448.00	$3,762.00	$314.00	9.11%	5.26%
GlaxoSmithKline PLC ADR (1)	$4,422.00	$4,691.00	$269.00	6.08%	5.23%
Great Northern Iron Ore (1)	$8,088.00	$7,457.00	$(631.00)	-7.80%	-2.94%
Home Loan Servicing Solutions	$2,302.00	$2,333.00	$31.00	1.35%	0.26%
Kinder Morgan Energy Partners LP (1)	$8,672.00	$8,977.00	$305.00	3.52%	5.10%
Linn Energy	$3,753.00	$3,797.00	$44.00	1.17%	-1.33%
LinkedIn	$17,046.00	$7,606.00	$560.00	3.29%	-0.45%
Macy's	$4,067.00	$4,184.00	$117.00	2.88%	0.41%
Northern Tier Energy LP Class A	$2,950.00	$2,990.00	$40.00	1.36%	-4.81%

Name (Pros in italics)	Purchase $ Value	3-29-13 $ Value	Total Net $ Gain/ Loss	Total Net % Gain/ Loss	Mth to Mth % Change
Oaktree Capital Group, LLC	$5,013.00	$5,102.00	$89.00	1.78%	0.73%
PVR Partners LP	$2,285.00	$2,411.00	$126.00	5.51%	5.75%
Samsung Electronics Co Ltd (1)	$150,000.00	$141,500.00	$(8,500.00)	-5.67%	-5.67%
Seaspan Corp	$1,930.00	$2,005.00	$75.00	3.89%	0.50%
Sunoco Logistics Partners LP	$6,258.00	$6,540.00	$282.00	4.51%	-3.14%
Terra Nitrogen Company	$23,461.00	$22,002.00	$(1,459.00)	-6.22%	-5.37%
TJX companies	$4,498.00	$4,675.00	$177.00	3.94%	4.10%
Triangle Capital Corporation	$2,971.00	$2,799.00	$(172.00)	-5.79%	-6.58%
Akre Focus Fund Retail	$1,630.00	$1,707.00	$77.00	4.72%	3.83%
Delaware Healthcare I	$1,355.00	$1,414.00	$59.00	4.35%	2.24%
Oceanstone Fund	$3,382.00	$3,408.00	$26.00	0.77%	1.25%
Fidelity Select Biotechnology Portfolio	$12,205.00	$13,239.00	$1,034.00	8.47%	4.13%
Fidelity Select IT Services Portfolio	$2,775.00	$2,889.00	$114.00	4.11%	2.08%
Wells Fargo Advantage Core Builder Ser M	$1,173.00	$1,168.00	$(5.00)	-0.43%	-0.17%
	$287,736.00	$281,065.00	$(6,671.00)	-2.32%	

Mom's Portfolio for March 2013

Name	Purchase $ Value	3-29-13 $ Value	Total Net $ Gain/Loss	Total Net % Gain/ Loss	Mth to Mth % Change
Altria Group	$3,349.00	$3,439.00	$90.00	2.69%	1.15%
AT&T Inc.	$3,601.00	$3,669.00	$68.00	1.89%	0.03%
Buckeye Partners LP	$5,611.00	$6,116.00	$505.00	9.00%	3.35%
Caterpillar Inc.	$9,136.00	$8,697.00	$(439.00)	-4.81%	-3.91%
Cleco Corp	$4,418.00	$4,703.00	$285.00	6.45%	5.42%
CMS Energy Corp	$2,645.00	$2,794.00	$149.00	5.63%	3.18%
Compass Securities	$1,574.00	$1,587.00	$13.00	0.83%	1.34%
Deluxe Corp	$3,965.00	$4,140.00	$175.00	4.41%	2.96%
Devon Energy Corp	$5,388.00	$5,642.00	$254.00	4.71%	0.32%
Dominion Res Inc. VA	$5,642.00	$5,818.00	$176.00	3.12%	4.13%
Duke Energy	$6,925.00	$7,259.00	$334.00	4.82%	4.24%
Enbridge Energy Partners	$2,763.00	$3,014.00	$251.00	9.08%	4.73%
Enterprise Products	$5,681.00	$6,029.00	$348.00	6.13%	4.40%
Exxon Mobile	$8,943.00	$9,011.00	$68.00	0.76%	1.28%
Frontier Communications Corp	$419.00	$399.00	$(20.00)	-4.77%	-1.97%
General Electric	$2,319.00	$2,312.00	$(7.00)	-0.30%	-2.73%
Great Plains Energy	$2,199.00	$2,319.00	$120.00	5.46%	2.47%
Hartford Financial Services Group	$2,368.00	$2,580.00	$212.00	8.95%	1.38%
Hudson City Bancorp	$858.00	$864.00	$6.00	0.70%	-0.69%
Integrys Energy Group	$5,610.00	$5,816.00	$206.00	3.67%	3.49%
Intel Corp	$2,103.00	$2,184.00	$81.00	3.85%	1.20%
Medical Property Trust	$1,483.00	$1,604.00	$121.00	8.16%	6.58%
Mondelez International	$2,781.00	$3,062.00	$281.00	10.10%	7.14%

Name	Purchase $ Value	3-29-13 $ Value	Total Net $ Gain/Loss	Total Net % Gain/ Loss	Mth to Mth % Change
Nat'l Grid Transco	$5,456.00	$5,801.00	$345.00	6.32%	5.95%
Nisource Inc.	$2,793.00	$2,934.00	$141.00	5.05%	3.71%
Occidental Petroleum	$8,265.00	$7,837.00	$(428.00)	-5.18%	-4.89%
Spyglass Resources Corp	$274.00	$283.00	$9.00	3.28%	2.54%
Pembina Pipeline	$2,821.00	$3,160.00	$339.00	12.02%	4.08%
Pepco	$2,053.00	$2,140.00	$87.00	4.24%	4.65%
Philip Morris	$9,144.00	$9,271.00	$127.00	1.39%	1.76%
Piedmont Natural Gas	$3,265.00	$3,288.00	$23.00	0.70%	-1.17%
Principle Financial Group	$3,155.00	$3,403.00	$248.00	7.86%	1.83%
Royal Dutch Shell PLC ADR	$6,578.00	$6,516.00	$(62.00)	-0.94%	-1.53%
Scana Corp	$4,906.00	$5,116.00	$210.00	4.28%	4.28%
Southern Co	$4,483.00	$4,692.00	$209.00	4.66%	3.53%
Spectra Energy	$2,881.00	$3,075.00	$194.00	6.73%	5.24%
Teco Energy	$1,735.00	$1,782.00	$47.00	2.71%	2.89%
US Bancorp	$3,401.00	$3,393.00	$(8.00)	-0.24%	-0.88%
Verizon Communications	$4,672.00	$4,915.00	$243.00	5.20%	2.48%
Wells Fargo	$3,539.00	$3,699.00	$160.00	4.52%	1.34%
DWS Core Equity Fund	$1,983.00	$2,062.00	$79.00	3.98%	1.33%
DWS S&P 500 Index Fund	$2,022.00	$2,083.00	$61.00	3.02%	0.77%
DWS Short Duration Fund	$931.00	$930.00	$(1.00)	-0.11%	-0.21%
Fidelity Contrafund	$8,122.00	$8,392.00	$270.00	3.32%	1.18%
Wellesley Income Fund	$2,479.00	$2,490.00	$11.00	0.44%	0.40%
	$174,739.00	**$180,320.00**	**$5,581.00**	**3.19%**	

APRIL

SECTOR IS AS SECTOR DOES

I will not be concerned at other men's not knowing me; I will be concerned at my own want of ability.

—Confucius

You know you're a novice investor when...

The market can easily dispose of your income.

Here's another example email expressing how 'they' can make me rich. And this one hit me up 3 times in the same week. *Maybe Prez Obama thinks she's the best looking investment advisor…*

From: Weather Orknot
Sent: Saturday, April 2, 2013 7:47 PM
To: Mark Slauter <markslauter@novice.investor>
Subject: TORNADO ALLEY!

A Highly Predictable "Twister" is Heading Your Way—Confined to a Narrow 21-Day Period Starting This Month.

If History Repeats, You'll Bank Mammoth Gains of +92%… +113%… +158%… and +243%. Just Like This Time Last Year!

Please Accept My Boldest Guarantee Ever:

Either You Double Your Cash by June 30—Or You Get It All Free!

April 3, 2013

The market's off 111 points today. Pundits are saying that investors may be in a holding pattern, waiting on a market correction. As I continue to check the news, I check one site and find the first article titled with pundit crap:

"Stocks Crater, Turnover Rises; Market Leaders Hit Hard"

Really??

The market loses 111 points (0.8%) and that constitutes a "crater"? So, if it went up 111 points would that be a volcanic rise? I'm pretty sure we can do without overzealous pundits relying on useless hyperbole. There were multiple media outlets attempting to create drama today.

April 15, 2013

Well, looks like today was a sell-off day. The market is down 266 points, hitting the Basic Materials sector hard. Okay, so once again the pundits are stating that the market "PLUMMETED." Come on folks. Why is a 1.5% decrease a "plummet"? Are you so insecure that you have to exaggerate reality? How would they describe a 1.5% increase?

While I find this type of drama annoying, I also find it interesting that the pundits aren't screaming about "meteoric" rises when the market moves up. On the 11th, the market gained 128 points; on the 16th, up 156 points; and on the 23rd, up 123 points - without a peep from the talking heads. I don't think I could work in these media environments with a bunch of drama queens.

Some days it seems like the market can be a self-fulfilling cesspool born from the Chicken Little gene pool. Apparently, if China farts or somebody hits the hookah too hard we all have to run for the hills. *Buy more guns and ammo. Stock up on non-perishable food. Get your nuclear bunker ready, because it's ANARCHY!! (See Sam Kinison as the history professor in the movie 'Back to School')*

Do I have the ability to conquer the unknown and become better for my attempts?

One month into my fantasy portfolio game, and I recognized that I would muddle through the learning process, stumbling and falling along the way only to get back up and try again. I found it weird and ironic that I was willing to put this much effort into taking care of Mom but haven't focused on my own financial health. *I can will change that.*

Early in April 2013, I was traveling for business, which made me realize a key question: How do I follow my portfolio when I'm not at home? Fortunately, I had my laptop and could attempt to keep up, but my late workdays cut into my available time to follow emails and any additional items of interest. Maybe less time was good for me; it became harder to chase smoky wisps of unknown information.

April was an interesting month for market movement and for making portfolio changes. By tracking my investments' performances, I recognized that some of my initial acquisitions were bad choices, so I sold and acquired several items to attempt repositioning myself. I also had to wade through some major market swings and determine which voices to pay attention to when the market fell and the talking heads went nuts.

So it came back to the question of ability: Am I able to tie together what I see happening with my portfolio with what the commentators say and with what the market was actually doing? Each aspect is a piece of the investing puzzle, and I wanted to know how the pieces were fitting together.

Of course, when analyzing my portfolio, part of the issue became knowing what puzzle pieces to even look for. At this point, I wasn't even sure if what I was looking at was important or not, and the only way to determine that was to read and look into as much as I could. I figured that, eventually, as I gained experience, all the pieces would come together.

WATCHING THE MARKET

As my second month began, I started seeing commentary on quarterly performance (January – March 2013). One email offered Morningstar's take on the first quarter of 2013:

> The broad stock market, as represented by the Morningstar U.S. Stock Market Index, rose 11%. The breadth of the rally since the heart of the financial crisis is remarkable. Stocks have now increased over 6% on average annually over the last five years.

I was happy to hear the positive perspective, but I was left wondering: *Am I in the money, too?* When I assessed where my picks stood a week prior at the end of March, my assumption was, *Nope!* When I read the article, Morningstar pointed out how the U.S. still hadn't addressed its long-term debt issue, nor had the European Union solved their debt crises. Both of these global economic factors left a huge unknown on the markets' future. This is why I wanted to know what the puzzle pieces were. If the global economy was unable to make positive progress, then any number of things could affect my investments. Maybe businesses would begin laying people off again, which meant there would be less consumer spending. For me, it was important to try and understand some of these big picture issues.

Following the market in April found me with some really nerve-wracking days. The market closed on the 15th down 266 points, and once again, the Basic Materials sector was hit hard. Basic Materials was getting beat up lately. However, in this type of sell-off, almost no sector went untouched, and it appeared that all sectors ended up with a loss on the day. This added to my worry of losing money. My only bright spot was that I sold my LinkedIn (LNKD) shares before this, and they closed down $10 below my sale price. I felt great about making money, but I also asked myself if I should buy LNKD back, since it dropped so much.

The rest of the 3rd week of April was a real see-saw ride. On the 16th, the market closed up 156 points! *Yippee!!* (I could hear the song by the Moody Blues "Ride My Seesaw"). On the 17th, the market was down 138 points followed by another 82 points drop the very next day, causing my portfolio to decline a little more. *I wondered how many traders take Prozac?* I didn't know yet if this level of movement was typical, but it sure was making me crazy.

As I started the fourth week of April, the market closed up 152 points on the 23rd. This was good as most sectors were trending up, but Utilities and Basic Materials struggled. I also noted that one of my technology stocks was continuing to decline. *Shit…Samsung is down another $175. That's it! Gotta go! That's the second Samsung sale for a loss! Yup, screwed the pooch on this one.* I still wanted a technology stock, so I bought Apple. Three of four sources I researched recommended it as a buy. And I saw it as a strong company. I had $130k from selling Samsung at a loss and acquiring 100 shares Apple cost me $39,354. Though having $90,646 remaining from the sale sounded awesome, I still had to determine what to do with it. *Great, now what do I do?*

UNDERSTANDING MARKET SECTORS

In addressing market sectors in April, I looked at some further commentary offered by Morningstar:

Sector-by-Sector Performance
The rising tide lifted most stock sectors in the quarter. Healthcare led the way (+14%) while Consumer Defensive (+10%) and Industrials (+9%) also posted double-digit increases. Basic Materials (-3%) had the worst quarter and was the only sector to lose ground.

Though I really didn't have much to go on at this point, I could at least have some understanding that my Healthcare, Consumer Defensive, and Industrial stock selections may have been a smart move. Of course, you have to take the good with the bad, just as I did with the Basic Materials.

Morningstar has its own valuation methodology that estimates a fair market value for stock prices. From their perspective, if you can acquire a stock at a discount (below what they think is the fair market value), then you have a buffer should the stock price go down. You can think of it as wiggle room. If the stock price goes up, then you're that much better off. Their current overall market estimate showed that the market was fully valued, because the median value was just about 1.

When the median value is above 1, the market is overvalued due to stock prices being above the estimated fair value. As an investor, this means you'll likely pay too much to acquire a stock, with no buffer against risk should the value decline. When the median value is below 1, you're more likely to find bargains, acquire stocks below fair market value, and have a risk buffer. If you had the choice between paying $20k or $15k for the same car, which dollar amount would you choose?

Reviewing the Sector information allows me to evaluate my portfolio to see what it's doing in relation to the broader market results. By looking at this information, I can compare my portfolio against broader trends. A valuable reason to track a portfolio's performance like this is *perspective.* Just because a particular sector is up or down doesn't automatically mean my holdings followed the trend.

For example, looking at the following table, it shows that the Basic Materials sector is down 3% in the first quarter of 2013 and Healthcare is up 14%. As I looked at my individual items, I saw that it was a mix of value increases and declines. For the three Basic Materials items I had, I was doing worse than the sector as a whole; mine ranged from 1.36% to -7.80%. The items I had in Healthcare ranged from 4.35% to 8.47%, which was not as good as the sector itself, but I was pleased with being on the positive side.

Sector	1st Quarter Performance
Basic Materials	-3%
Communications	+4
Consumer Cyclical	+9
Consumer Defensive	+10%
Energy	+4%

Sector	1st Quarter Performance
Financial Services	+8%
Healthcare	+14%
Industrials	+9%
Technology	+7%
Utilities	+6%

Apart from the Basic Materials sector, my portfolio returned to the positive. My portfolio also included two funds that invested across sectors and a municipal bond fund, but I wasn't sure how to place these from a sector standpoint and did not include them in the above table.

CHASING FOR INFORMATION

I have spent (and will continue to spend) a large chunk of time researching sources of information and individual investment opportunities. I find that having a specific type of fund in mind, like large- or mid-caps, etc., would be more useful to my search. There are so many listed funds that I need to focus my energy in order to save time and effort. Sometimes, different websites will categorize funds differently, which is confusing when trying to identify investment opportunities. I think the best approach to streamlining research is to find a third-party entity (such as Morningstar or the Wall Street Journal), because they both provide information on a long list of funds. In this way, you get the information you're seeking while also having two different sources to compare against.

During the first week of April, I decided *Okay, time to suck it up, and buy into some professional advice.* I felt that I wasn't getting enough information on my own. At this time, I'd received a discount deal on an annual subscription that gave me access to premium services. Since I'm definitely not the expert here, I felt that spending a few dollars for access to professional advice was worth the money. With so many different types of data and so many different ways to evaluate the data, I needed expert advice. I had neither the time nor the tools to do what they do.

As April 14 rolled around, I caught up on my emails. One discussed AeroVironment, the leading manufacturer of unmanned aerial vehicles (UAVs), as "a good bet now on the boom in pilot-less drones." The email discussed the potential growth for UAVs, a.k.a. "drones."

Piquing my interest, I decided I needed more information in order to form my own opinion. I found one source of information stating the company's stock value declined and hit a 52-week low. Another source, an investor, rated AeroVironment as a buy. After I checked other sources, I realized that the investor had the only "buy" recommendation. With deeper digging, I found that the stock was at about $18, roughly half its $35 high in 2010. The numbers showed it moderately profitable with no dividend. I decided to pass.

For me, the purpose of looking for information and doing research is to create and manage a portfolio that performs well. At the same time, looking for useful websites drove me crazy. With so many out there, choosing the useful ones became an exercise in patience. Of course, since I've been out of the market for decades, I'm not surprised. *Reality check: The last time I was "in" the market, the Internet and cell phones didn't exist, and I think we still had a black and white TV!*

Though I'd decided to acquire a subscription for better access to information, the real benefit was access to professional analyses. I still hadn't found a website that provided me with the ability to check various boxes for purposes of conducting my own research. For example, let's say I wanted to research stocks with a share price of $10-$20, a dividend of 4% or better, and an increasing annual profit of more than 5%. *Guess I'll keep looking.*

As I continued to look for and acquire information, I placed myself in a better position to understand and evaluate the fantasy portfolios. In turn, this translated into improving my decision-making ability in the world of real money.

MY PORTFOLIO

When I started my fantasy portfolio in March, I acquired stock in Atlantic Power (AT) based on a professional's buy recommendation. During this month, I came across a media report that a class action lawsuit was being initiated on AT. Since I bought my shares outside of the dates listed in the lawsuit, I wasn't directly part of it. However, much more was at stake. By the end of April, AT stock was down 33%, and though my investment was only $712, I got hammered. In hindsight, I realized that I should have dumped AT immediately. Better yet, I never should have bought it. *Thanks for the recommendation to buy AT, Pros!*

One option available to investors in the digital age is subscribing to email/text alerts for updates, just like for any other news feed. In hindsight, if I had signed up for alerts regarding AT, I may have been able to avoid or reduce my loss.

As an investor, I have to determine what my thresholds are:

How much risk is acceptable?

When do I take the loss?

Can I be emotionally removed from my investments?

For purposes of testing my emotions and relationship with loss and risk, I decided to retain AT in the portfolio, though I basically wrote off any hope for redemption. Had I decided to sell the stock, I would have done one of two things: 1) Look at where my successes were and consider putting the money into one of those, or 2) Look at other stocks within the same sector to maintain my desired level of diversity.

By April 14, I was already feeling some angst on my selections *(here come those emotions)* and decided to reposition my portfolio by selling off some big losers. All of these had some degree of support to buy from professionals. However, there were three that I acquired solely on their recommendation; the other three reflect where I made the choice.

Stock	Selected by	Loss/Gain in $	Loss/Gain in %
Aruba Networks: Technology sector	Pro	-$182	-7.3%
Atlantic Power Company: Utilities sector	Pro	-$207	-29.1%
Great Northern Iron Ore: Basic Materials sector	Me	-$1,144	-14.1%
LinkedIn: Technology sector	Me	$1,493	8.8%
Samsung: Technology sector	Me	-$12,500	-8.3%
Triangle Capital Corporation: Financial Services sector	Pro	-$252	-8.5%

I initially bought Great Northern due to the high dividend yield, which is somewhat pointless when the share value continues to decrease. It looked like the share price had leveled off, and the selection still had some support from the Pros, so I bought back the stock.

I took the same approach with Samsung but for an added reason: The company was gaining market share against competitors like Apple, and it appeared the company would continue to do so into the future. There was no dividend on this stock, and I did consider it a riskier investment.

The reason I sold LinkedIn was due to falling share price. It had a little support from the Pros when I bought it, but not much. As the price of shares started a downward movement, I didn't want to leave any money on the table, so I took my profit.

My total sales returned $168,525 into my pile of play money.

With the immediate buy back on Great Northern and Samsung, my cash balance dropped to $24,081 available to reinvest. Since LinkedIn was my only gain from the above list, my total loss from repositioning was $14,285. *Man, that really sucked.*

Since I wasn't tracking any potential new items, I acquired additional shares of items I already owned, zeroing out my cash balance.

○ **100 shares in GlaxoSmithKline (GSK) Healthcare sector:** The dividend was 2.76% and I thought there was additional potential for increasing share value from my perspective.

○ **100 shares of Kinder Morgan Energy (KMP) Energy sector:** The dividend was 5.16%. Though analysts ranked this as a hold and Morningstar showed it near the $92 fair estimate value, I saw some room for increasing share value.

○ **74 shares of Fidelity Select Biotech Portfolio (FBIOX) Mutual Fund:** The performance of this fund had been good, and looking at the stocks making up the fund I thought this to be a good fund selection.

With my new portfolio in play, I checked the market two days later on April 16, and it was up 156 points. Even the Basic Materials sector was up! Despite the semblance of good news, I had to check my portfolio and see if it aligned: up 0.33%. While checking, I noticed LinkedIn was up to $182.47 a share. *Maybe I should have repurchased LinkedIn.* The question was: Would I have been smart and savvy enough to place a sell order at the right level?

However, not all was rosy:

○ Great Northern (Basic Materials) was still moving down. What the hell is going on with this?

○ Northern Tier (Energy) was still moving down.

○ Samsung (Technology) was also down again.

I realized that these performances may have had something to do with the Great Northern stock price declining. Even though I was aware that this was a Royalty Trust that will terminate, I thought there was a larger issue. On April 6, 2015, GNI, by its terms, would dissolve, and all of its trusts would be terminated and shares canceled. At the end of the Trust on April 6, 2015, the certificates of beneficial interest (shares) in the Trust would cease to trade on the New York Stock Exchange.

On April 16, I also made six new acquisitions after selling Samsung for another loss ($7500) this month. This time, I was focusing on long-term revenue growth and dividends, and paying more attention to what my four primary professional sources were saying.

	Sector	Analyst Buy Recommendations	Dividend Yield	10-yr Avg for Revenue Growth	10-yr EPS
8x8, Inc.	Tech	4 of 4	0%	19.3%	N/A
Alliance Resource Partners LP	Basic Materials	3 of 4	6.1%	18.5%	14.7%
Legacy Reserves, LP	Energy	3 of 4	8.8%	44.0%	16.0%
Prudential PLC ADR	Financial	4 of 4	1.7%	21.6%	21.8%
Union Pacific Corp	Industrials	3 of 4	1.8%	5.3%	12.6%
Inventure Foods, Inc.	Consumer Defensive	4 of 4	0%	12.1%	9.7%

Alliance Resource Partners is a producer and marketer of coal mainly to major United States utilities and industrial users. Given that U.S. utilities were under pressure to reduce their coal usage, I did have some concern with owning this item, but I didn't think it would have any real effect on the company just yet.

As for Union Pacific, one of my reasons for acquiring the stock was that I currently had only one item in the sector and wanted to expand my holdings. Also, I thought that as the economy rebounded transportation activity would increase. The same rationalization applied to Prudential.

I also decided to make a tactical shift: Buy more mutual funds. I decided that I wanted to take advantage of the buying power (pooling of stocks to reduce risk) afforded by mutual funds. I chose Oakmark Global (OAKGX) and Vanguard Wellington Invest (VWELX), both of which were invested in large-cap companies (those with a market capitalization value more than $10 billion). These acquisitions cost me $6,257 and dropped my available cash amount to $55,289.

MOM'S PORTFOLIO

While working my fantasy portfolio, I was pulled into the original reason I started this project: Help mom. So, I dug up some information and details on a few of her portfolio's holdings. In particular, there was a report on Caterpillar (CAT) stating the projected growth was as high as 20% annually for the next several years and would be able to provide a 2% dividend yield. However, China was a major revenue source for CAT, and as the need for heavy machinery diminishes, so would the profits. So far, CAT was not performing well in Mom's fantasy portfolio.

I note that if I hadn't sucked it up and paid a subscription fee for professional information, I probably wouldn't know how susceptible CAT was to China's economy. Because China is a large global economic engine, if their economy begins to slow down, then several types of business will be negatively affected. Now that I knew a slowdown in the Chinese economy would impact CAT's profitability, I became more interested in paying attention to China.

MONTH IN REVIEW

Between March 29 and April 26, 2013, the Dow gained 134 points. Obviously, Mom's portfolio performed better than mine and slightly better than the DJIA.

	Weekly Return on Investment Stats		
	Dow Jones Industrial Average	Me	Mom
Week 5	3.37%	-4.93%	2.91%
Week 6	5.5%	-3.97%	4.87%
Week 7	3.25%	0.57%	3.40%
Week 8	4.42%	3.02%	5.30%

Overall for April, I had an unrealized gain of $6,408. While losses were primarily in the Basic Materials, Technology, and Utilities (because of Atlantic Power) sectors, the current losses in Terra Nitrogen Company and Samsung continued to weigh negatively against my portfolio. Mom had an unrealized gain of $9,257 this month. Mom experienced the same losses in the Energy and Utilities sectors.

COMPARISON

Just like last month, Mom won this round. She made more money and experienced fewer losses on a percentage basis than I did. And except for Spyglass Resources, her loss percentages were less than mine on individual items.

At this point, my portfolio had 17 items that I invested in based on recommendations from the Pros, which was about 46% (20 items were my picks). At month's end, the Pros had done much better than me in percentage terms. For value increases, only 65.0%

of my choices increased, while the Pros had 82.3% increase.

DIVIDENDS FOR APRIL

I received 11 payments totaling $461.51, which averaged $41.96 per payment. Mom received 10 payments for $357.65, which averaged $35.77 per payment. I made about 26% more than Mom with almost the same number of payments—a direct result from the advantage of chasing yield. However, my approach can (and did) come at a cost, since I lost a big chunk from selling losers. Making better investment decisions comes back to access to information, which allows me to invest in stocks with better prospects for increasing share value.

LESSONS LEARNED

Though some things made sense and were relatively clear to me, I knew that I still had a lot to learn and would only benefit from the experience of others.

○ **99% of email links lead down a rabbit hole that will want your money.** You just have to wade through the crap. There will always be someone asking you to buy into their surefire money-making system. The email example I present at the beginning of this chapter was sent by the same person three times in one week. But, there is an upside: Many contain some little morsel of information that actually contribute to your learning process.

○ **Cut and minimize your losses.** Taking this approach may be painful but probably more profitable in the long run. Don't hold on to items for emotional reasons.

○ **Do more research.** Hope is not a plan. Hoping you'll make money is like hoping for snow when you live near the equator. Don't hope for your future, plan for it.

The hardest one of these lessons learned was to being able cut my losses on a bad investment. Nobody wants to admit they made a bad decision and lost money. I lost $18k on my two sales of Samsung, and I was mad about losing fake money! Beware of the psychology in emotionally attaching to investments.

The following portfolio tables show what the current value (April 26) is compared to the purchase value. Value is presented in both dollar and percentage terms. The last column has the month-to-month (March to April) change as a percentage to show how items fluctuate monthly compared to the ever lengthening time between the start date and current values.

MY PORTFOLIO FOR APRIL 2013

Note: '0' in last column reflects ownership of less than a month.

Name (Pros in italics)	Purchase $ Value	4-26-13 $ Value	Total Net $ Gain/ Loss	Total Net % Gain/ Loss	Mar to Apr % Change
8x8, Inc.	$744.00	$723.00	$(21.00)	-2.8%	0
The AES Corporation	$1,193.00	$1,347.00	$154.00	12.9%	7.16%
Alliance Resource Partners LP	$6,725.00	$6,860.00	$135.00	2.0%	0
Apple Inc.	$39,354.00	$41,713.00	$2,359.00	6.0%	0
Coca-Cola Co	$3,870.00	$4,210.00	$340.00	8.8%	4.10%
Consolidated Communications	$1,637.00	$1,808.00	$171.00	10.4%	3.02%
El Paso Pipeline Partners LP	$4,140.00	$4,253.00	$113.00	2.7%	-3.03%
The GEO Group Inc.	$3,448.00	$3,734.00	$286.00	8.3%	-0.74%
GlaxoSmithKline PLC ADR (1)	$4,422.00	$5,216.00	$794.00	18.0%	11.19%
GlaxoSmithKline PLC ADR (2)	$4,847.00	$5,216.00	$369.00	7.6%	0
Great Northern Iron Ore (2)	$6,944.00	$6,873.00	$(71.00)	-1.0%	0
Home Loan Servicing Solutions	$2,302.00	$2,286.00	$(16.00)	-0.7%	-2.01%
Inventure Foods, Inc.	$726.00	$773.00	$47.00	6.5%	0
Kinder Morgan Energy Partners LP (1)	$8,672.00	$8,965.00	$293.00	3.4%	-0.13%
Kinder Morgan Energy Partners LP (2)	$9,025.00	$8,965.00	$(60.00)	-0.7%	0

Name (Pros in italics)	Purchase $ Value	4-26-13 $ Value	Total Net $ Gain/ Loss	Total Net % Gain/ Loss	Mar to Apr % Change
Legacy Reserves, LP	$2,773.00	$2,770.00	$(3.00)	-0.1%	0
Linn Energy	$3,753.00	$3,833.00	$80.00	2.1%	0.95%
Macy's	$4,067.00	$4,463.00	$396.00	9.7%	6.67%
Northern Tier Energy LP Class A (1)	$2,950.00	$2,544.00	$(406.00)	-13.8%	-14.92%
Oaktree Capital Group, LLC	$5,013.00	$5,257.00	$244.00	4.9%	3.04%
Prudential PLC ADR	$3,349.00	$3,468.00	$119.00	3.6%	0
PVR Partners LP	$2,285.00	$2,467.00	$182.00	8.0%	2.32%
Seaspan Corp	$1,930.00	$2,136.00	$206.00	10.7%	6.53%
Sunoco Logistics Partners LP	$6,258.00	$6,335.00	$77.00	1.2%	-3.13%
Terra Nitrogen Company	$23,461.00	$21,167.00	$(2,294.00)	-9.8%	-3.80%
TJX Companies	$4,498.00	$4,840.00	$342.00	7.6%	3.53%
Union Pacific Corp	$14,783.00	$14,752.00	$(31.00)	-0.2%	0
Akre Focus Fund Retail	$1,630.00	$1,725.00	$95.00	5.8%	1.05%
Delaware Healthcare I	$1,355.00	$1,486.00	$131.00	9.7%	5.09%
Oakmark Global I	$2,610.00	$2,616.00	$6.00	0.2%	0
Oceanstone Fund	$3,382.00	$3,545.00	$163.00	4.8%	4.02%
Fidelity Select Biotechnology Portfolio (1)	$12,205.00	$14,156.00	$1,951.00	16.0%	6.93%
Fidelity Select Biotechnology Portfolio (2)	$13,806.00	$10,475.44	$259.00	2.5%	0
Fidelity Select IT Services Portfolio	$2,775.00	$2,755.00	$(20.00)	-0.7%	-4.64%
Vanguard Wellington Inv	$3,647.00	$3,662.00	$15.00	0.4%	0
Wells Fargo Advantage Core Builder Series M	$1,173.00	$1,176.00	$3.00	0.3%	0.68%
	$212,162.44	$218,570.44	$6,408.00	3.02%	

MOM'S PORTFOLIO FOR APRIL 2013

Name	Purchase $ Value	4-26-13 $ Value	Total Net $ Gain/ Loss	Total Net % Gain/ Loss	Mar to Apr % Change
Altria Group Inc.	$3,349.00	$3,607.00	$258.00	7.70%	4.89%
AT&T Inc.	$3,601.00	$3,704.00	$103.00	2.86%	0.95%
Buckeye Partners LP	$5,611.00	$6,163.00	$552.00	9.84%	0.77%
Caterpillar Inc.	$9,136.00	$8,468.00	$(668.00)	-7.31%	-2.63%
Cleco Corp	$4,418.00	$4,815.00	$397.00	8.99%	2.38%
CMS Energy Corp	$2,645.00	$2,943.00	$298.00	11.27%	5.33%
Compass Diversified Holdings	$1,574.00	$1,678.00	$104.00	6.61%	5.73%
Deluxe Corp	$3,965.00	$3,859.00	$(106.00)	-2.67%	-6.79%
Devon Energy Corp	$5,388.00	$5,361.00	$(27.00)	-0.50%	-4.98%
Dominion Resources Inc.	$5,642.00	$6,101.00	$459.00	8.14%	4.86%
Duke Energy Corporation	$6,925.00	$7,486.00	$561.00	8.10%	3.13%
Enbridge Energy Partners LP	$2,763.00	$2,952.00	$189.00	6.84%	-2.06%
Enterprise Products Partners LP	$5,681.00	$6,079.00	$398.00	7.01%	0.83%
Exxon Mobil Corporation	$8,943.00	$8,800.00	$(143.00)	-1.60%	-2.34%
Frontier Communications Corp	$419.00	$408.00	$(11.00)	-2.63%	2.26%
General Electric Co	$2,319.00	$2,221.00	$(98.00)	-4.23%	-3.94%
Great Plains Energy Inc.	$2,199.00	$2,374.00	$175.00	7.96%	2.37%
Hartford Financial Services Group	$2,368.00	$2,712.00	$344.00	14.53%	5.12%
Hudson City Bancorp	$858.00	$822.00	$(36.00)	-4.20%	-4.86%
Integrys Energy Group	$5,610.00	$6,057.00	$447.00	7.97%	4.14%
Intel Corp	$2,103.00	$2,340.00	$237.00	11.27%	7.14%
Medical Property Trust	$1,483.00	$1,555.00	$72.00	4.86%	-3.05%
Mondelez International	$2,781.00	$3,156.00	$375.00	13.48%	3.07%
National Grid PLC ADR	$5,456.00	$6,239.00	$783.00	14.35%	7.55%
Nisource Inc.	$2,793.00	$3,082.00	$289.00	10.35%	5.04%
Occidental Petroleum Corp	$8,265.00	$8,611.00	$346.00	4.19%	9.88%
Spyglass Resources Corp	$274.00	$198.00	$(76.00)	-27.74%	-30.04%

Name	Purchase $ Value	4-26-13 $ Value	Total Net $ Gain/ Loss	Total Net % Gain/ Loss	Mar to Apr % Change
Pembina Pipeline Corp	$2,821.00	$3,170.00	$349.00	12.37%	0.32%
Pepco Holdings Inc.	$2,053.00	$2,218.00	$165.00	8.04%	3.64%
Philip Morris International Inc.	$9,144.00	$9,531.00	$387.00	4.23%	2.80%
Piedmont Natural Gas Co	$3,265.00	$3,383.00	$118.00	3.61%	2.89%
Principle Financial Group	$3,155.00	$3,574.00	$419.00	13.28%	5.02%
Royal Dutch Shell PLC ADR	$6,578.00	$6,678.00	$100.00	1.52%	2.49%
Scana Corp	$4,906.00	$5,320.00	$414.00	8.44%	3.99%
Southern Co	$4,483.00	$4,794.00	$311.00	6.94%	2.17%
Spectra Energy Corp	$2,881.00	$3,117.00	$236.00	8.19%	1.37%
Teco Energy Inc.	$1,735.00	$1,883.00	$148.00	8.53%	5.67%
US Bancorp	$3,401.00	$3,313.00	$(88.00)	-2.59%	-2.36%
Verizon Communications Inc.	$4,672.00	$5,363.00	$691.00	14.79%	9.11%
Wells Fargo & Co	$3,539.00	$3,788.00	$249.00	7.04%	2.41%
DWS Core Equity Fund	$1,983.00	$2,053.00	$70.00	3.53%	-0.44%
DWS S&P 500 Index Fund	$2,022.00	$2,102.00	$80.00	3.96%	0.91%
DWS Short Duration Fund	$931.00	$929.00	$(2.00)	-0.21%	-0.11%
Fidelity Contrafund	$8,122.00	$8,460.00	$338.00	4.16%	0.81%
Wellesley Income Fund	$2,479.00	$2,529.00	$50.00	2.02%	1.57%
	$174,739.00	$183,996.00	$9,257.00	5.30%	

May

Looking for More Goodies

If you are shopping for common stocks, choose them the way you would buy groceries, not the way you would buy perfume.

—Benjamin Graham

You know you're a novice investor when...

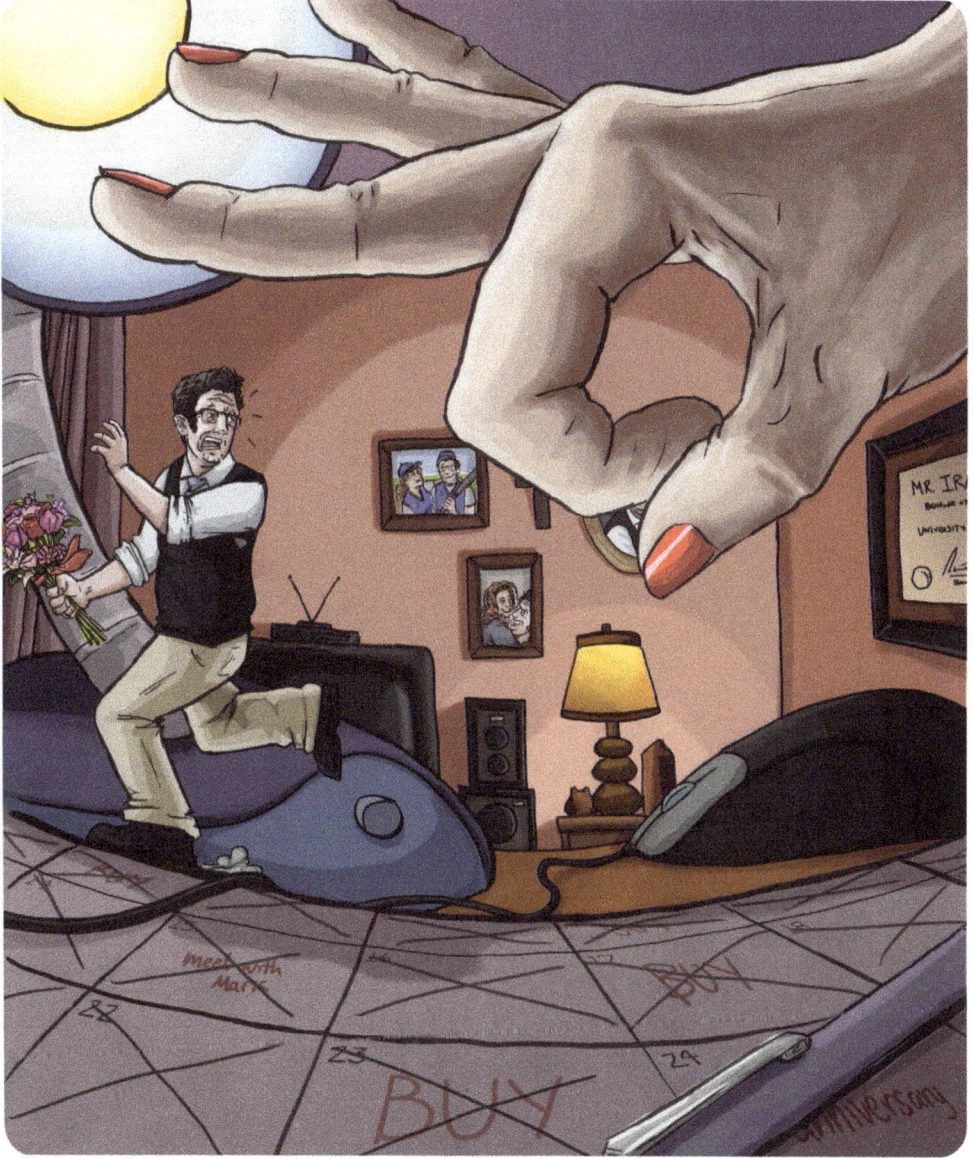

You remember the price of all your buy orders, but not your anniversary date.

From: Ban Krupt
Sent: Tuesday, April 20, 2013 7:47 PM
To: Mark Slauter <markslauter@novice.investor>
Subject: 80% of My Trades in the Next 12 Months Will Make You Money... or I'll Write You a Check for $697

In the last 9 months, we closed 25 winners in a row, with payouts like $4,000, $1,150 and $2,250... several times each month!

If you want to see these kinds of profits, too, all you have to do is make one simple change to your trading strategy...

...starting with your FREE trade right now. It could make you a quick $740.

Uh, yeah. I'll be sure to get on this right away. By the way, the check's in the mail. I can't wait to get my $740 from my free trade. Oh wait, you said could.

May 4, 2013

I came across the 'Financial Visualizations' FINVIZ website that has an interesting stock screener with over 60 filters. Definitely a lot of flexibility in trying to research a stock. Hot damn, I think I found my 'freebie' evaluation tool.

May 18, 2013

The market is up about 200 points over the past few days.

May 31, 2013

Looks like the profit taking was in bloom today; the market is down 200+ points. Crap.

Anyone who's ever invested in the markets knows one key fact: Time is a commodity. You can easily lose hours (or days!) analyzing investments, performance, research, etc. But, how you spend your time is within your control.

To get started, I suggest looking for something that you can relate to already or that has meaning in your life, whether it's clothes, food, or cars. For example, perhaps you love burritos from Chipotle, so start by checking out Chipotle stock. They're your investments, so it doesn't matter what you gravitate toward. But, by starting with companies you already care or know about, you'll maintain your interest in the markets and dedicate whatever time you feel is necessary to tracking them. Once you get to a point where you have a couple of news sources to read, you can easily spend only 20 minutes catching up. And if you're only tracking a few stocks, you can do that in less time than what you spend on social network websites. Then, once you become more sophisticated in your management, you can use websites that help you set up an online account to track your portfolio—so you can get back to the social media feeds. After all, your friends miss you.

WATCHING THE MARKET

The markets are temperamental beasts. One day, you may find things are all peachy keen, and then the very next, you have a rotten egg on your hands—and this fluctuation can even happen within a single day. If the markets were a person, I swear they'd have a personality disorder.

On the last day of April, the market moved up 106 points, dropped 139 points on May 1, only to turn around and rise 130 points on May 2. The very next day, it rose another 141 points to close out the week.

I'd been following Apple for several months, even before I started my game, and was already familiar with what the stock was doing.

The dividend was about two percent, and the company was both very profitable and a real powerhouse in the technology industry. I also felt that there was some additional room for growth in the share price.

The second week opened with the market down five points and oil prices moving up. I was prepared for a potential boost in my Basic Materials or Energy stocks, but nope, these were both mixed bags. But, two of my recent purchases looked good: Alaska Air (ALK) jumped up 5% and Qihoo 360 (QIHU) jumped up 8%. I ended the week feeling good. Nothing like watching a new purchase increase in value. *Hmm, am I beginning to think like an investor?*

By the end of the second week, the Dow reached another historic benchmark by closing above the magical 15k mark, which it hit midweek. Most of my recent acquisitions were up—with Qihoo 360 (QIHU) up 17%! Even though it had no dividend, that wasn't my focus; I chose Qihoo for growth in share price.

As I rolled through the third week of May, I was still suffering with my portfolio's biggest declines: my Basic Materials and Energy holdings. The week concluded with the Dow continuing its upward momentum and my healthcare focus maintained a positive position. I was winning and losing, but I reminded myself that my outlook had to be on how the individual parts perform to make the whole picture. I couldn't help but doubt some of my selections, and I started to hear a popular investing saying taunt me in my head: "Go away in May." Historically, the markets tend to perform poorly in May. *Not this time 'round!*

As the end of May approached, profit-taking seemed to be in bloom. The market moved down more than 200 points on the last day, thanks to some cloudy economic forecasts: concern with a variety of overseas issues, over-valued stocks, and a concern about the Federal Reserve scaling back on its quantitative easing (QE) activity (the massive monthly bond-buying program to get the U.S. out of recession).

While I was disappointed in my declining stocks (who wouldn't be?), I was more than pleased with my winners, in part because I felt that I had dodged the bullet of May's historical sell-off. Although the month ended by dropping 200 points, my view was that my portfolio was still making money and moving toward improving.

CHASING FOR INFORMATION

Research is an ongoing, continuous process when you're watching the markets. In the beginning of May, I found the Financial Visualizations (FINVIZ) website that has an interesting stock screener with over 60 filters. This tool definitely offers a lot of flexibility when trying to research a stock. *I think I found my freebie evaluation tool.* Even if you don't understand all that the website has to offer, I suggest you check it out.

As I prepared for doing research this month, I was also still trying to determine what do with the cash from my earlier sales. I wanted to use a more aggressive approach toward rising share value instead of chasing the dividends. As I originally stated, diversity among the various stock market sectors and stocks with opportunities for growth were part of my objectives. Up until this point, I've had good coverage and a fair degree of stability (and income) between my funds and my dividends. So, with this foundation beneath me, I became a little more comfortable with accepting some additional risk.

When thinking about risk, I felt the market's upward trend prodding me in the back of my mind. Given the market increase at the end of April, I expected to start seeing some profit taking by investors. The timing of a sale or acquisition is always unnerving. I returned back to pounding the beat for opportunities.

I started the month by reviewing information from the sources I follow as well as trying out the new website FINVIZ that I recently found. I use multiple sources because not everyone follows or provides recommendations on the same set of stocks. Since I paid for premium service with Morningstar, I had access to their screening tools. In this instance, I used their premium stock screener to look for those items Morningstar rates high. I also used the other websites to look at current and projected earnings per share (EPS) and the price/earnings ratio (P/E). Both of these contribute to my understanding of growth potential.

	Investor's Business Daily	Morningstar	The Street	Wall Street Journal
Protolabs (PRLB) Industrial sector	Buy	Buy	Hold	Buy (slight)
Alaska Air Group (ALK) Industrial sector	Buy	Buy	Buy	Buy
Qihoo 360 Technology Co., Ltd. ADR (QIHU) Technology sector	No	Buy	Hold	Buy
ARM Holdings (ARMH) Technology sector	Buy	Buy	N/A	Buy & hold (even split)
Cimarex Energy Company (XEC): Energy sector	No	Hold	Buy	Buy & hold (even split)
Navigant Consulting (NCI): Industrials sector	Buy (slight)	Hold	Buy (slight)	Buy (slight)
Mercadolibre, Inc. (MELI): Consumer Cyclical sector	Buy (slight)	Hold	Buy (slight)	Hold
Michael Kors Holdings Ltd (KORS): Consumer Cyclical sector	Buy	Buy	Hold	Buy
Noah Holdings Ltd. ADR (NOAH): Financial Services sector	Buy	Hold	Hold	Hold

NAVIGATING THE PRICE/EARNINGS RATIO (P/E)

Predicting an investment's potential for growth is truly an art—and one that takes experience to do correctly. You can never truly predict the markets. With so many variables out of our control that impact the markets (such as Greece's economic recovery), a fine line exists between true preparation and art.

In general, a high P/E suggests that investors are expecting higher earnings growth in the future compared to companies with a lower P/E. Chasing a high P/E is not necessarily a good idea. Sometimes, a stock becomes "hot" and the share price soars simply because investors see the price rising. In other words, no real intrinsic value exists with the increased share price when investors think they can get on a gravy train, which can falsely inflate the share value.

On the flip side, ignoring stocks with a low P/E is not necessarily good, either. A low P/E doesn't automatically equate to a bad company or a bad investment. In fact, it may represent a stock that's undervalued and therefore possible to buy cheaper. A good example of this is Utilities, which are typically slow or no growth, and sometimes ignored by investors. But think of Utilities this way: Many utility companies exist in an environment where what they charge customers and what they can pay out in dividends is regulated, which makes them more financially stable. Also, their stock prices usually are not subject to wild fluctuations in the market.

With all this said, you should not solely rely on using the EPS and P/E information to understand a stock or make a decision on whether to sell or acquire a stock. This is why I try to set aside time every day to quickly read national and international economic news, as well as look at more specific information on a company I'm interested in. The more information you find, the more well-rounded perspectives you gain.

As I caught up on emails and reports during the third week, I found a nugget of advice in an Investing Daily article stating that reviewing 13F filings is a great way to see what the professionals are doing—at least, those who have a very large investment portfolio. In other words, by reading these filings you can see both the successes and failures of more experienced investors. Pleased with this insight, I filed the advice into my growing library of resources. I then learned that the Securities and Exchange Commission (SEC) has a searchable database, EDGAR, that the public can use to view 13F filings. As I received an ever increasing amount of material and spent time looking for market news, one of the items I started seeing more frequently was references to big investors: folks who have hundreds of millions or billions of dollars invested. Warren Buffet is probably the most widely known.

These big investors must file Form 13F AND they're successful. So I thought to myself, *If I can see where they're putting their money, then it's likely a good thing?* I figure that anything to make my selections and portfolio better is worth looking into.

The drawback on waiting for the 13F filings is that investors submit them quarterly, which means that their investment decisions were probably made two or three months prior to the time you receive information. As a result, you're more likely to hear of a substantial move by a major investor in real time by checking in with the daily news. While 13F filings are not useful for real time or recent information sources, I came away from this resource seeing that they can be another tool for gaining additional insights.

ANALYZING THE PORTFOLIOS

In April, I sold seven stocks; since then, I was looking to expand my holdings in the Financial Services and Healthcare sectors. One of the best outcomes from selling my second Samsung purchase last month was that it returned a ton of cash back to me: $130,000, which equaled about 45% of my entire portfolio cash value. I quickly saw that this value was weighted way too heavily in one item.

Stupid! When thinking of diversity, I'm reminded that it not only applies to buying different stocks within different sectors, but also avoiding having too much cash in just one or two items.

I also began to realize that in order to create a fairer comparison between my portfolio and Mom's portfolio, I thought I should have about the same number of items, rather than fewer. So, using my available fantasy cash, I made some new acquisitions, which also altered the diversity of my portfolio.

As a result of my research, I now owned:

	Sector	Analyst Buy Recommendations	Dividend Yield	10-yr Avg for Revenue Growth	10-yr EPS
BlackRock Inc.	Financial Services	2 of 4	2.6%	32.0%	21.0%
Merck & Co Inc.	Healthcare	3 of 4	3.6%	-0.9%	-4.4%
Pfizer, Inc.	Healthcare	3 of 4	3.4%	6.2%	2.9%
Alaska Air Group	Industrial	4 of 4	0%	7.8%	23.3%[1]
Qihoo 360 Technology Co., Ltd	Technology	3 of 4	0%	16.8%[2]	102.7%[2]
Michael Kors Holdings Ltd	Consumer Cyclical	3 of 4	0%	62.5%[2]	136.4%[3]
Protolabs	Industrial	3 of 4	0%	42.2%[2]	8.9%[3]

1.   5-year average

2.   3-year average

3.   1-year average

While the growth and EPS numbers for Merck and Pfizer weren't great, I've learned through my research that the past few years were hard on some of the larger pharmaceutical companies, particularly as their drugs shifted into the generic brand market.

However, I stood by my belief that healthcare's bigger picture would advance in response to the federal healthcare law. Also, they both had a solid dividend yield.

Meanwhile, on the Chinese markets front, while some folks don't want to invest in China, some Chinese companies were exploding with growth. Whether or not Qihoo continued to grow and mature over time was anyone's guess. But if it did, I say that I had the potential to walk away very happy.

Though a little thin on historical information, Michael Kors was performing well and also added to my Consumer holdings.

With sales and acquisitions in the past several weeks, my portfolio's diversity changed. Excluding mutual funds, this is where Mom and I both started:

Market Sectors	My Portfolio		Mom's Portfolio	
	# of Items	Percentage	# of Items	Percentage
Basic Materials	3	13%	0	0%
Communications	1	4%	3	8%
Consumer Cyclical	2	9%	0	0%
Consumer Defensive	2	4%	3	8%
Energy	5	22%	10	25%
Financial Services	3	13%	5	13%
Healthcare	1	4%	0	0%
Industrials	2	9%	4	10%
Real Estate	0	0%	1	3%
Technology	3	13%	1	3%
Utilities	2	9%	13	33%
	23	100%	40	100%

With all of my changes, this is where we were in our portfolios. Communications Services, Real Estate and Utilities are the only sectors I'd not added to. In addition to the stocks, I had nine funds and Mom had five. I now had a total of 43 items, and she had 46, which meant that my comparison of how I was doing against Mom was more closely aligned. I didn't include the mutual funds in the table of stocks.

Market Sectors	My Portfolio		Mom's Portfolio	
	# of Items	Percentage	# of Items	Percentage
Basic Materials	4	12%	0	0%
Communications	1	3%	3	8%
Consumer Cyclical	5	15%	0	0%
Consumer Defensive	2	6%	3	8%
Energy	7	21%	10	25%
Financial Services	4	12%	5	13%
Healthcare	4	12%	0	0%
Industrials	3	9%	4	10%
Real Estate	0	0%	1	3%
Technology	3	9%	1	3%
Utilities	1	3%	13	33%
	23	100%	40	100%

Percentages do equal 100% due to rounding

MONTH IN REVIEW

Between April 26 and May 31, 2013, the Dow gained 403 points. Things turned around in May as the Dow led both Mom and me, but I stayed on the plus side and was slightly ahead of Mom. *Score!*

	Weekly Return on Investment Stats		
	Dow Jones Industrial Average	Me	Mom
Week 9	6.27%	4.19%	6.93%
Week 10	7.30%	6.32%	6.79%
Week 11	8.97%	5.89%	8.23%
Week 12	8.61%	5.86%	6.44%
Week 13	7.28%	4.43%	4.15%

Overall in May, I had an unrealized gain of $11,862. While my losses were primarily in the Energy and Utilities sectors, the

Consumer Cyclical and Technology sectors improved. Qihoo 360 (QIHU) was turning out to be a killer buy...so far. As for Mom, she had an unrealized gain of $7,243 this month. She experienced the same losses in the Energy and Utilities sectors but also had minor losses in the Industrial sector.

COMPARISON

Looks like I finally got ahead of Mom, but I also experienced wider top-to-bottom fluctuations on individual items. This volatility was due to the fact that some of my items were perceived as faster growth and subject to more activity by traders.

Currently, my portfolio had 21 items that I invested in based on recommendations from the Pros, which was about 49% (22 items were my picks). On a percentage basis, I came out ahead of the Pros this month as 72.7% of my items increased in value, but only 65.7% of the Pros items increased.

DIVIDENDS FOR MAY

I received 17 payments totaling $1,650.84, which averaged $97.11 per payment. Mom received 21 payments for $762.67, which averaged $36.32 per payment.

Having completed my first quarter of investing, I was in fair shape, considering:

o   My earlier sell-off of losses cost me about $22k.

o   My current value was up $11,861.50, and I'd received $2,487.18 in dividends. Better than Mom in both instances.

o   Mom's current value was up $7,243 plus $1,589.57 in dividends.

- I was still facing a loss of about $8k, overall.

- I was about equal with the Pros' picks for increases and decreases.

LESSONS LEARNED

Though my personal pick winners were leading losers this month, I still hadn't made back my earlier losses from sales of about $22k. Had I held onto those investments instead of selling when I did, the total loss would be about $30k, so I was ahead in this regard. I realized that the smart move was to reevaluate the non-performers. I was still looking for items to place on a watch list, but at some point, the list could become too big. As a result, mistakes were more likely to occur, so I decided to take a step back and consider my options for regrouping.

- **The market fluctuates.** Ignore the blips. Eat some food. Have a drink. Don't obsess over market changes. Be aware of them, but remember it's not all that exists in life.

- **There is no bullet train to wealth.** I think this email comment captures this sentiment quite well: "Most people who enter the market with the idea of becoming traders have a feeling of invincibility, superiority and no clue of what they are about to experience. The dream of quick money and financial success can very quickly become a living nightmare."

Though I have no delusion of being a professional trader anytime soon, I do feel an odd sense of superiority and thinking about "quick money." But, I have to recognize that this likely stems from a false sense of security driven by my lack of knowledge and experience. Remembering to keep emotions in check will do wonders for your ability to stay realistic and keep a level head.

The following portfolio tables show what the current value (May 31) is compared to the purchase value. Value is presented in both dollar and percentage terms. The last column has the month-to-month (April to May) change as a percentage to show how items fluctuate monthly compared to the ever lengthening time between the start date and current values.

MY PORTFOLIO FOR MAY 2013

Note: '0' in last column reflects ownership of less than a month.

Name (Pros in italics)	Purchase $ Value	5-31-13 $ Value	Total Net $ Gain/Loss	Total Net % Gain/ Loss	Apr to May % Change
8x8, Inc.	$744.00	$827.00	$83.00	11.2%	11.16%
The AES Corporation	$1,193.00	$1,220.00	$27.00	2.3%	-11.72%
Alaska Air Group	$6,273.00	$5,682.00	$(591.00)	-9.4%	0
Alliance Resource Partners LP	$6,725.00	$ 7,228.00	$503.00	7.5%	-2.07%
Apple Inc.	$39,354.00	$44,974.00	$5,620.00	14.3%	-0.05%
BlackRock Inc.	$26,500.00	$27,920.00	$1,420.00	5.4%	2.90%
Coca-Cola Co	$3,870.00	$3,999.00	$129.00	3.3%	-5.33%
Consolidated Communications	$1,637.00	$1,701.00	$64.00	3.9%	-5.60%
El Paso Pipeline Partners LP	$4,140.00	$4,109.00	$(31.00)	-0.7%	-3.32%
The GEO Group Inc.	$3,448.00	$3,482.00	$34.00	1.0%	-7.96%
GlaxoSmithKline PLC ADR (1)	$4,422.00	$5,177.00	$755.00	17.1%	1.03%
GlaxoSmithKline PLC ADR (2)	$4,847.00	$5,177.00	$330.00	6.8%	1.03%
Great Northern Iron Ore (2)	$6,944.00	$7,003.00	$59.00	0.8%	-2.23%
Home Loan Servicing Solutions	$2,302.00	$2,284.00	$(18.00)	-0.8%	1.02%
Inventure Foods, Inc.	$726.00	$752.00	$26.00	3.6%	0.80%

Name (Pros in italics)	Purchase $ Value	5-31-13 $ Value	Total Net $ Gain/Loss	Total Net % Gain/ Loss	Apr to May % Change
Kinder Morgan Energy Partners LP (1)	$8,672.00	$8,340.00	$(332.00)	-3.8%	-4.32%
Kinder Morgan Energy Partners LP (2)	$9,025.00	$8,340.00	$(685.00)	-7.6%	-4.32%
Legacy Reserves, LP	$2,773.00	$2,650.00	$(123.00)	-4.4%	1.49%
Linn Energy	$3,753.00	$3,290.00	$(463.00)	-12.3%	-14.41%
Macy's	$4,067.00	$4,834.00	$767.00	18.9%	4.56%
Merck & Co Inc.	$4,782.00	$4,670.00	$(112.00)	-2.3%	2.26%
Michael Kors Holdings Ltd	$5,804.00	$6,282.00	$478.00	8.2%	0
Northern Tier Energy LP Class A (1)	$2,950.00	$2,375.00	$(575.00)	-19.5%	-6.61%
Oaktree Capital Group, LLC	$5,013.00	$5,215.00	$202.00	4.0%	-2.74%
Pfizer Inc.	$3,043.00	$2,723.00	$(320.00)	-10.5%	-5.97%
Proto Labs Inc.	$5,505.00	$5,524.00	$19.00	0.3%	0
Prudential PLC ADR	$3,349.00	$3,381.00	$32.00	1.0%	-6.63%
PVR Partners LP	$2,285.00	$2,576.00	$291.00	12.7%	2.02%
Qihoo 360 Technology Co., Ltd.	$3,440.00	$4,381.00	$941.00	27.4%	0
Seaspan Corp	$1,930.00	$2,292.00	$362.00	18.8%	1.24%
Sunoco Logistics Partners LP	$6,258.00	$6,054.00	$(204.00)	-3.3%	0.10%
Terra Nitrogen Company	$23,461.00	$21,178.00	$(2,283.00)	-9.7%	3.81%
TJX Companies	$4,498.00	$5,061.00	$563.00	12.5%	2.14%
Union Pacific Corp	$14,783.00	$15,462.00	$679.00	4.6%	3.47%

Name (Pros in italics)	Purchase $ Value	5-31-13 $ Value	Total Net $ Gain/Loss	Total Net % Gain/ Loss	Apr to May % Change
Akre Focus Fund Retail	$1,630.00	$1,829.00	$199.00	12.2%	2.35%
Delaware Healthcare I	$1,355.00	$1,571.00	$216.00	15.9%	4.73%
Oakmark Global I	$2,610.00	$2,738.00	$128.00	4.9%	2.43%
Oceanstone Fund	$3,753.00	$3,753.00	$371.00	11.0%	5.51%
Fidelity Select Biotechnology Portfolio (1)	$14,631.00	$14,631.00	$2,426.00	19.9%	2.70%
Fidelity Select Biotechnology Portfolio (2)	$10,826.94	$10,826.94	$610.50	6.0%	2.70%
Fidelity Select IT Services Portfolio	$2,985.00	$2,985.00	$210.00	7.6%	3.72%
Vanguard Wellington Inv	$3,707.00	$3,707.00	$60.00	1.6%	0.22%
Wells Fargo Advantage Core Builder Series M	$1,167.00	$1,167.00	$(6.00)	-0.5%	-1.02%
	$267,509.44	**$279,370.94**	**$11,861.50**	**4.43%**	

Mom's Portfolio for May 2013

Name	Purchase $ Value	5-31-13 $ Value	Total Net $ Gain/Loss	Total Net % Gain/ Loss	Apr to May % Change
Altria Group Inc.	$3,349.00	$3,610.00	$261.00	7.8%	0.08%
AT&T Inc.	$3,601.00	$3,499.00	$(102.00)	-2.8%	-5.53%
Buckeye Partners LP	$5,611.00	$6,614.00	$1,003.00	17.9%	7.32%
Caterpillar Inc.	$9,136.00	$8,580.00	$(556.00)	-6.1%	1.32%
Cleco Corp	$4,418.00	$4,551.00	$133.00	3.0%	-5.48%
CMS Energy Corp	$2,645.00	$2,695.00	$50.00	1.9%	-8.43%
Compass Diversified Holdings	$1,574.00	$1,725.00	$151.00	9.6%	2.80%
Deluxe Corp	$3,965.00	$3,740.00	$(225.00)	-5.7%	-3.08%
Devon Energy Corp	$5,388.00	$5,685.00	$297.00	5.5%	6.04%
Dominion Resources Inc.	$5,642.00	$5,655.00	$13.00	0.2%	-7.31%
Duke Energy Corporation	$6,925.00	$6,693.00	$(232.00)	-3.4%	-10.59%
Enbridge Energy Partners LP	$2,763.00	$2,951.00	$188.00	6.8%	-0.03%
Enterprise Products Partners LP	$5,681.00	$5,939.00	$258.00	4.5%	-2.30%
Exxon Mobil Corporation	$8,943.00	$9,047.00	$104.00	1.2%	2.81%
Frontier Communications Corp	$419.00	$414.00	$(5.00)	-1.2%	1.47%
General Electric Co	$2,319.00	$2,332.00	$13.00	0.6%	5.00%
Great Plains Energy Inc.	$2,199.00	$2,257.00	$58.00	2.6%	-4.93%
Hartford Financial Services Group	$2,368.00	$3,063.00	$695.00	29.3%	12.94%
Hudson City Bancorp	$858.00	$850.00	$(8.00)	-0.9%	3.41%
Integrys Energy Group	$5,610.00	$5,753.00	$143.00	2.5%	-5.02%

Name	Purchase $ Value	5-31-13 $ Value	Total Net $ Gain/Loss	Total Net % Gain/ Loss	Apr to May % Change
Intel Corp	$2,103.00	$2,428.00	$325.00	15.5%	3.76%
Medical Property Trust	$1,483.00	$1,484.00	$1.00	0.1%	-4.57%
Mondelez International	$2,781.00	$2,948.00	$167.00	6.0%	-6.59%
National Grid PLC ADR	$5,456.00	$5,956.00	$500.00	9.2%	-4.54%
Nisource Inc.	$2,793.00	$2,873.00	$80.00	2.9%	-6.78%
Occidental Petroleum Corp	$8,265.00	$9,207.00	$942.00	11.4%	6.92%
Spyglass Resources Corp	$274.00	$208.00	$(66.00)	-24.1%	5.05%
Pembina Pipeline Corp	$2,821.00	$3,129.00	$308.00	10.9%	-1.29%
Pepco Holdings Inc.	$2,053.00	$2,077.00	$24.00	1.2%	-6.36%
Philip Morris International Inc.	$9,144.00	$9,091.00	$(53.00)	-0.6%	-4.62%
Piedmont Natural Gas Co	$3,265.00	$3,379.00	$114.00	3.5%	-0.12%
Principle Financial Group	$3,155.00	$3,785.00	$630.00	20.0%	5.90%
Royal Dutch Shell PLC ADR	$6,578.00	$6,637.00	$59.00	0.9%	-0.61%
Scana Corp	$4,906.00	$5,044.00	$138.00	2.8%	-5.19%
Southern Co	$4,483.00	$4,390.00	$(93.00)	-2.1%	-8.43%
Spectra Energy Corp	$2,881.00	$3,057.00	$176.00	6.1%	-1.92%
Teco Energy Inc.	$1,735.00	$1,761.00	$26.00	1.5%	-6.48%
US Bancorp	$3,401.00	$3,506.00	$105.00	3.1%	5.83%
Verizon Communications Inc.	$4,672.00	$4,848.00	$176.00	3.8%	-9.60%
Wells Fargo & Co	$3,539.00	$4,055.00	$516.00	14.6%	7.05%
DWS Core Equity Fund	$1,983.00	$2,137.00	$154.00	7.8%	4.09%

Name	Purchase $ Value	5-31-13 $ Value	Total Net $ Gain/Loss	Total Net % Gain/ Loss	Apr to May % Change
DWS S&P 500 Index Fund	$2,022.00	$2,171.00	$149.00	7.4%	3.28%
DWS Short Duration Fund	$931.00	$927.00	$(4.00)	-0.4%	-0.22%
Fidelity Contrafund	$8,122.00	$8,714.00	$592.00	7.3%	3.00%
Wellesley Income Fund	$2,479.00	$2,517.00	$38.00	1.5%	-0.47%
	$174,739.00	**$183,996.00**	**$7,243.00**	**4.15%**	

JUNE

THE ROLLER COASTER SHOW

*Investing is like sex. Past results are no guarantee
of future performance.*

—Mark Slauter

You know you're a novice investor when...

Your investment charts move like a hooker's skirt.

From:	Jeremy Astro
Sent:	Saturday, April 14, 2013 3:12 PM
To:	Mark Slauter <markslauter@novice.investor>
Subject:	The Jetsons Is Now A Reality—And It's Your Ticket To Big Profits!

"What once seemed conceivable only on The Jetsons is real... The future of American homes is now." —USA Today

Dude,
What a great email. You know George personally? Cool....

Regards,
Mark

June 20, 2013

Holy crap! The market is off about 560 points in 2 days. The Federal Reserve intimated they will be reducing the bond buying if the economy continues to improve. Here's the dilemma: I like what I have and don't want to sell—emotion says hold, but the head says sell; think I'll sell on those that are still up. Maybe this will afford me an opportunity to buy some of them back cheaper. Part of the problem is the flight mentality of investors... "Well, if others are selling then I'd better sell too!"

Of course, this also means I'll have to find other new stocks to invest in. With bond rates creeping up a little I would expect my bond fund to improve but it has continued to fall. If I sell the winners, I'm stuck with the losers.

June 21, 2013

Decided to hold off on mass sale of equities thinking that my emotion was driving the decisions. Yesterday, I identified 20 items that could be sold, which would be about one-half of my portfolio. Since I decided not to sell, I wanted to know what the outcome could have been - keeping in mind that I like what I own and part of my consideration was to buy back what was sold.

For the 20 items I had marked to sell (and repurchase), here's what could have happened:

- 4 (20%) of the 20 did not get to my sell price. I anticipated another drop in share price and set the sell price below Thursday's close price. Not only do I still own them, but they increased.
- 8 (40%) of the 20 did hit my sell price. However, they turned around and closed above my sell price. Depending on what the market does in the coming days and weeks, it's possible that my desire to repurchase them would have been costlier than holding onto them in the first place.
- 8 (40%) of the 20 did hit my sell price...and then continued to decline.

The bottom line: 60% increased and 40% decreased. Holding was the better choice...whew!

In order to achieve a balance in your portfolio (and really, overall in life), it's important to have proper perspective. Selling at what may appear to be the appropriate time does not always result in your intended outcome. And just because someone says gadgets from the Jetson's is a reality, doesn't make it real. Look beyond the sales pitch and daily market fluctuations before making a decision.

WATCHING THE MARKET

June picked up where May left off, and the first week was choppy at best. June 3 was another roller coaster day, but the Dow came out on top, gaining 138 points. On the same day, the Institute for Supply Management (ISM) also released its report showing that the manufacturing activity index fell to 49.0 from April's reading of 50.7 (readings above 50 are seen as positive.). This reading was worse than expected and the lowest since November 2012. As an indication of economic activity, traders may view this as a reason to sell or reposition their investments. After all this action, the market closed the first week by dropping 217 points on June 6 and bouncing back up by 80 points on the 7th, returning to just over the 15000 mark.

By the second week of June, volatility was reaching a few-weeks-long high. Investors were quite concerned with what the Federal Reserve would do regarding the monthly bond buying program known as quantitative easing (QE), which has been the factor in keeping lending rates historically low. Once the Fed reduces or stops the QE effort, interest rates would rise, meaning borrowing money costs more. In looking ahead, when the Fed starts tapering QE, I have every expectation that investors will grab their profits. When this happens, the market value will drop, which means that my stocks will have less value, which means that I make less profit, which means my wife will be mad that I didn't sell earlier, which means I'm not as happy as I could be.

In other words, this scenario can create a whole lotta *which means*.

Somehow, even in this volatile environment, the market rose 181 points on June 13. *Go figure.* On the 14th, the second week closed with the market dropping 106 points, appearing to be just another downhill stretch of the roller coaster. I couldn't find any particular economic reason for this decline and suspected that there weren't many undervalued stocks available, since selection was fairly thin. My takeaway from the whole experience was that once the Fed introduced the idea of reducing its bond-buying mania, folks decided to take profits where they could.

As I transitioned from the third to fourth week of June, the market dropped another 148 points on the 24th as a reaction to news regarding China's monetary policy (alleged currency manipulation) and our own Federal Reserve statements from the previous week. Although the Dow gained about 265 points through the week, it fell back again on June 28 to close out the month below the magical 15000 at 14910.

June was definitely one wild ride.

CHASING FOR INFORMATION

By this point in the process, I was getting more used to seeing the charts available online and the metrics of individual stocks—but was still struggling to fully understand what I was looking at. So, I decided I must lay out some of the key terms I needed to know, as well as a series of charts regarding one of my stocks. (Note: Never view metrics in isolation. All details work together to form the bigger picture you need to pay attention to.)

The definitions listed below (from Morningstar.com and Investopedia.com.) are the typical key metrics you'll find on websites when you pull up an individual stock. Remember, details found from metrics are not the only factors to consider but do hold primary relevance.

o **Price/Earnings (P/E) Ratio:** A valuation ratio of a company's current share price compared to its per-share earnings.

I'm interested in this because... A high number typically indicates that investors hold a high expectation of positive future growth; a low number typically indicates that investors hold low expectations. But watch out: A number that's too high could signify an unjustified expectation. A number too low may signify an unjustified perception.

o **Price/Book Ratio:** Used to compare a stock's market value to its book value.

I'm interested in this because... If the ratio is a high number, then it's likely that the stock may be overvalued from a market perspective. If the number is lower, it may indicate the company is undervalued from a market perspective and is therefore a good buying opportunity.

○ **Price/Sales Ratio** (Note: This may be represented as price/sales TTM.): An indicator of the value placed on each dollar of a company's sales or revenues.

I'm interested in this because... If Company A's peers (which should be within the same industry) are trading at an average P/S ratio of 1.5, compared with Company A's 2.2, it suggests a premium valuation for Company A. One reason for this could be that the future revenue growth for Company A is expected to be better than what's expected for its peers.

○ **Net Margin** (Note: This may be represented as Net Margin% TTM.): The ratio of net profits to revenues for a company or business segment—typically expressed as a percentage—that shows how much of each dollar earned by the company translates into profits for the preceding 12 months.

I'm interested in this because... It tells me how much money the company makes after expenses. For example, if a company sells an item for $10 but it costs $9 to make, then their profit is $1 after expenses or 10%. If I was interested in a company and could see that its net margin declined from 7.7% to 2.9% over a four-year period (with the most recent year showing a further decline to 2.5%) it may indicate that the company is becoming less profitable. And, if it is becoming less profitable, then the potential for me to make money by investing in it diminishes.

○ **Return on Assets (ROA)** (Note: This may be represented as ROA TTM.): The percentage a company earns on its assets in a given year (Year 1, 2, etc.) and indicates how much profit a company generates on its asset base. The company's net income is found in the annual income statement. The company's total assets are found in the annual balance sheet.

I'm interested in this because… The better the company, the more profit it generates as a percentage of its assets. For example, a major software company was earning 20% on its assets, which means that for every $1 of assets, the company was able to produce $0.20 of profits.

○ **Return On Equity (ROE)** (Note: This may be represented as ROE TTM.): The percentage a company earns on its total equity in a given year (Year 1, 2, etc.) and indicates how much profit a company generates on the money shareholders have invested in the firm.

I'm interested in this because… For example, a major pharmaceutical company earned 37% on its shareholders' equity. This means that for every $1 shareholders had invested in the company, the company produced $0.37 worth of profit.

○ **Operating Margin** (Note: This may be represented as Operating Margin% TTM.): A measurement of what proportion of a company's revenue remains after paying for variable production costs, such as wages, raw materials, etc.

I'm interested in this because… A healthy operating margin is required for a company to be able to pay for its fixed costs, such as interest on debt.

There are other criteria you can consider when looking into a stock, but you're likely to see these stats most often. Now that I've listed these out, the next section shows how I attempted to use the information available to me from Morningstar.

PUTTING INFORMATION INTO ACTION

In May, I noticed that I had a dilemma with my Terra Nitrogen stock. So far, it was losing money from the share price declining. In retrospect, I asked myself if I should have made the purchase to begin with. I questioned my judgment. Now that I was reevaluating Terra Nitrogen, I was also looking at other stocks in the same industry. How would you approach this?

Metric	Industry Avg	Terra Nitrogen	Monsanto	Syngenta
Price/Earnings TTM	9.3	4.4	22.6	19.4
Price/Book	3.1	11.7	4.3	4.2
Price/Sales TTM	2.0	4.7	3.9	2.6
Rev Growth (3 Yr Avg)	4.9	15.4	4.9	8.9
Net Income Growth (3 Yr Avg)	-0.8	98.1	-0.8	10.0
Operating Margin% TTM	27.1	74.7	25.2	16.1
Net Margin% TTM	18.3	105.4	17.2	13.2
ROA TTM	13.6	230.3	12.6	10.2
ROE TTM	27.7	302.2	21.6	23.1
Debt/Equity	0.3	—	0.2	0.3

	10-yr Average for Revenue Growth	10-yr EPS	Growth Rating	Profitability Rating	Dividend Yield	Analyst Rating
Terra Nitrogen	9.1%	48.37%	A	C	8.18%	None
Monsanto	11.59%	18.57%	C	D	1.35%	Buy
Syngenta AG	8.65%	48.14	C	C	1.66%	None

What I noted was that Terra Nitrogen showed a better return on assets, return on equity, better margins, and growth. These tend to be driven by past performance. All three stocks had a low debt amount.

That left me looking at the price/earnings, price/book, and price/sales, which were also historical as presented above, but with a twist. Investors tend to make investments based on what they expect the future to be. If they expect the price of oil to be higher in three months, then buying the shares now makes more sense (and cents!), because they're less expensive. However, this rationale only plays out if the price of oil really does increase and share prices really do go up. With Monsanto and Syngenta, investors appeared to have higher expectations for future earnings and were willing to pay a higher share price.

For the price/book line item, Terra Nitrogen investors appeared to be paying a premium over the other two as compared to the industry average. In other words, if Terra Nitrogen sold at the exact moment I was analyzing its metrics, the value of its shares would be 11.7 times greater than the company's actual book value, which could be viewed as the company being over-valued based on share price. For the price/sales line item there was a similar situation where Terra Nitrogen investors appeared to be paying a premium. In the above table, the value of Terra Nitrogen shares showed as 4.7 times greater than their sales.

Bottom line? I saw Terra Nitrogen as historically more profitable than Monsanto or Syngenta and with higher returns on assets (ROA), equity (ROE), and on the margin percentages. However, investors put more confidence in Monsanto and Syngenta for future earnings (P/E).

Well, one of us was wrong—and I suspected it was me.

ANALYZING THE PORTFOLIOS

Since I wasn't in this experiment for day trading, I focused my concern on longer term economic conditions. However, by tracking my investments in a weekly format, I was able to look for trending results. Obviously, the websites provided information in charts, but doing it my way ensured I got what I wanted, because I could see the data in a way that made sense to me. This is a very helpful tool to keep in mind: When you keep track of information in a way that you understand the data is more useful.

During June, I noticed that I had a few items drop significantly from what would have been very profitable highs. And, I had a few items that would have been profitable had I been more attuned with daily fluctuations and patterns. For example, I purchased Alaska Air Group (ALK) at $62.73 and saw the following performance during the first three weeks that I owned it:

o   End of first week, ALK was up 5.5%.

o   End of second week, ALK was still up 4%.

o   End of the third week, ALK was down -6.4%.

When assessing performance and whether to hold, some pros recommend a 10% rule: Minimize your losses at -10% or take your gains at +10%. So, if I'd sold ALK after the first week, I would have had a profit of $342 (excluding taxes and trade transaction fees). But, with the 10% rule in mind, at week six, ALK was down -10.7%. *Should I hold? Should I sell?* I didn't receive any dividend for this stock. And in relation to the industry, this stock was a better buy—and the analysts were being consistent in their buy recommendations. *So many voices to listen to!* Ultimately, I decided to hold onto it for a longer period of time.

As the month progressed, I was looking at selling my stake in:

o   Apple (AAPL).

o   Michael Kors Holdings Ltd (KORS).

o   Protolabs Inc. (PRLB).

o   Qihoo 360 Technology Co (QIHU).

o   Union Pacific Corp (UNP).

Only Apple and Union Pacific had dividends. Though bond funds were generally taking a beating during this time period, the Wells Fargo CoreBuilder Series M (WFCMX) fund was still doing well compared to other bond funds. I also noticed that Apple was on another downward trend that could support buying back shares at a reasonable price.

I decided to search for suitable replacements that would support my objective of growth if I sold the other items. This led me to the following potential new opportunities:

o   HCP Inc. (Real Estate—focused on healthcare properties).

o   NTT DoCoMo Inc. (Communications Services).

○ Bank of Nova Scotia (Financial Services).

○ British American Tobacco PLC (Consumer Defensive).

○ BHP Billiton PLC ADR (Basic Materials).

○ Sonoco Products Company (Consumer Cyclical).

I felt driven to change my portfolio in response to avoid declining share value. *Wait, what am I doing?...reconsider the above. Is this the smart move or a response to an apparent death spiral from market volatility? The market changes, and I have to decide the best course of action.*

Okay, deep breath...

I decided to stick with the sale of Apple, because it made sense to me, and sell Union Pacific, so I could take the profit and look for another opportunity. I also decided to stick with $40k reserve from these sales to repurchase Apple because I believed it was a strong company and any fall in share price would be temporary. The remaining funds were applied to the purchase of:

	HCP Inc.	NTT DoCoMo Inc.	Bank of Nova Scotia	Sonoco Products Company
Sector	Real Estate	Communication Services	Financial Services	Consumer Cyclical
10-yr EPS	7.01%	-3.48%	12.21%	5.46%
10-yr Average for Revenue Growth	18.12%	-1.97%	5.52%	3.23%
Dividend Yield	5.1%	3.6%	4.1%	4.1%
Analyst Buy Recommendations	1 of 4	1 of 4	3 of 4	1 of 4

While the numbers for NTT DoCoMo Inc. weren't good, they weren't necessarily bad either when I looked at similar companies. Buying this was a little riskier than the other three acquisitions here. After acquiring these new items, I still had enough cash to repurchase Apple when the price dropped enough on June 25 for me to buy at $395/share for $39,500—and I even had a little cash remaining.

MONTH IN REVIEW

	Weekly Return on Investment Stats		
	Dow Jones Industrial Average	Me	Mom
Week 14	8.22%	4.92%	4.58%
Week 15	6.96%	3.40%	4.21%
Week 16	5.03%	0.42%	1.95%
Week 17	5.81%	1.52%	3.38%

Between May 31 and June 28, 2013, the Dow lost 206 points. Both Mom and I fell farther behind the DJIA.

Overall, in June I had an unrealized gain of $4,057. Generally, there were losses across the board, though Energy seemed to improve a bit as well as a couple of other individual stocks. Qihoo took a substantial leap upward. Mom had an unrealized gain of $5,900 this month. Mom experienced the same losses as me, but some of her Industrial stocks gained a little.

COMPARISON

Looks like I was beat up more than Mom this month as we're both behind the DJIA, but mine really moved down.

Currently, my portfolio had 21 items that I invested in based on recommendations from the Pros, which was about 45% (26 items were my picks). On a percentage basis, I came out ahead of the

Pros this month as 68.0% of my items increased in value, but only 61.9% of the Pros items increased.

DIVIDENDS FOR JUNE

I received 9 payments totaling $615.35, which averaged $68.37 per payment and Mom received 20 payments for $718.66, which averaged $35.93 per payment. I did substantially better than Mom on my dividends this month. However, I still had a long way to go to recoup my earlier losses. My decision to chase after Samsung when I started really, really screwed me.

LESSONS LEARNED

Simply put: I was not ready for June. This month became hellacious on my sense of well-being, and I felt like a rat tied to the mizzenmast on a sinking ship! If I had Buffet's cash position, I'd probably be less skittish about my position. Of course, if I had Buffet's financial head, I'd probably be doing something else right now.

And in typical life-goes-on fashion, we all have other things that require our attention. Here we were, my sister and I, 10 months after Dad's death, still working on getting accounts straight, still working on getting Mom's medications and health plan into a stable fashion, trying to sell a house that had lost about 35% of its sale value due to the housing crisis and in an area where no one was really buying houses. Life always dishes up something to divert your attention. But, I found that by making reviewing my financial situation a regular activity, I was able to create a new habit that will ultimately provide a higher degree of financial security.

- **Always question the data and the pundits!** Different professionals have different opinions and perspectives. Find second and third opinions before making decisions.

○ **Be happy but wary.** You can always find something lurking behind the shadows. There's no reason for paranoia, but do pay attention.

○ **The market can be a scary place.** It will test your nerves, your resolve, and your confidence. Just think for a moment how you might feel when your $1000 investment is only worth $750. Now imagine it's a month later and your investment is worth $1250. Whether you invest on your own or through a broker, you're very likely to have this experience. Finding patience and calm during the market mayhem becomes essential.

○ **Have a valid reason for buying.** You have to live with the consequences. These are your choices, which affect your life in one way or another. Be sure you always consider the possible outcomes. Try focusing on long- term outcomes versus short-term gratifications. Identifying and evaluating your options and outcomes will help you improve your financial health.

Emotions are a strong factor in investing. If you see the market fall by several hundred points and watch your selections go down as well, you can't help but feel a desire to do something. By acquiring resolve and confidence in your decisions, you'll go a long way toward finding valid reasons for the decisions you make.

The following portfolio tables show what the current value (June 28) is compared to the purchase value. Value is presented in both dollar and percentage terms. The last column has the month-to-month (May to June) change as a percentage to show how items fluctuate monthly compared to the ever lengthening time between the start date and current values.

MY PORTFOLIO FOR JUNE 2013

Note: '0' in last column reflects ownership of less than a month.

Name (Pros in italics)	Purchase $ Value	6-28-13 $ Value	Total Net $ Gain/Loss	Total Net % Gain/Loss	May to June % Change
8x8, Inc.	$744.00	$824.00	$80.00	10.8%	-0.36%
The AES Corporation	$1,193.00	$1,199.00	$6.00	0.5%	-1.72%
Alaska Air Group	$6,273.00	$5,200.00	$(1,073.00)	-17.1%	-8.48%
Alliance Resource Partners LP	$6,725.00	$7,063.00	$338.00	5.0%	-2.28%
Apple Inc. (2)	$39,354.00	$39,604.00	$104.00	0.3%	0
Bank of Nova Scotia	$5,341.00	$5,355.00	$14.00	0.3%	0
BlackRock Inc.	$26,821.00	$25,685.00	$(815.00)	-3.1%	-8.01%
Coca-Cola Co	$3,870.00	$4,011.00	$141.00	3.6%	0.30%
Consolidated Communications	$1,637.00	$1,741.00	$104.00	6.4%	2.35%
El Paso Pipeline Partners LP	$4,140.00	$4,367.00	$227.00	5.5%	6.28%
The GEO Group Inc.	$3,448.00	$3,395.00	$(53.00)	-1.5%	-2.50%
GlaxoSmithKline PLC ADR (1)	$4,422.00	$4,997.00	$575.00	13.0%	-3.48%
GlaxoSmithKline PLC ADR (2)	$4,847.00	$4,997.00	$150.00	3.1%	-3.48%
Great Northern Iron Ore (2)	$6,944.00	$6,890.00	$(54.00)	-0.8%	-1.61%
HCP Inc.	$4,325.00	$4,544.00	$219.00	5.1%	0

Name (Pros in italics)	Purchase $ Value	6-28-13 $ Value	Total Net $ Gain/Loss	Total Net % Gain/Loss	May to June % Change
Home Loan Servicing Solutions	$2,302.00	$2,397.00	$95.00	4.1%	4.95%
Inventure Foods, Inc.	$726.00	$836.00	$110.00	15.2%	11.17%
Kinder Morgan Energy Partners LP (1)	$8,672.00	$8,540.00	$(132.00)	-1.5%	2.40%
Kinder Morgan Energy Partners LP (2)	$9,025.00	$8,540.00	$(485.00)	-5.4%	2.40%
Legacy Reserves, LP	$2,773.00	$2,660.00	$(113.00)	-4.1%	0.38%
Linn Energy	$3,753.00	$3,318.00	$(435.00)	-11.6%	0.85%
Macy's	$4,067.00	$4,800.00	$733.00	18.0%	-0.70%
Merck & Co Inc.	$4,782.00	$4,645.00	$(137.00)	-2.9%	-0.54%
Michael Kors Holdings Ltd	$5,804.00	$6,202.00	$398.00	6.9%	-1.27%
Northern Tier Energy LP Class A (1)	$2,950.00	$2,402.00	$(548.00)	-18.6%	1.14%
NTT DoCoMo Inc.	$1,505.00	$1,565.00	$60.00	4.0%	0
Oaktree Capital Group, LLC	$5,013.00	$5,255.00	$242.00	4.8%	0.77%
Pfizer Inc.	$3,043.00	$2,801.00	$(242.00)	-8.0%	2.86%
Proto Labs Inc.	$5,505.00	$6,497.00	$992.00	18.0%	17.61%
Prudential PLC ADR	$3,349.00	$3,272.00	$(77.00)	-2.3%	-3.22%
PVR Partners LP	$2,285.00	$2,730.00	$445.00	19.5%	5.98%
Qihoo 360 Technology Co., Ltd.	$3,440.00	$4,617.00	$1,177.00	34.2%	5.39%
Seaspan Corp	$1,930.00	$2,075.00	$145.00	7.5%	-9.47%
Sonoco Products Co	$3,407.00	$3,457.00	$50.00	1.5%	0

Name (Pros in italics)	Purchase $ Value	6-28-13 $ Value	Total Net $ Gain/Loss	Total Net % Gain/Loss	May to June % Change
Sunoco Logistics Partners LP	$6,258.00	$6,395.00	$137.00	2.2%	5.63%
Terra Nitrogen Company	$23,461.00	$21,399.00	$(2,062.00)	-8.8%	1.04%
TJX Companies	$4,498.00	$5,006.00	$508.00	11.3%	-1.09%
Akre Focus Fund Retail	$1,630.00	$1,816.00	$186.00	11.4%	-0.71%
Delaware Healthcare I	$1,355.00	$1,568.00	$213.00	15.7%	-0.19%
Oakmark Global I	$2,610.00	$2,667.00	$57.00	2.2%	-2.59%
Oceanstone Fund	$3,753.00	$3,765.00	$383.00	11.3%	0.32%
Fidelity Select Biotechnology Portfolio (1)	$14,631.00	$14,175.00	$1,970.00	16.1%	-3.12%
Fidelity Select Biotechnology Portfolio (2)	$10,826.94	$10,489.50	$273.06	2.7%	-3.12%
Fidelity Select IT Services Portfolio	$2,985.00	$2,990.00	$215.00	7.7%	0.17%
Vanguard Wellington Inv	$3,707.00	$3,633.00	$(14.00)	-0.4%	-2.00%
Wells Fargo Advantage Core Builder Series M	$1,167.00	$1,123.00	$(50.00)	-4.3%	-3.77%
	$267,540.44	$271,507.50	$4,057.06	1.52%	

Mom's Portfolio for June 2013

Name	Purchase $ Value	6-28-13 $ Value	Total Net $ Gain/Loss	Total Net % Gain/ Loss	May to June % Change
Altria Group	$3,349.00	$3,499.00	$150.00	4.48%	-3.07%
AT&T Inc.	$3,601.00	$3,540.00	$(61.00)	-1.69%	1.17%
Buckeye Partners LP	$5,611.00	$7,016.00	$1,405.00	25.04%	6.08%
Caterpillar Inc.	$9,136.00	$8,249.00	$(887.00)	-9.71%	-3.86%
Cleco Corp	$4,418.00	$4,643.00	$225.00	5.09%	2.02%
CMS Energy Corp	$2,645.00	$2,717.00	$72.00	2.72%	0.82%
Compass Securities	$1,574.00	$1,753.00	$179.00	11.37%	1.62%
Deluxe Corp	$3,965.00	$3,465.00	$(500.00)	-12.61%	-7.35%
Devon Energy Corp	$5,388.00	$5,188.00	$(200.00)	-3.71%	-8.74%
Dominion Res Inc. VA	$5,642.00	$5,682.00	$40.00	0.71%	0.48%
Duke Energy	$6,925.00	$6,750.00	$(175.00)	-2.53%	0.85%
Enbridge Energy Partners	$2,763.00	$3,049.00	$286.00	10.35%	3.32%
Enterprise Products	$5,681.00	$6,215.00	$534.00	9.40%	4.65%
Exxon Mobile	$8,943.00	$9,035.00	$92.00	1.03%	-0.13%
Frontier Communications Corp	$419.00	$405.00	$(14.00)	-3.34%	-2.17%
General Electric	$2,319.00	$2,319.00	-	0.00%	-0.56%
Great Plains Energy	$2,199.00	$2,254.00	$55.00	2.50%	-0.13%
Hartford Financial Services Group	$2,368.00	$3,092.00	$724.00	30.57%	0.95%
Hudson City Bancorp	$858.00	$918.00	$60.00	6.99%	8.00%
Integrys Energy Group	$5,610.00	$5,853.00	$243.00	4.33%	1.74%
Intel Corp	$2,103.00	$2,423.00	$320.00	15.22%	-0.21%
Medical Property Trust	$1,483.00	$1,432.00	$(51.00)	-3.44%	-3.50%
Mondelez International	$2,781.00	$2,853.00	$72.00	2.59%	-3.22%

Name	Purchase $ Value	6-28-13 $ Value	Total Net $ Gain/Loss	Total Net % Gain/ Loss	May to June % Change
Nat'l Grid Transco	$5,456.00	$5,667.00	$211.00	3.87%	-4.85%
Nisource Inc.	$2,793.00	$2,864.00	$71.00	2.54%	-0.31%
Occidental Petroleum	$8,265.00	$8,923.00	$658.00	7.96%	-3.08%
Spyglass Resources Corp	$274.00	$182.00	$(92.00)	-33.58%	-12.50%
Pembina Pipeline	$2,821.00	$3,062.00	$241.00	8.54%	-2.14%
Pepco	$2,053.00	$2,016.00	$(37.00)	-1.80%	-2.94%
Philip Morris	$9,144.00	$8,662.00	$(482.00)	-5.27%	-4.72%
Piedmont Natural Gas	$3,265.00	$3,374.00	$109.00	3.34%	-0.15%
Principle Financial Group	$3,155.00	$3,745.00	$590.00	18.70%	-1.06%
Royal Dutch Shell PLC ADR	$6,578.00	$6,380.00	$(198.00)	-3.01%	-3.87%
Scana Corp	$4,906.00	$4,910.00	$4.00	0.08%	-2.66%
Southern Co	$4,483.00	$4,413.00	$(70.00)	-1.56%	0.52%
Spectra Energy	$2,881.00	$3,446.00	$565.00	19.61%	12.72%
Teco Energy	$1,735.00	$1,719.00	$(16.00)	-0.92%	-2.39%
US Bancorp	$3,401.00	$3,615.00	$214.00	6.29%	3.11%
Verizon Communications	$4,672.00	$5,034.00	$362.00	7.75%	3.84%
Wells Fargo	$3,539.00	$4,127.00	$588.00	16.61%	1.78%
DWS Core Equity Fund	$1,983.00	$2,074.00	$91.00	4.59%	-2.95%
DWS S&P 500 Index Fund	$2,022.00	$2,134.00	$112.00	5.54%	-1.70%
DWS Short Duration Fund	$931.00	$921.00	$(10.00)	-1.07%	-0.65%
Fidelity Contrafund	$8,122.00	$8,564.00	$442.00	5.44%	-1.72%
Wellesley Income Fund	$2,479.00	$2,457.00	$(22.00)	-0.89%	-2.38%
	$174,739.00	$180,639.00	$5,900.00	3.38%	

July

I Can Get Paid for Owning Stock?

No stock market crash here. Our assets are liquid.
—Unknown Liquor Store Owner

You know you're a novice investor when...

You don't quite understand the concept of combining "financial" and "planning."

From:	Penny McMillyun
Sent:	Tuesday, July 8, 2013 8:25 PM
To:	Mark Slauter <markslauter@novice.investor>
Subject:	I Want To Make You $102,392 Richer!

To Make It Happen I'm Going To Pair This Golden Opportunity With The Most Ridiculous Price We've Ever Offered.

And I asked myself how much will this cost me?

July 13, 2013

Wow! ...what an up week for the Dow, which closed today at 15464. I'm not sure how badly I may have damaged my portfolio from selling a few items a couple of weeks back when the market stumbled. Given that my new acquisitions are up and have better dividends, I should come out ahead in the long run.

July 26, 2013

Apple jumped this week after its positive earnings report. It was at about $419 and topped out at just north of $444. Investors who played this made about 6% on their money.

The market feels stretched like a rubber band about to snap. It appeared that undervalued stocks were harder to come by and traders were also considering some profit taking. I didn't see any indications of the economy doing anything more than stumbling along just above neutral. If true, traders may continue to hold out on equities and shy away from bonds. U.S. traders still appeared somewhat jittery regarding overseas markets and economies.

WATCHING THE MARKET

Part of the news commentary in July focused on the apparent "Goldilocks" economy: an economy with growth that is not too strong and not too weak, but just right. From my perspective, this meant there was more hope in the market than actual value and that investors were hoping the Federal Reserve will keep money cheap. However, at this point in my fantasy portfolio experience, I believed that the market would continue to be a roller coaster moving slowly upward until the Fed stated a specific date for ending its QE2 efforts.

Meanwhile, the media was also speculating that trading was light due to traders waiting on economic news and company quarterly reports. Apart from the week ending on July 13th, the Dow bounced around the neutral line: up a few points, down a few points. Compared to the market, I found it interesting that my portfolio appeared to experience a bigger decrease and bigger increase as a percentage than the Dow did. There is an element to investing that can make it appear to be a crap shoot in the sense that even when you do your homework, a company can experience an unforeseen circumstance.

As the month came to a close, the media was focusing on the fact that the market was moving very little either up or down, with some profit taking in play. One item garnering almost daily comment was the apparent high valuation of stocks and how that could be a cause of concern for traders. Notably, there didn't appear to be any major sell-offs or panic selling; some analysts looked at this minor level of activity as a consolidation. After going through all the different viewpoints and perspectives, I emerged feeling like I wasn't sure if I should be glad or concerned about how things were playing out.

CHASING FOR INFORMATION

No matter how much experience you gain in the markets, never stop researching and gathering information—especially from analyst reports. These professionals are extremely well versed in the industry and have tools to evaluate companies that I (and probably most novice investors) don't have. Without some professional insights, I'd really be screwed. The sooner you admit this and allow yourself to rely on professionals' wisdom, the better off you'll be in the long run. Analyst reports can cover a variety of issues, such as what valuation they give the company, what's preventing or supporting its future outlook, what are the risk factors, etc. Assessing them all individually and collectively becomes an invaluable process when chasing for information.

As I looked for information on items I owned I saw this Morningstar analyst evaluation of Bank of Nova Scotia (BNS):

> Bank of Nova Scotia, or Scotiabank, is the third largest of the big six Canadian banks that collectively hold almost 90% of that nation's banking assets. The firm has earned returns on equity averaging nearly 19% over the past 10 years. Much of this record was achieved through careful expense management.
>
> Canadian household debt as a percentage of disposable income has risen to an all-time high of 160% from 50% in the mid-1980s and 90% in 1990. Low interest rates have also contributed to a housing bubble in Canada, which will put stress on borrowers once the Bank of Canada raises rates. We think the Canadian consumer's limited ability to take on more debt will have a materially negative effect on Canadian banks', including Scotiabank's, ability to expand their loan books or increase net interest income.
>
> In light of Canada's highly leveraged consumers, lower interest rates, and the current housing bubble in Canada, we are concerned about Scotiabank's near-term profitability. While we like how well Scotiabank has been managed and

has performed in the past, we are cautious with regard to these economic conditions and their potential impacts on Scotiabank's net income.

Hmmm, interesting to see how much consumer's behaviors with debt is impacting Canada's banks. Caution duly noted.

As I reviewed the analyst report further, I also looked at what the Bulls (call them market optimists) and the Bears (call them market pessimists) have to say. This way I got both viewpoints.

Morningstar's Bulls & Bears...

Topic	Bulls Say...	Bears Say...
Canadian Economy	Canadian market remains attractive, with high returns protected by the barriers to entry enacted by the Canadian government.	Net interest margin will continue to be under pressure in this low-rate environment.
International Segments	International segment's exposure to higher-growth emerging markets in Latin America and Asia will offset Scotiabank's slower growth in North America.	The higher-growth international banking segment earns a lower return on capital than the Canadian banking segment.
Banking Segment	Without one dominant business segment, Scotiabank has achieved superior returns on capital relative to its peers over an extended time.	The Canadian banking segment is unlikely to achieve the growth that it has experienced over the past 10 years.

After reviewing the analyst report and the countering perspectives, I concluded that if I wanted to glean any profit from my Scotiabank holding, I had to pay attention to the potential housing bubble and general economy in Canada. Within three weeks of acquiring this investment in June, I was up 2.8%. To truly know value, the long-term environment matters—and I realized I had to address this moving forward. Maybe because I tend to be optimistic, but I thought the Bulls had the better argument and perspective here. Also, I wasn't looking at BNS in a vacuum. I was considering it as I compared it to other stocks in the Financial Services sector.

Again, all the pieces form a united picture. Remember to connect them together!

ANALYZING THE PORTFOLIOS

Overall, I was growing worried about a few items in my fantasy portfolio. Some holdings weren't performing how I'd expected.

Specifically, Linn Energy had been problematic for several weeks, and I came across the following information from an article in Investing Daily early in the month:

Linn Energy, LinnCo, Berry Petroleum and the SEC
by David Dittman
7/8/2013

When the deal was first announced, on February 21, 2013, Linn Energy LLC (LINE) and affiliate LinnCo (LNCO) expected their billion acquisition of Berry Petroleum Co (BRY) to close by July 1, 2013.

The Linn entities offered 1.25 shares of LinnCo for every one Berry share; the day before the deal's announcement, February 20, 2013, LinnCo closed at $36.99, putting a preliminary value on the deal, including assumed debt, of $4.4 billion, or $46.2375 per Berry share.

On July 1, however, after the market close, Linn Energy and LinnCo announced that the Securities and Exchange Commission (SEC) has commenced an inquiry into the entities' accounting practices with regard to their hedge program as well as their proposed merger with Berry.

If I had been receiving alerts regarding my investments, I probably would have known these perspectives sooner and would have sold Linn immediately. However, I didn't receive alerts (I felt that I got enough email already and didn't need news feeds on 90 more items!) and decided to let it play out for a while. But, seeing how valuable this information was to me right now, I was reminded as to how this was exactly why I signed on to email lists. Without receiving these background details, it could have been months later before I learned about this. And in an investment-timing world, a month passing can mean loads of money lost.

Further, I noticed new movement from my Alaska Air Group (ALK) holding, it was now providing a dividend. Their last movement in this area was a 2:1 stock split in March 2012 (which means, if you owned 10 shares of ALK prior to the split, you'd own 20 shares afterwards). I'd been considering selling ALK because it had fallen below my purchase price. So, my strategy was to shoot for breaking even—or at least minimizing my loss as much as possible. Now that ALK was providing a dividend, I decided to hold onto it for a while longer.

I did manage to find a bright spot during this time: My holding, Legacy, made it back to the plus side of the column by 0.1% or $3.00—the first time in seven weeks. *Woo hoo! I'm in de money!*

DIVIDENDS

Oh, the wild world of dividends. Okay, maybe not so *wild* themselves. But navigating dividends can be a whirlwind if you aren't prepared for the journey.

Remember, dividends are payments to you as an owner of shares in a company. But keep in mind, not all companies provide dividends. If a company does pay dividends, it will usually announce in advance when the payment date is—though I've seen a few companies be sneaky and tell you after the date has passed. A company arrives at the date of a dividend payment by reviewing its financials and deciding that it will pay a dividend based on the share value for a particular date. For example, they'll make an announcement on March 5 that they'll pay a dividend on March 29 based on the share price from March 7. They'll also state the yield as a percentage.

As you navigate the world of dividends, you should be aware of the following key terms (these are from www.dividend.com):

Ex-dividend Date. The ex-dividend date is the day on which all shares bought and sold no longer come attached with the right to be paid the most recently declared dividend. This is an important date for any company that has many stockholders, including those that trade on exchanges, as it makes reconciliation of who is to be paid the dividend easier. It is just as important for investors, however, since you must own a stock before the ex-dividend date in order to receive the next scheduled dividend.

Record Date. Shareholders who properly registered their ownership on or before the record date (or "date of record") will receive the dividend. Shareholders who are not registered as of this date will not receive the dividend. Registration in most countries is essentially automatic for shares purchased before the ex-dividend date.

Payment Date. The payment date (or "pay date") is the day when the dividend checks will actually be mailed to the shareholders of a company or credited to brokerage accounts.

Declaration Date. The declaration date is the day on which a company's board of directors announces its next dividend payment.

Also known as the "announcement date," this is the least important date for dividend investors to consider.

While knowing the key terms is essential, so too is your ability to listen to the noise surrounding dividends. For example, as I was again scouring through my inbox trying to keep up with email, I came across a one-liner claiming, "Dividends are FREE money. Companies pay YOU to own them. What could be better!?"

I smelled bullshit. Not only was this company spamming me and trying to get me to buy their newsletter, I knew their claim was a straight-up lie: Dividends ARE NOT free money.

Why?

○ Dividends cannot be guaranteed.

○ Stock prices cannot be guaranteed.

○ Company value cannot be guaranteed.

○ My money and my future carry an equal risk to that of the company's.

Plus, you have to use *your* money to invest in companies that even pay dividends. So, remind me again: What part of dividends is free?! Ultimately, the whole point of investing is to increase the value of your money, either through dividends or increased share value. And it does cost you to make the money you earn.

So, with all these factors on the table, don't forget:

○ You decide the level of risk you can bear.

○ You decide where to invest your money.

○   You decide to buy an ownership stake in a company.

If I'm going to invest, you'd better believe I'm going into it expecting a company to be able to pay back my money with interest. Otherwise, there's no point, and I may as well just stick my money under the mattress.

MONTH IN REVIEW

Between June 28 and August 2, 2013, the Dow gained 748 points. All three really moved upward this month, and I was now ahead of Mom. *Woo hoo!*

	Weekly Return on Investment Stats		
	Dow Jones Industrial Average	Me	Mom
Week 18	7.42%	3.10%	3.91%
Week 19	9.75%	6.47%	7.20%
Week 20	10.32%	7.25%	8.18%
Week 21	10.40%	8.29%	7.97%
Week 22	11.10%	9.39%	6.42%

Overall for July, I had an unrealized gain of $25,100. Generally, I had losses across the board, with the Energy and Basic Materials sectors still lagging. On the flip side, Technology and Consumer Defensive sectors were holding up well. Meanwhile, Mom had an unrealized gain of $13,917. Mom's losses were in the Energy and Utilities sectors, but the Financial Services sector was performing well.

I still had a fair percentage of individual losses across the board, although most items improved a bit. And my Qihoo 360 investment kept rockin'. *Really, really? A 96% increase!!! Hey Mom, I think I know a good investment for you…how do I find another one of these???* I suspected part of the driving force in this advance of Qihoo was a trifold effect:

○ The lack of easy pickings for undervalued equities as discussed by the media.

○ The appearance of rapid growth (and investor expectation).

○ The lack of alternatives.

Meanwhile, the bond market remained in the crapper. I couldn't find any good bond funds and the ones we owned continued to go down in share value.

COMPARISON

We both improved in July, but I improved more and moved ahead of Mom rather than being behind her as I was in June. Ultimately, however, the Dow was still beating both of us and had an unrealized gain of 11.10%.

At this point, my portfolio had 21 items that I invested in based on recommendations from the Pros, which was about 46% (25 items were my picks). On a percentage basis, I came out behind the Pros this month as 72.0% of my items increased in value, but 76.2% of the Pros items increased.

DIVIDENDS FOR JULY

I received 10 payments totaling $494.31, which averaged $49.43 per payment. Mom received 10 payments for $328.83, which averaged $32.88 per payment. I made 54% more money than Mom did this month. *Now that's a substantial difference!*

LESSONS LEARNED

Though investors seem to be taking a break—"consolidating" as the media referred to it— I felt I was on the right path. My investments appeared to be turning to the positive, in part because I sold some of my losers and acquired new stocks.

○ **Don't be afraid to sell.** There's nothing wrong with selling, whether you make or lose money. The object is to not lose money and it's better to sell a loss early.

○ **What you own does not necessarily move in the same direction as the market or in the direction you want it to.** After evaluating whether or not there was a relationship between the market movement and my investments, I was unable to find a valid correlation. However, chances are likely that if a sector is moving up or down, your items will eventually do the same.

○ **It takes many pieces to complete a puzzle.** You wouldn't buy a car without looking at it. So, why make an investment if you haven't looked at it?

○ **You can have an increase in losses and still be ahead.** What I'm seeing in my portfolio is that sometimes I have several items decreasing in value but the portfolio is profitable. Invest from the big picture, but don't ignore the smaller details.

One thing I had been looking for was a correlation of the market's movement to my stocks' movement. I wasn't seeing any patterns yet, and I wasn't sure if it was even worth chasing after, but I felt it could be one of the pieces to the puzzle worth paying attention to. To me, investing is similar to a puzzle. Each piece of information contributes to the whole picture. But, often it feels like putting a puzzle together with no completed picture to use as a reference! What'll drive you crazy is when you don't know you're missing a piece of the puzzle until someone gives it to you. And that's just the nature of the beast.

The following portfolio tables show what the current value (August 2) is compared to the purchase value. Value is presented in both dollar and percentage terms. The last column has the month-to-month (June to July) change as a percentage to show how items fluctuate monthly compared to the ever lengthening time between the start date and current values.

MY PORTFOLIO FOR JULY 2013

Note: '0' in last column reflects ownership of less than a month.

Name (Pros in italics)	Purchase $ Value	8-2-13 $ Value	Total Net $ Gain/ Loss	Total Net % Gain/ Loss	June to July % Change
8x8, Inc.	$744.00	$945.00	$201.00	27.0%	10.79%
The AES Corporation	$1,193.00	$1,266.00	$73.00	6.1%	6.75%
Alaska Air Group	$6,273.00	$6,312.00	$39.00	0.6%	20.73%
Alliance Resource Partners LP	$6,725.00	$7,482.00	$757.00	11.3%	4.61%
Apple Inc. (2)	$39,354.00	$46,254.00	$6,754.00	17.1%	10.81%
Bank of Nova Scotia	$5,341.00	$5,611.00	$270.00	5.1%	6.88%
BlackRock Inc.	$26,821.00	$28,662.00	$2,162.00	8.2%	11.43%
Coca-Cola	$3,870.00	$4,022.00	$152.00	3.9%	-0.74%
Consolidated Communications Inc.	$1,637.00	$1,781.00	$144.00	8.8%	0.11%
El Paso Pipeline Partners LP	$4,140.00	$4,088.00	$(52.00)	-1.3%	-6.15%
The GEO Group Inc.	$3,448.00	$3,449.00	$1.00	0.0%	-0.81%
GlaxoSmithKline PLC ADR (1)	$4,422.00	$5,222.00	$800.00	18.1%	1.99%
GlaxoSmithKline PLC ADR (2)	$4,847.00	$5,222.00	$375.00	7.7%	1.99%
Great Northern Iron Ore (2)	$6,944.00	$6,775.00	$(169.00)	-2.4%	-5.03%
HCP Inc.	$4,325.00	$4,281.00	$(44.00)	-1.0%	-3.69%
Home Loan Servicing Solutions	$2,302.00	$2,504.00	$202.00	8.8%	7.88%
Inventure Foods, Inc.	$726.00	$956.00	$230.00	31.7%	8.51%

Name (Pros in italics)	Purchase $ Value	8-2-13 $ Value	Total Net $ Gain/ Loss	Total Net % Gain/ Loss	June to July % Change
Kinder Morgan Energy Partners LP (1)	$8,672.00	$8,198.00	$(474.00)	-5.5%	-3.87%
Kinder Morgan Energy Partners LP (2)	$9,025.00	$8,198.00	$(827.00)	-9.2%	-3.87%
Legacy Reserves, LP	$2,773.00	$2,720.00	$(53.00)	-1.9%	6.92%
Linn Energy	$3,753.00	$2,687.00	$(1,066.00)	-28.4%	14.58%
Macy's	$4,067.00	$4,946.00	$879.00	21.6%	0.57%
Merck & Co Inc.	$4,782.00	$4,854.00	$72.00	1.5%	2.93%
Michael Kors Holdings Ltd	$5,804.00	$6,880.00	$1,076.00	18.5%	9.26%
Northern Tier Energy LP Class A (1)	$2,950.00	$2,398.00	$(552.00)	-18.7%	7.68%
NTT DoCoMo Inc.	$1,505.00	$1,568.00	$63.00	4.2%	1.62%
Oaktree Capital Group, LLC	$5,013.00	$5,394.00	$381.00	7.6%	3.57%
Pfizer Inc.	$3,043.00	$2,937.00	$(106.00)	-3.5%	5.01%
Proto Labs Inc.	$5,505.00	$6,859.00	$1,354.00	24.6%	4.73%
Prudential PLC ADR	$3,349.00	$3,657.00	$308.00	9.2%	9.75%
PVR Partners LP	$2,285.00	$2,563.00	$278.00	12.2%	-8.82%
Qihoo 360 Technology Co., Ltd.	$3,440.00	$6,740.00	$3,300.00	95.9%	39.54%
Seaspan Corp	$1,930.00	$2,122.00	$192.00	9.9%	4.84%
Sonoco Products Co	$3,407.00	$3,941.00	$534.00	15.7%	11.42%
Sunoco Logistics Partners LP	$6,258.00	$6,103.00	$(155.00)	-2.5%	-4.30%
Terra Nitrogen Company	$23,461.00	$21,800.00	$(1,661.00)	-7.1%	-0.10%
TJX Companies	$4,498.00	$5,393.00	$895.00	19.9%	5.91%
Akre Focus Fund Retail	$1,630.00	$1,916.00	$286.00	17.5%	3.40%
Delaware Healthcare I	$1,355.00	$1,685.00	$330.00	24.4%	6.24%
Oakmark Global I	$2,610.00	$2,882.00	$272.00	10.4%	6.03%

Name (Pros in italics)	Purchase $ Value	8-2-13 $ Value	Total Net $ Gain/ Loss	Total Net % Gain/ Loss	June to July % Change
Oceanstone Fund	$3,753.00	$3,888.00	$506.00	15.0%	3.57%
Fidelity Select Biotechnology Portfolio (1)	$14,631.00	$16,805.00	$4,600.00	37.7%	11.91%
Fidelity Select Biotechnology Portfolio (2)	$10,826.94	$16,805.00	$2,219.26	21.7%	11.91%
Fidelity Select IT Services Portfolio	$2,985.00	$2,407.96	$479.00	17.3%	5.75%
Vanguard Wellington Inv	$3,707.00	$3,792.00	$145.00	4.0%	3.75%
Wells Fargo Advantage Core Builder Series M	$1,167.00	$1,103.00	$(70.00)	-6.0%	-1.25%
	$267,450.44	$292,550.70	$25,100.26	9.39%	

MOM'S PORTFOLIO FOR JULY 2013

Name	Purchase $ Value	8-2-13 $ Value	Total Net $ Gain/ Loss	Total Net % Gain/ Loss	June to July % Change
Altria Group	$3,349.00	$3,568.00	$219.00	6.54%	1.97%
AT&T Inc.	$3,601.00	$3,577.00	$(24.00)	-0.67%	1.05%
Buckeye Partners LP	$5,611.00	$7,192.00	$1,581.00	28.18%	2.51%
Caterpillar Inc.	$9,136.00	$8,430.00	$(706.00)	-7.73%	2.19%
Cleco Corp	$4,418.00	$4,886.00	$468.00	10.59%	5.23%
CMS Energy Corp	$2,645.00	$2,852.00	$207.00	7.83%	4.97%
Compass Securities	$1,574.00	$1,802.00	$228.00	14.49%	2.80%
Deluxe Corp	$3,965.00	$4,227.00	$262.00	6.61%	21.99%
Devon Energy Corp	$5,388.00	$5,596.00	$208.00	3.86%	7.86%
Dominion Res Inc. VA	$5,642.00	$5,943.00	$301.00	5.33%	4.59%
Duke Energy	$6,925.00	$7,175.00	$250.00	3.61%	6.30%
Enbridge Energy Partners	$2,763.00	$3,089.00	$326.00	11.80%	1.31%
Enterprise Products	$5,681.00	$6,209.00	$528.00	9.29%	-0.10%
Exxon Mobile	$8,943.00	$9,195.00	$252.00	2.82%	1.77%
Frontier Communications Corp	$419.00	$448.00	$29.00	6.92%	10.62%

Name	Purchase $ Value	8-2-13 $ Value	Total Net $ Gain/ Loss	Total Net % Gain/ Loss	June to July % Change
General Electric	$2,319.00	$2,470.00	$151.00	6.51%	6.51%
Great Plains Energy	$2,199.00	$2,460.00	$261.00	11.87%	9.14%
Hartford Financial Services Group	$2,368.00	$3,203.00	$835.00	35.26%	3.59%
Hudson City Bancorp	$858.00	$977.00	$119.00	13.87%	6.43%
Integrys Energy Group	$5,610.00	$6,355.00	$745.00	13.28%	8.58%
Intel Corp	$2,103.00	$2,322.00	$219.00	10.41%	-4.17%
Medical Property Trust	$1,483.00	$1,414.00	$(69.00)	-4.65%	-1.26%
Mondelez International	$2,781.00	$3,194.00	$413.00	14.85%	11.95%
Nat'l Grid Transco	$5,456.00	$6,008.00	$552.00	10.12%	6.02%
Nisource Inc.	$2,793.00	$3,109.00	$316.00	11.31%	8.55%
Occidental Petroleum	$8,265.00	$8,892.00	$627.00	7.59%	-0.35%
Spyglass Resources Corp	$274.00	$173.00	$(101.00)	-36.86%	-4.95%
Pembina Pipeline	$2,821.00	$3,120.00	$299.00	10.60%	1.89%
Pepco	$2,053.00	$2,061.00	$8.00	0.39%	2.23%
Philip Morris	$9,144.00	$8,959.00	$(185.00)	-2.02%	3.43%
Piedmont Natural Gas	$3,265.00	$3,469.00	$204.00	6.25%	2.82%
Principle Financial Group	$3,155.00	$4,437.00	$1,282.00	40.63%	18.48%
Royal Dutch Shell PLC ADR	$6,578.00	$6,425.00	$(153.00)	-2.33%	0.71%
Scana Corp	$4,906.00	$5,222.00	$316.00	6.44%	6.35%
Southern Co	$4,483.00	$4,434.00	$(49.00)	-1.09%	0.48%
Spectra Energy	$2,881.00	$3,599.00	$718.00	24.92%	4.44%
Teco Energy	$1,735.00	$1,778.00	$43.00	2.48%	3.43%
US Bancorp	$3,401.00	$3,777.00	$376.00	11.06%	4.48%
Verizon Communications	$4,672.00	$5,025.00	$353.00	7.56%	-0.18%
Wells Fargo	$3,539.00	$4,449.00	$910.00	25.71%	7.80%
DWS Core Equity Fund	$1,983.00	$2,233.00	$250.00	12.61%	7.67%
DWS S&P 500 Index Fund	$2,022.00	$2,274.00	$252.00	12.46%	6.56%
DWS Short Duration Fund	$931.00	$922.00	$(9.00)	-0.97%	0.11%
Fidelity Contrafund	$8,122.00	$9,192.00	$1,070.00	13.17%	7.33%
Wellesley Income Fund	$2,479.00	$2,514.00	$35.00	1.41%	2.32%
	$174,739.00	**$188,656.00**	**$13,917.00**	**7.96%**	

AUGUST

LISTENING TO THE PROS

All my money is in a savings account. My dad has explained the stock market to me maybe 75 times. I still don't understand it.

—John Mulaney

You know you're a novice investor when...

Investing is more emotional than all of your weddings combined.

From:	Count DeMoney
Sent:	Friday, July 31, 2013 7:17 PM
To:	Mark Slauter <markslauter@novice.investor>
Subject:	The Little Lies of the CPI

The Consumer Price Index (CPI) recently announced inflation was at 1.4%. But that's a lie. They rig the inflation-calculating formula to keep it artificially low. According to the CPI, milk prices haven't changed in 5 years. That's not true at my grocery store, and I bet it isn't at yours. If you were to truly calculate inflation, it would be a whopping 9.2%! The government lies so you won't freak out. Don't freak out.

I don't know about the 9.2% claim to inflation in this email, but it's easy to see how all of our daily expenses have continued to rise through the recession: gas, food, clothing…hell, even our property taxes have increased! So it begs the question: What is the true rate of inflation?

August 5, 2013

Not much in the way of economic news. Jobless claims are down, which appears to be due to people dropping out of the job search rather than a reflection of more people being hired.

August 18, 2013

As the market declined this week I was once again tempted to sell off and take profit where I thought I should. One item that I almost pulled the trigger on was Qihoo when it dropped from just over 100% to the mid-80% ROI. Glad I didn't as it came back up and landed slightly higher than last week's close. I was also considering (and still am) selling the Fidelity Biotech. It's dropped 13 points in 3 weeks and

I don't know if it will continue or if this is just leveling off. It's this type of slow loss that suddenly creeps up on you and one day realize you've lost 50% of your gains!

No matter what happens with the Affordable Care Act and "Obamacare," healthcare will continue to increase in cost and likely in profits. I also anticipate a marketplace consolidation in the next five years as profits may thin out and companies will be looking for value added mergers or acquisitions. However, I still viewed the healthcare sector as a great place to put some money. So, I continued to hunt for those opportunities.

WATCHING THE MARKET

Truly reading the market is probably not possible unless you do this for a living. However, if you spend some time every day to get an overview of what is occurring, you'll at least know something— and something is always better than nothing.

During the month of August, one of the apparent oddities in the market climate was traders frequently ignoring bad news or just reacting like they don't care. The market is 'too hot to miss out on'. One media explanation for investor behavior was the fact that if bad news emerges, then the QE2 bond-buying program wouldn't be altered, which meant money would stay cheap and investors could make more money.

At first glance this may seem counterintuitive, but remember that investors make decisions based on future scenarios. So, if the economy doesn't improve (think rising unemployment), the Fed won't make a change. If the Fed doesn't make a change, then borrowing money remains cheap. (I'm sure there's a conspiracy theorist somewhere claiming that investment firms are colluding to ruin the economy so they can make more money.) If borrowing remains inexpensive, then maybe consumers will spend a little more—which is what makes the world go 'round.

However, throughout August, the Federal Reserve was not clear about their approach to end QE2 and investors got nervous. *No one wants to be hanging out to dry when the ball drops.* Specifically, the week of August 12 became a sell-off week that appeared to be a reaction to the uncertainty surrounding the Federal Reserve's decision on the QE2 program. The worry stemmed from the fact that if the Fed scaled back, then interest rates would go up, making money more expensive and cutting into company profits. The QE2 program keeps interest rates artificially low, and investors like that.

And if that wasn't enough to dampen moods, the report on falling jobless claims moved the market in early August. Usually, fewer people looking for work would be a good sign; unfortunately, it seemed to mostly stem from people dropping out of the job search effort rather than more people being hired. When people stop looking for jobs, hiring statistics are skewed—which I interpreted as creating a false jobless claims report. But no one wants to talk about the job participation rate, and investors don't appear to be concerned about it. Instead, they saw a lower jobless claims number as good for the economy. Being good for the economy would make more sense to me if I saw a commensurate increase in the number of people being hired, but I didn't see any report trying to reconcile the two statistics.

As a result of this uncertainty and other global factors—such as concerns about China's economy slowing down and declines in durable goods orders—the Dow fell more than 800 points this month. There were several days that I felt like I had to sell stocks just so I wouldn't lose my profits, but I didn't. And sticking to my watch-and-wait position was far from easy. Especially when throughout the month, media was reporting that the market remained skittish due to stock valuations being high and that only a small bit of bad news could make stocks go down. I also saw frequent chatter around how the Bulls (the optimists) proved to be resilient as they kept pushing the market higher. Every time stocks would start to decline the Bulls would start buying. One day the Dow drops 130 points only to see the Bulls bring it back up 195 points the next day.

When watching the market feels like a ticking time bomb, throwing your hands in the air can be completely tempting. And it'll drive you bonkers in the process.

ANALYZING THE PORTFOLIOS

As the market declined during the week of August 12, I was once again tempted to sell and take profit where I thought I should. One item that I almost pulled the trigger on was the high performer Qihoo 360 (QIHU) when it dropped from just over a 100% unrealized gain to the mid-80s. *Glad I didn't let emotions get the best of me!* Qihoo rebounded and landed slightly higher than the previous week's close. This experience was a good practice in patience. Sometimes, you can get trigger-happy and over-react to the markets. Had I sold at Qihoo's low point, I would have lost out on some major bucks. In times like this, the saying "patience is a virtue" is so true.

But, I kept a watchful eye on other holdings I owned. I considered selling (and continued to for a while) one of my Fidelity Select Biotechnology Portfolio (FBIOX) holdings. Over a three-week period, it dropped 13 points; I didn't know if the loss would continue or if it was just leveling off. Sitting on performance like this is when patience as a virtue can be tricky. Unless you're keeping up with the markets, this type of slow loss can suddenly creep up on you, and one day, you realize you've lost 50% of your potential profit! This is when I needed to pay close attention to the stock. I was still on the plus side, but I didn't want to miss out on any profit. Since I'd already experienced the markets' yo-yo effect, and I didn't see any real reason to sell, I decided to wait.

The reason why I analyze the portfolios is to understand how they are doing. Are we going up or down? What's the possible future outcome? I'm trying to understand and make sense of what I see. It's no different than why a person sees a doctor, or has maintenance work done on a car or house. To a novice investor, the market can be a whirlwind. Though Mom and I were still in positive territory, we'd lost some momentum this month. Mom's portfolio had dropped from an unrealized gain of 7.97% to 3.86% - losing about 50% of its value in three weeks! Since the beginning of this game, her best week of being positive was 8.23%, while mine was 9.39%. Three weeks ago I was up 8.29% and now it's 8.43%; an almost imperceptible increase, but I was still to the plus side, which is where I wanted to be.

An element of my analysis is doing research to identify opportunities. Many people discuss and suggest having a watch list. So, if I owned automotive stocks but was learning that computer security might be or was becoming a major concern, I would be looking into computer security stocks. If I find any of interest, I'll watch them for a while and learn more about the company. And if the opportunity presents itself, I can buy the computer stock with available cash or by selling stock I already own. I wanted to replace my non-performers and boost the dividends I received and growth in share value.

As a result of my sleuthing, I found a few items of interest and decided to dig a little deeper. I had developed several watch lists already, but this was the latest one.

○ ECA Marcellus Trust I

○ Box Ships Inc.

○ Navios Maritime Partners L.P.

○ TICC Capital Corp BDC

○ EQT Midstream Partners LP

o   Anika Therapeutics

o   PDL BioPharma, Inc.

o   GasLog Ltd

Of course, doing research on my own would (and continues to) only get me so far. That's why I've signed up for emails and pay for a premium online service. I wanted some expert advice and insight to keep informed and in the loop.

LISTENING TO ADVICE FROM "MY ADVISORS"

During August, I was reminded of my ever-present need to understand what Mom and I owned, as well as my desire to keep looking for other opportunities. In part, the desire was driven by having available cash, but mainly it was because I wanted to do better. I want to be successful at investing; but this desire (emotions) can also get in the way and result in bad decisions. So, in pursuit of success and to balance my emotions with logic, I read a lot of emails and pay attention to certain sources and experts.

Receiving expert advice is critical for me to achieve better success. For example, during August, I was reading about the AES Corporation (Utilities sector) holding in my portfolio and came across the following analysis from Morningstar:

AES Corporation (AES) reported 2013 second-quarter adjusted earnings per share of $0.32 versus $0.18 in the same period last year. The strong results were driven by a lower effective income tax rate, the commercial startup of the 71%-owned 270 MW Ventanas IV coal-fired plant in Chile, higher plant availability in Chile and Argentina, and favorable tariff impacts in Brazil.

We continue to believe that AES shares will provide investors with at least a 6% total return through 2015, the lower end of management's 6%-8% forecast and well below the company's long-term growth potential. Our fair value estimate of $13 per share is unchanged.

At the moment, my holding was profitable. So, my takeaway from reading their analysis was:

○ Recent earnings of AES were better this year than last year, and why.

○ Morningstar told me what they expect for a return on my investment.

○ Morningstar also gave me what they thought was a fair value estimate for a stock share.

So, now I was able to use information in two ways: Recognize that my holding was currently profitable, and combine it with perspectives from the experts. Had I only relied on the face-value of what I saw in my portfolio (profit), I would have only seen one side of the coin. With deeper insight guiding me, I decided to hold onto AES. However, I'd also be looking for updated information on this in the future.

Another analyst update example from Morningstar was a stock that Mom owned, Frontier Communications Corp (Communications Services sector). I'd been unimpressed from the outset, and based on these comments, I wasn't holding my breath.

Frontier Communications made considerable progress during the second quarter, but it continues to lag in the business services market. With two straight quarters of solid customer gains, consumer revenue is starting to show signs of stabilizing. However, business services revenue failed to rebound from a weak first quarter, declining 4% year over year. We believe Frontier's competitive position overall continues to erode.

The key piece of information here was that although Frontier had some recent success, the professional advice suggested just the opposite into the near future. *Again, here are those differing voices!* Since I didn't want to make any changes to Mom's portfolio, I decided that we would just have to ride it out; otherwise, I would have been inclined to sell.

Ultimately, looking for advice and insight isn't limited to what you own. Your research should include what's going on around what you own as well. You can think of it similar to predicting the weather: You don't just step outside your backyard and judge how weather is across your entire city or state. Chances are you also look at the news reports to gain a better perspective on the current and future weather to expect.

During August, one of the national issues constantly talked about was the Affordable Care Act (ACA) or "Obamacare." After reading through pundits' opinions and market analyses, I concluded that no matter what happened with the ACA, healthcare would continue to increase in cost and likely in profits. I also anticipated a marketplace consolidation over the next five years as profits may thin out and companies will be looking for value-added mergers or acquisitions.

As an example, here is an excerpt from an InvestorPlace article discussing healthcare and investing associated with Baby Boomers and Millennials.

This is where we are today. America's baby boomers are now on the downward slope of the consumer life cycle. Since the 1960s, they've provided economic tailwinds; but those tailwinds have now turned into some pretty harsh headwinds.

In truth, there is not much you can "do" about demographics—they are the future that has already been written. But you can invest accordingly. Understand that top-line sales growth will probably not be as robust as in years past. Earnings-per-share growth will come disproportionately from share buybacks—as has been the case for the past several years.

Where possible, look for growth in companies that target emerging-market consumers and young American families. The millennials are starting to enter the family formation stage, and this generation will be the primary engine of domestic growth for the next 30 years.

First and foremost, the takeaway message here is to pay attention to demographics. When people are younger, their need for healthcare services is less than when they're older. What's being described here is that the Baby Boomers will require more services, creating a drain on the system; whereas Millennials will be paying for services they're less likely to use, thereby allowing companies to be more profitable. In essence, the article suggests investing in companies that are servicing Millennials versus Baby Boomers. However, based on my experience, I add that you should look to companies servicing the Boomers just as much as you would for the Millennials. Knowing firsthand what it takes to support elder care, I decided to definitely look into those companies.

This last example I include for two reasons: 1) I stated under the discussion of AES above that I look for updated information, and 2) I've previously discussed the Bank of Nova Scotia (Scotiabank) as one of my current holdings. As I continued searching for insight from the Pros, I came across information from Morningstar on the bank, which I acquired in June. Since then, my position had ranged from being down -1.7% to being up 6.6%, and currently sat at 3.9%. To date, I'd received one dividend payment of about $32. *Rolling in the dough, now!*

Here's what Morningstar had to say:

Diversified Income Streams Keep Scotiabank In An Enviable Competitive Position

As Canada's most international bank, Scotiabank has consistently demonstrated its ability to earn high returns through a variety of channels over a long period. With a well-diversified income stream from each business segment (Canadian banking, international, capital markets, and wealth management), Scotiabank's overall capital generation has been resilient but faces nearer-term headwinds.

We are increasing our fair value estimate to $64 per share from $61 as we incorporate recent financial performance. We project average annual organic loan growth of 5.7% from 2014 to 2017 compared with 12.0% over the past seven years. We anticipate that Scotiabank' tangible equity/assets ratio will equal 5.5% for 2013-17. Overall, we expect average returns on equity to dip slightly to 16.3% for 2013 and then rising to 17.5% for 2017, comfortably above our 10% cost of equity.

I was relieved to see that Morningstar analysts also saw the company in a positive light, since I was having doubts about the long-term prospects. My problem was trying to reconcile the projected rise in earnings with the "nearer-term headwinds" and the still very real possibility that Canada, the U.S., or any other number of countries could experience an economic downturn.

Yes, searching for information from the Pros in August was truly essential to my investment success.

MONTH IN REVIEW

Between August 2 and August 30, 2013, the Dow lost 848 points. I finally advanced beyond the Dow and Mom *(heh, heh)*, and was leading the pack.

Weekly Return on Investment Stats			
	Dow Jones Industrial Average	**Me**	**Mom**
Week 23	9.48%	8.69%	6.75%
Week 24	7.03%	8.43%	3.86%
Week 25	6.54%	9.35%	4.23%
Week 26	5.11%	7.69%	2.55%

Overall, for August, I had an unrealized gain of $20,558. Mom had an unrealized gain of $4,448 this month. Generally, there were losses across the board and no sector escaped the sell-off.

COMPARISON

We both got hammered this month, but mine was not as bad as Mom's. She was behind the market with an unrealized gain of only 2.55%, and I finished out the month in the lead at 7.69%—more than double Mom's.

At this point, my portfolio had 21 items that I invested in based on recommendations from the Pros, which was about 46% (25 items were my picks). On a percentage basis, I came out behind the Pros this month as 64.0% of my items increased in value, but 71.4% of the Pros items increased.

DIVIDENDS FOR AUGUST

August was a great month for dividends. By month's end, I received 20 payments totaling $1,706.98, which averaged $85.35 per payment. Meanwhile, Mom received 19 payments totaling $722.18, which averaged $38.01 per payment.

After completing my second quarter of investing, I felt that I was in fair shape, considering…

○ My earlier sell-off of losses cost me about $22,000.

○ My current value was up $20,558, and I'd received $5,305 in dividends. Mom was up $4,448 with $3,664 in dividends.

○ I'd received 74 dividend payments for an average of $71.69 per payment. Mom had received 99 payments for an average of $37.01 per payment.

○ Overall, I was profitable.

○ I was exceeding Mom's unrealized gains value at greater than a 3-to-1 ratio.

○ I felt I was competitive with the Pros.

LESSONS LEARNED

I came away from August with two major reminders: 1) Keep up to speed with the Healthcare sector, and 2) It pays to look around me for inspiration. *What do I buy every day? What do my friends buy? What about my parents and their friends?* As I've previously stated, a company exists behind the products you see and use every day. Research them and find the viable investment options. Man, what I would give to be able to buy Microsoft, Apple, or Google stock when it was newly issued.

○ **Maybe I am doing something correctly, though the market is still confusing.** While it appeared that I was achieving some level of success, there are many things I still didn't understand. I'm not sure I could explain why I was having some success.

○ **Managing investments is stressful...particularly when you make daily evaluations.** I think there is some level of hazard in reviewing the entire portfolio every day because you expose yourself to myriad minor fluctuations of the individual stocks. It's easy to get wrapped up in something that won't be an issue next week, next month, or maybe even until next year. Most stuff isn't worth stressing over.

○ **Have a stash of cash to take advantage of opportunities. You don't have to invest all your money.** Just because you have cash doesn't mean it should be burning a hole in your pocket. Either you or your broker will have a few items outside your portfolio being tracked on a watch list. Having some cash on hand is good for those situations where you've tracked the stock and find that now is good time to buy.

Remember: You don't have to change your lifestyle or become an economics geek to find investment ideas. By just paying a little more attention to the things going on around you, you'll immediately become more aware of all the investment potential surrounding every aspect of your life.

The following portfolio tables show what the current value (August 30) is compared to the purchase value. Value is presented in both dollar and percentage terms. The last column has the month-to-month (July to August) change as a percentage to show how items fluctuate monthly compared to the ever lengthening time between the start date and current values.

MY PORTFOLIO FOR AUGUST 2013

Note: '0' in last column reflects ownership of less than a month.

Name (Pros in italics)	Purchase $ Value	8-30-13 $ Value	Total Net $ Gain/Loss	Total Net % Gain/ Loss	July to Aug % Change
8x8, Inc.	$744.00	$925.00	$181.00	24.3%	-2.12%
The AES Corporation	$1,193.00	$1,271.00	$78.00	6.5%	0.39%
Alaska Air Group	$6,273.00	$5,662.00	$(611.00)	-9.7%	-10.30%
Alliance Resource Partners LP	$6,725.00	$7,528.00	$803.00	11.9%	0.61%
Apple Inc. (2)	$39,354.00	$48,722.00	$9,222.00	23.3%	5.34%
Bank of Nova Scotia	$5,341.00	$5,550.00	$209.00	3.9%	-1.09%
BlackRock Inc.	$26,821.00	$26,032.00	$(468.00)	-1.8%	-9.18%
Coca-Cola Co	$3,870.00	$3,818.00	$(52.00)	-1.3%	-5.07%
Consolidated Communications	$1,637.00	$1,668.00	$31.00	1.9%	-6.34%
El Paso Pipeline Partners LP	$4,140.00	$4,173.00	$33.00	0.8%	2.08%
The GEO Group Inc.	$3,448.00	$3,121.00	$(327.00)	-9.5%	-9.51%
GlaxoSmithKline PLC ADR (1)	$4,422.00	$5,089.00	$667.00	15.1%	-2.55%
GlaxoSmithKline PLC ADR (2)	$4,847.00	$5,089.00	$242.00	5.0%	-2.55%
Great Northern Iron Ore (2)	$6,944.00	$7,051.00	$107.00	1.5%	4.07%
HCP Inc.	$4,325.00	$4,073.00	$(252.00)	-5.8%	-4.86%

Name (Pros in italics)	Purchase $ Value	8-30-13 $ Value	Total Net $ Gain/Loss	Total Net % Gain/ Loss	July to Aug % Change
Home Loan Servicing Solutions	$2,302.00	$2,280.00	$(22.00)	-1.0%	-8.95%
Inventure Foods, Inc.	$726.00	$902.00	$176.00	24.2%	-5.65%
Kinder Morgan Energy Partners LP (1)	$8,672.00	$8,156.00	$(516.00)	-6.0%	-0.51%
Kinder Morgan Energy Partners LP (2)	$9,025.00	$8,156.00	$(869.00)	-9.6%	-0.51%
Legacy Reserves, LP	$2,773.00	$2,698.00	$(75.00)	-2.7%	-0.81%
Linn Energy	$3,753.00	$2,111.00	$(1,642.00)	-43.8%	-21.44%
Macy's Inc.	$4,067.00	$4,443.00	$376.00	9.2%	-10.17%
Merck & Co Inc.	$4,782.00	$4,729.00	$(53.00)	-1.1%	-2.58%
Michael Kors Holdings Ltd	$5,804.00	$7,409.00	$1,605.00	27.7%	7.69%
Northern Tier Energy LP Class A (1)	$2,950.00	$2,083.00	$(867.00)	-29.4%	-13.14%
NTT DoCoMo Inc.	$1,505.00	$1,603.00	$98.00	6.5%	2.23%
Oaktree Capital Group, LLC	$5,013.00	$5,180.00	$167.00	3.3%	-3.97%
Pfizer Inc.	$3,043.00	$2,821.00	$(222.00)	-7.3%	-3.95%
Protolabs Inc.	$5,505.00	$7,104.00	$1,599.00	29.0%	3.57%
Prudential PLC ADR	$3,349.00	$3,356.00	$7.00	0.2%	-8.23%
PVR Partners LP	$2,285.00	$2,321.00	$36.00	1.6%	-9.44%
Qihoo 360 Technology Co., Ltd.	$3,440.00	$7,793.00	$4,353.00	126.5%	15.62%
Seaspan Corp	$1,930.00	$2,133.00	$203.00	10.5%	0.52%
Sonoco Products Co	$3,407.00	$3,723.00	$316.00	9.3%	-5.53%
Sunoco Logistics Partners LP	$6,258.00	$6,424.00	$166.00	2.7%	5.26%
Terra Nitrogen Company	$23,461.00	$21,382.00	$(2,079.00)	-8.9%	-1.92%

Name (Pros in italics)	Purchase $ Value	8-30-13 $ Value	Total Net $ Gain/Loss	Total Net % Gain/ Loss	July to Aug % Change
TJX Companies	$4,498.00	$5,272.00	$774.00	17.2%	-2.24%
Akre Focus Fund Retail	$1,630.00	$1,832.00	$202.00	12.4%	-4.38%
Delaware Healthcare I	$1,355.00	$1,645.00	$290.00	21.4%	-2.37%
Oakmark Global I	$2,610.00	$2,772.00	$162.00	6.2%	-3.82%
Oceanstone Fund	$3,753.00	$3,925.00	$543.00	16.1%	0.95%
Fidelity Select Bio-technology Portfolio (1)	$14,631.00	$16,118.00	$3,913.00	32.1%	-4.09%
Fidelity Select Biotechnology Portfolio (2)	$10,826.94	$16,118.00	$1,710.88	16.7%	-4.09%
Fidelity Select IT Services Portfolio	$2,985.00	$3,175.00	$400.00	14.4%	-2.43%
Vanguard Wellington Inv	$3,707.00	$3,678.00	$31.00	0.9%	-3.01%
Wells Fargo Advantage Core Builder Series M	$1,167.00	$1,085.00	$(88.00)	-7.5%	-1.63%
	$267,450.44	$288,008.32	$20,557.88	7.69%	

Mom's Portfolio for August 2013

Name	Purchase $ Value	8-30-13 $ Value	Total Net $ Gain/Loss	Total Net % Gain/Loss	July to Aug % Change
Altria Group	$3,349.00	$3,388.00	$39.00	1.16%	-5.04%
AT&T Inc.	$3,601.00	$3,383.00	$(218.00)	-6.05%	-5.42%
Buckeye Partners LP	$5,611.00	$7,000.00	$1,389.00	24.75%	-2.67%
Caterpillar Inc.	$9,136.00	$8,254.00	$(882.00)	-9.65%	-2.09%
Cleco Corp	$4,418.00	$4,516.00	$98.00	2.22%	-7.57%
CMS Energy Corp	$2,645.00	$2,653.00	$8.00	0.30%	-6.98%
Compass Securities	$1,574.00	$1,728.00	$154.00	9.78%	-4.11%

Name	Purchase $ Value	8-30-13 $ Value	Total Net $ Gain/Loss	Total Net % Gain/Loss	July to Aug % Change
Deluxe Corp	$3,965.00	$3,935.00	$(30.00)	-0.76%	-6.91%
Devon Energy Corp	$5,388.00	$5,709.00	$321.00	5.96%	2.02%
Dominion Res Inc. VA	$5,642.00	$5,835.00	$193.00	3.42%	-1.82%
Duke Energy	$6,925.00	$6,560.00	$(365.00)	-5.27%	-8.57%
Enbridge Energy Partners	$2,763.00	$2,982.00	$219.00	7.93%	-3.46%
Enterprise Products	$5,681.00	$5,942.00	$261.00	4.59%	-4.30%
Exxon Mobile Corporation	$8,943.00	$8,716.00	$(227.00)	-2.54%	-5.21%
Frontier Communications Corp	$419.00	$433.00	$14.00	3.34%	-3.35%
General Electric Co	$2,319.00	$2,314.00	$(5.00)	-0.22%	-6.32%
Great Plains Energy	$2,199.00	$2,192.00	$(7.00)	-0.32%	-10.89%
Hartford Financial Services Group	$2,368.00	$2,960.00	$592.00	25.00%	-7.59%
Hudson City Bancorp	$858.00	$919.00	$61.00	7.11%	-5.94%
Integrys Energy Group	$5,610.00	$5,592.00	$(18.00)	-0.32%	-12.01%
Intel Corp	$2,103.00	$2,198.00	$95.00	4.52%	-5.34%
Medical Property Trust	$1,483.00	$1,155.00	$(328.00)	-22.12%	-18.32%
Mondelez International	$2,781.00	$3,067.00	$286.00	10.28%	-3.98%
Nat'l Grid Transco	$5,456.00	$5,756.00	$300.00	5.50%	-4.19%
Nisource Inc.	$2,793.00	$2,926.00	$133.00	4.76%	-5.89%
Occidental Petroleum Corp	$8,265.00	$8,821.00	$556.00	6.73%	-0.80%

Name	Purchase $ Value	8-30-13 $ Value	Total Net $ Gain/Loss	Total Net % Gain/Loss	July to Aug % Change
Spyglass Resources Corp	$274.00	$168.00	$(106.00)	-38.69%	-2.89%
Pembina Pipeline Corp	$2,821.00	$3,108.00	$287.00	10.17%	-0.38%
Pepco Holdings Inc.	$2,053.00	$1,894.00	$(159.00)	-7.74%	-8.10%
Philip Morris International Inc.	$9,144.00	$8,344.00	$(800.00)	-8.75%	-6.86%
Piedmont Natural Gas Co	$3,265.00	$3,226.00	$(39.00)	-1.19%	-7.00%
Principle Financial Group	$3,155.00	$4,092.00	$937.00	29.70%	-7.78%
Royal Dutch Shell PLC ADR	$6,578.00	$6,459.00	$(119.00)	-1.81%	0.53%
Scana Corp	$4,906.00	$4,812.00	$(94.00)	-1.92%	-7.85%
Southern Co	$4,483.00	$4,162.00	$(321.00)	-7.16%	-6.13%
Spectra Energy Corp	$2,881.00	$3,311.00	$430.00	14.93%	-8.00%
Teco Energy Inc.	$1,735.00	$1,653.00	$(82.00)	-4.73%	-7.03%
US Bancorp	$3,401.00	$3,613.00	$212.00	6.23%	-4.34%
Verizon Communications Inc.	$4,672.00	$4,738.00	$66.00	1.41%	-5.71%
Wells Fargo & Co	$3,539.00	$4,108.00	$569.00	16.08%	-7.66%
DWS Core Equity Fund	$1,983.00	$2,139.00	$156.00	7.87%	-4.21%
DWS S&P 500 Index Fund	$2,022.00	$2,176.00	$154.00	7.62%	-4.31%
DWS Short Duration Fund	$931.00	$920.00	$(11.00)	-1.18%	-0.22%
Fidelity Contrafund	$8,122.00	$8,870.00	$748.00	9.21%	-3.50%
Wellesley Income Fund	$2,479.00	$2,460.00	$(19.00)	-0.77%	-2.15%
	$174,739.00	$79,187.00	$4,488.00	2.55%	

SEPTEMBER

DIVERSITY & REALIGNMENT

When a fool has made up his mind the market has gone by.
—Spanish Proverb

You know you're a novice investor when...

You learn your broker's favorite restaurant is named 'Rumours.'

From: Richard Kraneyum
Sent: Monday, August 29, 2013 9:19 AM
To: Mark Slauter <markslauter@novice.investor>
Subject: Urgent message!

Dear Fellow Investor,

I put this message together quickly, to get it to you ASAP. So, please forgive me if there are typos. It concerns a rapidly developing investment opportunity you can get into today for less than $5 per share. But as you'll see, that price is about to double -- and then double again by year end simply because it's...

Ok...I'm putting this one out here solely because of the first sentence. Really?? You expect me to follow your advice when you slap something together and apologize for typos?

September 11, 2013

A day of remembrance...

The market was climbing again today (11th), but Apple is getting smacked. It was up over $500 two days ago and closed today at $467. That hurts my bottom line. Interesting that while the market went up, several of my items decreased. I sold Apple on the 12th and took my 18% profit, which was good, because it dropped another $15 on the 16th. I think Apple will edge close to the $450 mark again as investors just don't seem too impressed with the company, though I think it's a solid buy.

September 23, 2013

So I start my day listening to the TV news and, at one point, there is a short piece of business news stating that the Dow is down 200 points in the pre-market! I think, "oh crap," in part because I had thought of selling a couple items today. Not only does the market have a somewhat contained case of the jitters because of the Fed potentially easing off their bond-buying program—but now it's the Republicans in the House saying they'll agree to increase the debt ceiling if the Democrats kill Obamacare.

Investing can be a fool's paradise. Around every bend of the market, within every voice yelling at you in an email—despite not giving a hoot about typos—contradictory information may confuse and undermine your efforts. You can foolishly think you're swimming in money when the bottom's about to drop out of the market. Or you can feel like a fool missing opportunities when you're really in the right place. There aren't any "right" answers, but there's definitely one wrong, surefire way to be a fool: Chase every bit of info that comes your way. So, I was determined to not be played a fool, whether by mine or another's actions.

In my opinion, there's no point in chasing after the market. Usually, by the time you read an email or analyst report, the stock value has already changed. In fact, investing is no different than keeping up with the daily news; by the time you hear about something, it's already happened. With that said, many articles point to a future position of an investment—and that's where the rubber meets the road. A stock's share price has a future time value already in place, which is why investors can make sudden shifts in their buying or selling. Investors will try to get in or out early due to a current action that may affect the future of a company.

NAVIGATING DIVERSITY

Once you start investing, you'll hear a key word over and over again: diversification.

Part of the whole reason I decided to create my fantasy portfolio was to better understand diversity within my Mom's portfolio and how we can maximize her financial strength. With my sister and I responsible for her personal and financial well-being, I felt that this approach would provide me with an educated perspective, improving my ability to meet her needs. Knowing how to diversify a portfolio was crucial to my experiment.

Being too heavy in a sector means you have too many eggs in one basket and are over-exposed to the sectors' fluctuations. If you're heavy in a sector that goes up, then you can pour the champagne. But, if you're heavy in a sector that plummets, you'll start looking at selling your pets for scientific experiments to generate income. Meanwhile, being light in a sector means you're underexposed. While underexposure can be a good thing if the sector value moves down, you'll be mad when it goes up, because you "could have had more." Remember, investing is all about balance. Whatever you do, make the effort to avoid situations you think will stress you out.

Diversifying your portfolio has no hard-and-fast rules. Your portfolio's diversification can be as varied and unique as the markets themselves. The key is to research, stay up to date on performance, and always look for opportunities.

So, how did diversification compare between me and Mom?

I didn't really think about this when I first started, but as I learned more I found myself interested in other possible market metrics. Without some degree of difficulty, I don't think you could align yourself perfectly with the current diversity represented by market sectors. Frankly, I see no point in trying to do so. However, you should have some understanding of what your portfolio looks like compared to the market.

Sector	Current Market Diversity %	Me	Mom	Me	Mom
		Where We Started		Current	
Basic Materials	3.16%	13.64%	0%	12.20%	0%
Consumer Goods	10.18%	4.55%	7.14%	4.88%	7.32%
Consumer Services	13.45%	9.09%	2.38%	14.63%	0%
Energy	9.68%	22.73%	23.81	14.63%	24.39%
Financial Services	18.37%	13.64%	14.29%	12.20%	12.20%
Healthcare	11.94%	4.55%	0%	9.76%	0%
Industrial	13.06%	9.09%	9.52%	9.76%	9.76%
Technology	14.61%	9.09%	2.38%	12.20%	4.88%
Telecommunications	2.25%	4.55%	7.14%	4.88%	7.32%
Utilities	3.31%	9.09%	30.95%	2.44%	31.71%
Real Estate	3.79%	0%	2.38%	2.44%	2.44%

Though we somewhat aligned in a couple of sectors, we weren't even close for many of them. Mom was most overexposed in Utilities, and I was mostly overexposed in Basic Materials. Mom was underexposed in Basic Materials and Healthcare, for me it was Healthcare. Being overexposed creates a bigger negative impact if the stock value drops. However, if the stock value increases, you'll be quite happy. Since I wasn't trying to exactly match the sector percentages, I wasn't concerned with where I was. However, knowing where I was overexposed was a signal for me to re-evaluate a few holdings to ensure I really wanted to retain them.

WATCHING THE MARKET

As September moved forward, the media was reporting that investors had not been very active due to the possible actions of the Federal Open Market Committee (FOMC)—resulting in the market hovering around the neutral line. Any negative comments after the FOMC's meeting on this topic could have sent stocks down. Plus, the U.S. Congress was looking to defund Obamacare; the

Republican trade-off was: If the President postponed the program for one year, then they would agree to raise the federal debt ceiling. *Why do these folks keep getting voted in?* As a result, investors were quite skittish about the potential outcome of all of this, which was making me nervous.

On September 18, the FOMC meeting ended and reported that it would maintain the QE program for now. As a result, investors gained back some confidence and pushed the market up 147 points, supporting improvement in all sectors. And just like that, the market shrugged off the Federal Reserve, ignored Congress, and jumped upward. Imagine being a day trader on days like this! Meanwhile, I was going out of my mind as I watched the value of our portfolios move like a yo-yo in response. It made me think of someone in one of those baby bungee chairs you hang in a doorway, so the baby can bounce up and down. I was quite pissed off that my financial livelihood was dependent upon Congress.

The question became: Would the market hold? Or did we just enter a bona fide profit-taking opportunity? Only time would tell…

CHASING FOR INFORMATION

To make the most of your investment experience, never, ever, ever stop searching for insight. You'll have several variables to consider when investing. So, the more you know, the more confident you'll be with your decisions.

Inflation is just one detail I realized I must pay attention to. I must also understand and factor other issues into my investment strategy—and I needed to know what they mean. For example, I must know when I take a profit or loss, what my income is, any changes in tax laws, etc. You pay less taxes on investments held longer than one year. With all of the selling and buying I was doing, I have no doubt someone would say I lost some of my profits to taxes due to selling so quickly. And these taxes add up! *And they make*

Uncle Sam happy in the process.

Examples provided in this article show how a nominal increase in value of more than 10% erodes to less than 6% due to other factors. No matter how I slice this up, losing 30% or more—particularly when it comes as a result of politicians doing stupid shit—just plain sucks. Read the Morningstar article titled "A Study of Real Real Returns: Always look beyond nominal returns to what investments generate after inflation, taxes, and expenses: the real real return."

Think about whether or not you have an investment philosophy. I kind of do…and then again, I kind of don't—I'm learning. Reading this article by Christine Benz of Morningstar on having an investment philosophy was useful: "The Error-Proof Portfolio: Why You Need an Investment Philosophy: Having conviction in your belief system can help you act with discipline."

As I was mulling over what my philosophy is, I continued looking for investing opportunities. I came across an article on the Quebec train derailment where rail cars full of oil crashed, exploded, burned several buildings, and resulted in several deaths. While reading, I realized that this type of accident can result in new regulations. So, I researched who manufactures DOT 111 tankers, which the article highlighted, and eventually found details regarding five manufacturers. Turned out, a few of the companies were way up for the one-year trend. *It's good to sleuth?* Though I decided not to invest in these companies at this point, I knew I had to watch these developments in the coming months. In particular, I was waiting on what the political fallout would be. If the politicos started jabbering about this and the need for new regulations, such as thicker walls on the tankers, then the manufacturing companies would have to build new ones and the transportation companies would have to buy them.

And this is why it's good to sleuth for potential investment opportunities. It pays to pay attention to the world around you.

ANALYZING THE PORTFOLIOS

On September 7, I made some changes I felt would help my portfolio and the day after was nerve racking. It's like wondering if you've won your five-card draw poker hand. Applying information I'd previously learned, I almost sold The AES Corporation (AES) stock but held onto it as it was running a 10% return from a slight increase over these past few weeks. Good decision! AES jumped up to over 11% a couple days later. Then on September 9, the market rose 141 points. Five of the six new acquisitions increased with the rally—and one dropped $1. I was glad I sold the second acquisition of GlaxoSmithKline PLC ADR (GSK), as it dropped again. Since I had more wiggle room from the first buy, I felt okay with its performance, for now.

Man, what a difference a rally can make! Almost every item improved. But, I remembered to not let my emotions get the best of me and grounded myself by keeping in mind what's ahead. At least I tried.

AAHHRRRGGG...Ok, it'll be done. Crappy bond funds...still can't find a good one.

I became very frustrated with the lack of performance and decided to sell my Wells Fargo Advantage Core Builder Series M (WFCMX) holdings for a $94 loss. Not a big loss, but who likes losing money? I also sold my Legacy Reserves, LP (LGCY) holdings for a loss, though I did get a few bucks from dividends. Initially, Legacy had support from the Pros, but it had since lost that support. Also, selling this for a minimal loss reduced my overexposure in the Energy sector.

With my increased cash reserves I made the following acquisitions this month:

	Sector	Analyst Buy Recommendations	Dividend Yield	10-yr Avg for Revenue Growth	10-yr EPS
Anika Therapeutics	Healthcare	4 of 4	0%	18.39%	5.12%[1]
GasLog Ltd.	Industrial	3 of 4	3.1%	100.31%[2]	-80.56%[3,4]
Navios Maritime Holdings Inc.	Industrial	3 of 4	3.3%	36.85%	-10.03%[1]
Omnicell, Inc.	Technology	3 of 4	0%	13.61%	-18.16%[1]
Orchids paper Products Company	Basic Materials	2 of 4	0%	10.08%	-24.16%[1]
RF Industries, Ltd.	Technology	1 of 4	4.4%	12.99%	22.41%

1. 5-year average
2. 3-year average
3. 1-year average
4. The year-over-year average for earnings per share was -80.56% (but moving up from 0.07 in 2012 to 0.91 in 2013)

Despite the Pros not preferring Orchids Paper and RF Industries, I went with my interpretation of the data and picked them anyway. Four of the six stocks listed above had dividends and all six appeared to be growing. But I also chose these investments because they improved my sector diversity. A quote I once read explains this rationale perfectly (paraphrased):

> I look for some degree of diversification in my portfolio to minimize the impact of the bad decisions I will inevitably make.

At the other end of this argument is Warren Buffet who basically says people pursue diversity because they don't know what they're doing. Another fine example of hearing two opposite perspectives. *Yeah, it's like that.*

By the middle of September, three of my holdings were big losers: Linn Energy (LINE), Northern Tier Energy (NTI), and Terra Nitrogen (TNH). Though they paid me big dividends, they were equally matched with big losses. So, I had to analyze these from a loss-gain ratio. If the dividends weren't even close to covering the losses, I decided to drop them. Since TNH dividends covered about two-thirds of its losses, I kept that and dumped the others. *You gotta start somewhere!*

By September 28, I was curious to look back at a few of my previous sales to see where I'd be if I had kept them:

Item	Acquired Price	Sold Price	Closing Price	Sentiment
Apple (1st purchase)	$393.54	$413.50	$482.75	Should have kept this one.
Aruba Networks	$25.00	$23.16	$16.60	Glad I took the loss when I did.
GlaxoSmithKline (2nd purchase)	$48.47	$51.67	$50.48	Came out farther ahead on profit. Plus, my first purchase was at $44.22, and I'm still up 14.2%.
Northern Tier Energy	$29.50	$19.89	$19.82	I should have taken the loss earlier.

My losses were double my gains from sales. *Ouch!* The upshot was that I was doing okay with dividends, the value of my portfolio was up, and I had about $33k in cash. Not too shabby.

MONTH IN REVIEW

Between August 30 and September 27, 2013, the Dow gained 448 points. I still had the lead but the Dow had closed the gap a little from last month.

Weekly Return on Investment Stats			
	Dow Jones Industrial Average	Me	Mom
Week 27	5.91%	9.09%	2.43%
Week 28	9.13%	8.86%	3.83%
Week 29	9.66%	9.22%	5.51%
Week 30	8.29%	9.90%	4.79%

Overall, for September, I had an unrealized gain of $23,939. Though there were no real loss leaders this month, Energy and Basic Materials were lagging. Mom had an unrealized gain of $8,367 this month.

COMPARISON

For this month, I was about 1.5 points ahead of the market and about 5 points ahead of Mom. Across the board, this was a better month for all three. Even with the sniping and pettiness of Congress, the market was able to shake them off and move forward.

At this point, my portfolio had 22 items that I invested in based on recommendations from the Pros, which was about 48% (24 items were my picks). On a percentage basis, I came out behind the Pros this month as 75.0% of my items increased in value, but 86.3% of the Pros items increased. Looks like the Pros have decided to step up to the plate and show me how it's done.

DIVIDENDS FOR SEPTEMBER

My dividend payments in September dipped below August's dividends performance, which made me a bit bummed, but hey, at least I was still receiving income!

Though I received fewer payments this month compared to last month, it's not uncommon. The timing of dividend payments all depends on the fiscal cycle of the company. Not all companies use the same fiscal calendar or payment intervals. Hey, so what, Mom and I are still making money.

I received 11 payments totaling $520.72, which averaged $47.34 per payment. Mom received 20 payments totaling $556.55, which averaged $27.83 per payment. Though she made more in total, my value per payment was greater by a substantial $20! So, this is a great example of how the quality of dividend yield may be a factor in your investment selections.

LESSONS LEARNED

For a short week (after Labor Day), it sure felt like a long one and the first two weeks consisted of agonizing over what to sell and what to buy. The urge to sell and buy felt like an itch I couldn't scratch, which told me that I was probably falling subject to some emotional element caused by an illusion of inaction—I felt the "need for speed." I attempted to temper my need by spending more time evaluating what to sell and buy. I altered my short list about 10 times, before deciding which selections to make.

o **Not every itch should or can be scratched.** Just because you think you've found a good deal, or have cash not currently invested, or you're just feeling antsy, doesn't mean you have to take action. Sometimes the smarter and harder decision is to do nothing.

o **A few portfolio items can determine being ahead or behind as applied against the market rate of return.** It's the law of averages. If you have some stocks that are performing really well or very poorly, they can drive your overall percentage of profit or loss. I find it useful to keep this in mind. As September closed, my best performing stock was up about 144%. My worst performer was down about 13%—everything else fell in between.

○ **Dividends don't equate to increasing value.** Some folks present chasing dividends as the path to success. Avoid the argument as it's nothing more than the lure of easy money. I want a good return on my investment, but some poorly based decisions cost me much more than I gained. Getting a 10% dividend on a stock whose value has dropped 30% is a losing proposition.

○ **Confidence and knowledge are not necessarily interchangeable.** There is always the chance that confidence will outstrip knowledge. This line is tricky because the emotion of confidence may override the brain saying (in opposition) you don't really know something.

Willpower. I think that's a good word to describe this month.

The following portfolio tables show what the current value (September 27) is compared to the purchase value. Value is presented in both dollar and percentage terms. The last column has the month-to-month (August to September) change as a percentage to show how items fluctuate monthly compared to the ever lengthening time between the start date and current values.

MY PORTFOLIO FOR SEPTEMBER 2013

Note: '0' in last column reflects ownership of less than a month.

Name (Pros in italics)	Purchase $ Value	9-27-13 $ Value	Total Net $ Gain/ Loss	Total Net % Gain/ Loss	Aug to Sept % Change
8x8, Inc.	$744.00	$1,036.00	$292.00	39.2%	12.00%
The AES Corporation	$1,193.00	$1,347.00	$154.00	12.9%	5.98%
Alaska Air Group	$6,273.00	$6,359.00	$86.00	1.4%	12.31%
Alliance Resource Partners LP	$6,725.00	$7,473.00	$748.00	11.1%	-0.73%
Anika Therapeutics	$2,417.00	$2,450.00	$33.00	1.4%	0
Apple Inc.(3)	$39,354.00	$48,275.00	$2,721.00	6.0%	0
Bank of Nova Scotia	$5,341.00	$5,738.00	$397.00	7.4%	3.39%
Coca-Cola Co	$3,870.00	$3,840.00	$(30.00)	-0.8%	0.58%
Consolidated Communications Inc.	$1,637.00	$1,726.00	$89.00	5.4%	3.48%
El Paso Pipeline Partners LP	$4,140.00	$4,186.00	$46.00	1.1%	0.31%
GasLog Ltd	$1,432.00	$1,486.00	$54.00	3.8%	0
The GEO Group Inc.	$3,448.00	$3,334.00	$(114.00)	-3.3%	6.82%
GlaxoSmithKline PLC ADR (1)	$4,422.00	$5,048.00	$626.00	14.2%	-0.81%
Great Northern Iron Ore (2)	$6,944.00	$7,235.00	$291.00	4.2%	2.61%
HCP Inc.	$4,325.00	$4,155.00	$(170.00)	-3.9%	2.01%
Home Loan Servicing Solutions	$2,302.00	$2,200.00	$(102.00)	-4.4%	-3.51%
Inventure Foods, Inc.	$726.00	$1,051.00	$325.00	44.8%	16.52%

Name (Pros in italics)	Purchase $ Value	9-27-13 $ Value	Total Net $ Gain/ Loss	Total Net % Gain/ Loss	Aug to Sept % Change
Kinder Morgan Energy Partners LP (1)	$8,672.00	$7,983.00	$(689.00)	-7.9%	-2.12%
Kinder Morgan Energy Partners LP (2)	$9,025.00	$7,983.00	$(1,042.00)	-11.5%	-2.12%
Macy's Inc.	$4,067.00	$4,352.00	$285.00	7.0%	-2.05%
Merck & Co Inc.	$4,782.00	$4,779.00	$(3.00)	-0.1%	1.06%
Michael Kors Holdings Ltd	$5,804.00	$7,445.00	$1,641.00	28.3%	0.49%
Navios Maritime Holdings Inc.	$719.00	$721.00	$2.00	0.3%	0
NTT DoCoMo Inc.	$1,505.00	$1,615.00	$110.00	7.3%	0.75%
Oaktree Capital Group, LLC	$5,013.00	$5,415.00	$402.00	8.0%	4.54%
Omnicell, Inc.	$2,318.00	$2,361.00	$43.00	1.9%	0
Orchids Paper Products Co	$2,724.00	$2,801.00	$77.00	2.8%	0
Pfizer Inc.	$3,043.00	$2,888.00	$(155.00)	-5.1%	2.38%
Protolabs Inc.	$5,505.00	$7,632.00	$2,127.00	38.6%	7.43%
Prudential PLC ADR	$3,349.00	$3,747.00	$398.00	11.9%	11.65%
PVR Partners LP	$2,285.00	$2,287.00	$2.00	0.1%	-1.46%
Qihoo 360 Technology Co., Ltd.	$3,440.00	$8,393.00	$4,953.00	144.0%	7.70%
RF Industries, Ltd	$636.00	$722.00	$86.00	13.5%	0
Seaspan Corp	$1,930.00	$2,450.00	$520.00	26.9%	14.86%
Sonoco Products Co	$3,407.00	$3,924.00	$517.00	15.2%	5.40%
Sunoco Logistics Partners LP	$6,258.00	$6,679.00	$421.00	6.7%	3.97%
Terra Nitrogen Company	$23,461.00	$20,350.00	$(3,111.00)	-13.3%	-4.83%
TJX Companies	$4,498.00	$5,647.00	$1,149.00	25.5%	7.11%
Akre Focus Fund Retail	$1,630.00	$1,948.00	$318.00	19.5%	6.33%
Delaware Healthcare I	$1,355.00	$1,723.00	$368.00	27.2%	4.74%
Oakmark Global I	$2,610.00	$2,991.00	$381.00	14.6%	7.90%
Oceanstone Fund	$3,753.00	$4,122.00	$740.00	21.9%	5.02%

Name (Pros in italics)	Purchase $ Value	9-27-13 $ Value	Total Net $ Gain/ Loss	Total Net % Gain/ Loss	Aug to Sept % Change
Fidelity Select Biotechnology Portfolio (1)	$14,631.00	$17,620.00	$5,415.00	44.4%	9.32%
Fidelity Select Biotechnology Portfolio (2)	$10,826.94	$13,038.80	$2,822.36	27.6%	9.32%
Fidelity Select IT Services Portfolio	$2,985.00	$3,384.00	$609.00	21.9%	6.58%
Vanguard Wellington Inv	$3,707.00	$3,754.00	107.00	2.9%	2.07%
	$241,754.44	$265,693.80	$23,939.36	9.90%	

Note: The primary reason for my doing better this month is because I realigned my portfolio, which resulted in me selling stocks for more money than what I reinvested. Last month's Purchase Value was about $271k.

MOM'S PORTFOLIO FOR SEPTEMBER 2013

Name	Purchase $ Value	9-27-13 $ Value	Total Net $ Gain/ Loss	Total Net % Gain/ Loss	Aug to Sept % Change
Altria Group	$3,349.00	$3,471.00	$122.00	3.64%	2.45%
AT&T Inc.	$3,601.00	$3,398.00	$(203.00)	-5.64%	0.44%
Buckeye Partners LP	$5,611.00	$6,578.00	$967.00	17.23%	-6.03%
Caterpillar Inc.	$9,136.00	$8,380.00	$(756.00)	-8.27%	1.53%
Cleco Corp	$4,418.00	$4,493.00	$75.00	1.70%	-0.51%
CMS Energy Corp	$2,645.00	$2,621.00	$(24.00)	-0.91%	-1.21%
Compass Securities	$1,574.00	$1,787.00	$213.00	13.53%	3.41%
Deluxe Corp	$3,965.00	$4,122.00	$157.00	3.96%	4.75%
Devon Energy Corp	$5,388.00	$5,871.00	$483.00	8.96%	2.84%
Dominion Res Inc. VA	$5,642.00	$6,243.00	$601.00	10.65%	6.99%
Duke Energy	$6,925.00	$6,690.00	$(235.00)	-3.39%	1.98%
Enbridge Energy Partners	$2,763.00	$3,034.00	$271.00	9.81%	1.74%
Enterprise Products	$5,681.00	$6,090.00	$409.00	7.20%	2.49%

Name	Purchase $ Value	9-27-13 $ Value	Total Net $ Gain/ Loss	Total Net % Gain/ Loss	Aug to Sept % Change
Exxon Mobile Corporation	$8,943.00	$8,690.00	$(253.00)	-2.83%	-0.30%
Frontier Communications Corp	$419.00	$429.00	$10.00	2.39%	-0.92%
General Electric Co	$2,319.00	$2,405.00	$86.00	3.71%	3.93%
Great Plains Energy	$2,199.00	$2,228.00	$29.00	1.32%	1.64%
Hartford Financial Services Group	$2,368.00	$3,127.00	$759.00	32.05%	5.64%
Hudson City Bancorp	$858.00	$912.00	$54.00	6.29%	-0.76%
Integrys Energy Group	$5,610.00	$5,582.00	$(28.00)	-0.50%	-0.18%
Intel Corp	$2,103.00	$2,298.00	$195.00	9.27%	4.55%
Medical Property Trust	$1,483.00	$1,225.00	$(258.00)	-17.40%	6.06%
Mondelez International	$2,781.00	$3,180.00	$399.00	14.35%	3.68%
Nat'l Grid Transco	$5,456.00	$5,940.00	$484.00	8.87%	3.20%
Nisource Inc.	$2,793.00	$3,067.00	$274.00	9.81%	4.82%
Occidental Petroleum Corp	$8,265.00	$9,446.00	$1,181.00	14.29%	7.09%
Spyglass Resources Corp	$274.00	$157.00	$(117.00)	-42.70%	-6.55%
Pembina Pipeline Corp	$2,821.00	$3,306.00	$485.00	17.19%	6.37%
Pepco Holdings Inc.	$2,053.00	$1,845.00	$(208.00)	-10.13%	-2.59%
Philip Morris International Inc.	$9,144.00	$8,733.00	$(411.00)	-4.49%	4.66%
Piedmont Natural Gas Co	$3,265.00	$3,266.00	$1.00	0.03%	1.24%
Principle Financial Group	$3,155.00	$4,319.00	$1,164.00	36.89%	5.55%
Royal Dutch Shell PLC ADR	$6,578.00	$6,588.00	$10.00	0.15%	2.00%
Scana Corp	$4,906.00	$4,603.00	$(303.00)	-6.18%	-4.34%
Southern Co	$4,483.00	$4,123.00	$(360.00)	-8.03%	-0.94%
Spectra Energy Corp	$2,881.00	$3,417.00	$536.00	18.60%	3.20%
Teco Energy Inc.	$1,735.00	$1,651.00	$(84.00)	-4.84%	-0.12%
US Bancorp	$3,401.00	$3,650.00	$249.00	7.32%	1.02%

Name	Purchase $ Value	9-27-13 $ Value	Total Net $ Gain/ Loss	Total Net % Gain/ Loss	Aug to Sept % Change
Verizon Communications Inc.	$4,672.00	$4,700.00	$28.00	0.60%	-0.80%
Wells Fargo & Co	$3,539.00	$4,159.00	$620.00	17.52%	1.24%
DWS Core Equity Fund	$1,983.00	$2,242.00	$259.00	13.06%	4.82%
DWS S&P 500 Index Fund	$2,022.00	$2,249.00	$227.00	11.23%	3.35%
DWS Short Duration Fund	$931.00	$921.00	$(10.00)	-1.07%	0.11%
Fidelity Contrafund	$8,122.00	$9,383.00	$1,261.00	15.53%	5.78%
Wellesley Income Fund	$2,479.00	$2,487.00	$8.00	0.32%	1.10%
	$174,739.00	$183,106.00	$8,367.00	4.79%	

Mark Slauter

OCTOBER

PATIENCE & UNDERSTANDING

October: This is one of the particularly dangerous months to invest in stocks. Other dangerous months are July, January, September, April, November, May, March, June, December, August and February.

—Mark Twain

You know you're a novice investor when...

You realize that the market is just a menagerie of animals: chickens, bulls, bears, dogs, pigs, and asses.

From:	Dee Faughlt
Sent:	Thursday, September 21, 2013 2:29 PM
To:	Mark Slauter <markslauter@novice.investor>
Subject:	We All Love Wendy's!

This Message is Urgent!

Burger chain Wendy's (WEN) has soared almost 60% so far in 2012, but remains under $10 a share and is still a decent buy for investors looking at low-priced options right now.

At least they're correct that the stock is under $10. However, it wasn't 2012 and the stock was up 84% year-to-date. Holy crap! The price earnings/trailing twelve months (PE/TTM) was 232.6!!!!

October 4, 2013

The market has steadily moved downward, primarily from the shutdown of the federal government. My portfolio has been a mixed bag of increases and decreases, more down than up. But, I'm still faring better on percentages as I'm at 9.25% and the market is at 6.44%. Another looming issue is the need for Congress to make a decision on the debt limit by Oct 17th. Obviously, these monkeys are from a different barrel than the one I had as a kid…

October 8, 2013

The continued government shutdown has unsettled investors as they are showing less desire for higher growth, riskier stocks. Some media are calling recent investor moves the "flight to safety" mentality. I think that once Congress gets its shit together (relatively speaking) the market will roar back up. I'd refer to the current Congressional activity as mental masturbation but that would infer a point of completion.

October brought another strange period for my portfolio, which is why the month became my time for focusing on patience and understanding. The market dropped, market rose, market went serial—challenging the state of mind we call "sane."

A multitude of political happenings were influencing the market—and while I couldn't find a discernible pattern for all the ebbs and flows, I did notice a major theme: When the market dropped, many of my holdings increased in value; when the market rose, my portfolio experienced a mixed bag of increases and decreases. Of course, Congressional asses kept butting heads, which didn't help market consistency. I found myself taking deep breaths and consoling my anxiety with the humorous idea that if Congress wasn't so divided, the market volatility surely wouldn't be as fun. Right?

Up to this point, my top three losers were (and had been) the Kinder Morgan (EPB & KMP) and Terra Nitrogen (TNH) items. I started realizing that it was going to take substantial investor action to raise the share price and get me to my break-even point, let alone the profit point. If I was at the break-even point on these three, my overall unrealized gain would increase from 11.8% to 12.9%—about a 9% difference, which is significant.

WATCHING THE MARKET

As the soap opera on Capitol Hill played to its own members (*surely, they weren't doing this on my behalf*), the markets continued their roller-coaster style. However, the markets eventually moved up once Congress reached a temporary agreement on the debt ceiling limit. Add to this some good quarterly earnings reports plus China's economy still growing, and investors were willing to jump back in. There was still some concern over what the Federal Reserve would do with the monthly bond-buying efforts.

Meanwhile, I was watching my biggest winner, Qihoo 360, get whittled away a little at a time. I wasn't too worried about the mutual funds as they tend to absorb the impact better than individual equities. I was still two points better than the Dow based on my start date, but it was painful to watch the drop.

My big dilemma became: Should I sell some big winners and take the gains with the forethought to buy them back when they bottom out—or should I hold on and wait?

I felt my decision relied less on being smart enough to do this and more on being confident enough in my own smarts. There's a fine line among confidence, arrogance, intelligence, and ignorance, with little effort needed to easily cross from one into another. As with any decision, the wrong one can be disastrous. Knowing I don't have all of the information forces me to question whether or not the amount of information I do have is sufficient to make a decision. There's a difference between buying a car you think will work versus buying one where you've turned the key to prove it starts.

With some of my holdings' values falling rapidly, I feared that these items would continue losing value as investors pulled out and took their profit. Following the herd can be easy with a lot of emotions flying around, but patience and understanding are key components of investing.

Here are a few examples of how fast changes can occur within a portfolio. The focus here is on how the value of an unrealized gain can quickly degrade.

Name	Oct 4 Profit Value	Oct 4 Profit %	Oct 8 Profit Value	Oct 8 Profit %	Dollar Change	Percentage Change
Michael Kors Holdings Ltd (KORS)	$1831	31.6%	$1288	22.2%	-$543	-29.7%
Protolabs Inc. (PRLB)	$2542	46.2%	$1795	32.6%	-$747	-29.4%
Qihoo 360 Technology Co (QIHU)	$5177	150.1%	$4284	124.5%	-$893	-17.1%

Between Friday October 4 and Thursday October 8, these three items dropped from an unrealized gain of $9550 down to $7367 for an averaged loss of 22.9%—about $2200. To say this made me nervous is an understatement.

By the time October 24 rolled around, the markets had completely shifted into a new direction, creeping upward in value. I kept hearing James Brown celebrating in my head, *"I feel good! Bada dada dada da. The way that I should now…"* I felt like I had turned a corner, even if only temporarily, and that provided a small boost to my confidence and took away a bit of the stress I was experiencing.

CHASING FOR INFORMATION

As I continued to acquire a better understanding of my investments, I made more of an effort to seek out and read analyst updates and media reports. By October, I started feeling like I had a good start with the knowledge I'd gained—and needed to dive into deeper waters. I wanted to know the companies better, I wanted to know more of what the professionals thought, and I wanted to protect my money.

A topic I've not yet touched upon is buybacks. Many companies provide dividend distributions as a primary way to return cash to shareholders. Another way to do this is by using their cash to buy back the stock, thus removing those shares from the marketplace. With fewer shares available, the ones you own constitute a larger percentage of ownership.

For example, is it better to own 100 shares of a company with 10,000 shares in the marketplace or 100 shares in a company with only 5,000 shares available in the marketplace? With 10,000 shares available, your ownership stake is 1.0 percent. With only 5,000 shares available, your ownership stake is worth 2.0%.

The take away? Being subject to buybacks is good for your investments, especially if you retain the shares. However, this change is not as simple as it sounds.

When a company purchases its shares back from the market, it can also affect other metrics applied to the company's performance, such as earnings per share (EPS). In other words, they can increase the EPS simply because the number of shares available to purchase is reduced—without improving the company's underlying fundamentals. As a result, an increased EPS doesn't necessarily mean the company is doing better or is more profitable.

So, if you don't dig deeper, you might be investing in a company thinking performance has improved, when really, nothing fundamentally changed.

To help investors out, some organizations have a process for estimating a "fair" share value. I found the Morningstar fair value estimate to be quite useful. Since I didn't have the knowledge or tools to determine a stock's value, I realized that paying a subscription fee for this information was worth it. While plenty of free sources of investment information exist, they don't have the level of detail provided by Morningstar or similar subscription services.

Here's an example from Morningstar.com:

> **Merck & Co Inc. (MRK)**: Further, while the restructuring will likely save $2.5 billion a year, we don't expect any major changes to our fair value estimate of $52 per share, as we had already projected a portion of these savings. We continue to view Merck as slightly undervalued, as we believe investors under-appreciate the company's early-stage pipeline.

In my findings, I noted that Morningstar recommended considering fair value estimates in conjunction with other factors, such as a company's "economic moat." Like a water moat protecting a castle from outside invasion, analyzing a company's economic moat can help you understand how well protected a company is from outside influences—and whether or not they're positioned to stay ahead of competitors. Their definition is:

Economic Moat: (Economic Moat is a proprietary Morningstar data point.) The idea of an economic moat refers to how likely a company is to keep competitors at bay for an extended period. One of the keys to finding superi- or long-term investments is buying companies that will be able to stay one step ahead of their competitors, and it's this characteristic-think of it as the strength and sustainability of a firm's competitive advantage-that Morningstar is trying to capture with the economic moat rating.

According to Morningstar, the following data points reveal a company with economic moat:

○ Historical financial performance

○ Market share

○ Production costs

○ Patents

○ Copyrights or other forms of government approval or license

○ Corporate culture

○ Customer switching costs

○ Network effect (to consumers and other businesses)

Once they've analyzed these data points, Morningstar organizes companies into three categories according to moat size:

○ **Wide Moat**. Companies with the strongest competitive advantage

○ **Narrow Moat.** Those with some competitive advantage

○ **No Moat.** Those with no sustainable competitive advantage

Here are two examples of moat ratings from Morningstar:

Apple Inc. (AAPL): We will maintain our $600 fair value estimate and narrow moat rating for Apple after the company announced its lineup of refreshed iPads and Macs. We believe Apple has a narrow economic moat based on modest, but not insurmountable, customer switching costs.

GlaxoSmithKline PLC ADR (GSK): GlaxoSmithKline reported third-quarter results largely in line with our expectations and those of consensus....Core to our valuation and wide moat rating is the company's pipeline, which continues to make strong strides. Glaxo holds a wide economic moat on the basis of patents, a powerful distribution network, economies of scale, and diverse operations.

I view economic moat as an indicator of strength, and understanding the strength of the company should put me in a better position to make profitable decisions. But, it still comes down to my objectives. Just because Apple (APPL) has a narrow moat and GlaxoSmithKline (GSK) has a wide moat doesn't automatically equate to one being a better investment than the other. Apple meets my purpose of having a stock with rising share value; that's where the profit is. GSK has slower rising share value but a better dividend and good prospects for stable long-term growth.

Now, if I compare narrow moat Apple to wide moat Microsoft I have to ask the same question of my objectives. Maybe owning both is a good thing. Regardless of the moat rating, an item either fits or doesn't fit into my portfolio objectives—and that's the bottom line.

Here's a good story regarding economic moat that was written by Matt Coffina who is the Editor of Morningstar's StockInvestor and manages the two portfolios he writes about.

Starting with the Basics: A Lemonade Stand

The most important quantitative evidence that an economic moat may be present is a high return on invested capital, or ROIC. Investors – both shareholders and creditors – require a certain level of return in exchange for providing a company the funds it needs to run its business. This is called the weighted average cost of capital, or WACC. A company generates excess returns if its ROIC consistently exceeds its WACC.

For example, imagine little Joe wants to open a lemonade stand. He needs $100 up front to buy a table, a pitcher, lemons, sugar, ice, and cups. This is his invested capital. Joe borrows $50 from Mom, and promises to pay her 5% interest ($2.50).

Dad has a higher risk tolerance, so he buys $50 worth of common stock in Joe's lemonade stand. Dad expects a 10% return (this is called the cost of equity).

The lemonade stand's invested capital is funded with 50% equity and 50% debt. The weighted average cost of capital is exactly what it sounds like, a weighted average of the cost of equity and debt capital. It is calculated as:

$$0.5 \times 5\% + 0.5 \times 10\% = 7.5\%$$

If Joe's lemonade stand were just any ordinary business,

we would expect its return on invested capital to match its WACC. But Joe is an exceptional salesman, and when the day is done he has earned a $10 operating profit, after paying himself a reasonable wage and replenishing his stock of lemons, sugar, ice, and cups. The lemonade stand's ROIC is 10% ($10/$100), and Joe has achieved excess returns on capital.

Beware of Competitors

At this point, Joe is feeling pretty satisfied, and his Dad is ecstatic. After paying Mom's $2.50 in interest, Joe has $7.50 left over to either reinvest in the business or distribute to Dad as a dividend. Dad's return on equity is 15% ($7.50 divided by his $50 investment), well ahead of the 10% cost of equity he was expecting. It's good to be a stockholder.

Unfortunately, Joe's lemonade stand lacks an economic moat. His sister Julie hears about his successful business venture, and decides she wants in. Mom and Dad can hardly show favoritism to one child over the other, so they agree to fund Julie with the same $50 in debt and $50 in equity. Julie sets up shop the next morning right next to Joe.

When Joe and Julie count their day's take, they find that each has earned a profit of $6. ROIC has fallen to 6% ($6/$100), and both Joe and Julie have failed to earn their cost of capital. Mom is still doing OK, collecting 4% of interest and her $100 total investment. But now there is only $7 left for Dad: a 7% return on his $100 investment. Dad had been expecting to earn at least 10% - the sleepless night he spent worrying about his equity investment wasn't worth the measly 7% return. Joe wished he could push Julie into a real moat.

ANALYZING THE PORTFOLIOS

While October helped me focus on patience and understanding, I was challenged to fully understand what was happening in my portfolio. Out of what seemed to be nowhere, my HCP Inc. (HCP) holding dropped by almost 10%. Digging deeper into the details, I learned from a company press release that they fired the CEO for "lack of confidence in leadership not performance." Apparently, several executive staff had left in recent years, prompting the Board to make a change. *A good reminder of how who works at a company can impact how it's viewed by investors.*

I had been sitting on the fence patiently biding my time for Northern Tier Energy (NTI) and BlackRock (BLK) share prices to drop a little more. By October 8, the price had dropped sufficiently for me to only reacquire BLK at $265.

I also decided it was time to bring my Wells Fargo (WFCMX) bond fund back. Bond values/rates were minimally trending up, signaling to me that it appeared to be a good time to get back in. Even with Congress' recent fiscal screw up, I didn't think the Fed would greatly extend the timeframe of its current bond-buying efforts—even though a slight downward trend on 3rd and 4th quarter economic stats was possible. *Sometimes, you just gotta trust your gut, even if it leads you through surprising turns.*

Looking back, this may have been an example of "sell at the loss" and "buy back at that price." Had I done so, the value would be to the positive side by 2%, but I waited to see what the market would do. In this instance, buying the fund earlier than I did would have increased my profit, but there's no point in trying to time the market. Buying and selling is a personal judgment.

A surprise this month was learning that PVR Partners L.P. (PVR) agreed to be acquired by Regency Energy Partners for roughly $5.6 billion, including the assumption of debt. *Oohhh... could be good for me...*You never know what might occur with an investment, companies are bought and sold constantly. The unknown was whether or not holding onto the Regency shares would be a good decision.

But, the roller coaster ride of deciding when/if to buy and when/ if to hold ended on a surprisingly positive note: The market closed on the plus side each week, which really helped our portfolios. A substantial number of items improved in value during the second week in both my and Mom's portfolio; in fact, almost every one of Mom's investments improved. By October 22, only five of my investments were in the red. Either I was getting the hang of this investment roller coaster, or I was damn lucky. I think just as you must have both patience and understanding to make sound judgments and decisions on your market timing, so too must you have equal amounts of perseverance and prudence to guide you.

In one week, market improvements provided some big percentage changes for my portfolio:

Name	Oct 11 Profit Value	Oct 11 Profit %	Oct 18 Profit Value	Oct 18 Profit %	Dollar Change	Percentage Change
8x8, Inc. (EGHT)	$317	42.6%	$451	60.6%	$134	42.3%
Anika Therapeutics (ANIK)	$108	4.5%	$445	18.4%	$337	308.0%
Qihoo 360 Technology Co (QIHU)	$4852	141.0%	$6027	175.2%	-$893	24.3%

Between October 11 and October 18, these three items improved from an unrealized gain of $5227 up to $6923 for an averaged gain of 32.4%—about $1700. To say this made me happy is an understatement.

Interestingly, while Mom's portfolio did turn around in October, none of her investments returned the same type of value as mine.

I think this was primarily due to what appeared to be a slight decline in interest for Utility and Energy stocks. Also, this pointed to her slow and steady investment approach. Mom's portfolio was not as volatile as mine and not subject to some of the wide variations in share value that mine was; I had the Hare approach and Mom had the Tortoise, fast versus slow and steady. This is precisely why I wanted and needed to compare the different approaches.

MONTH IN REVIEW

Between September 27 and November 1, 2013, the Dow gained 358 points. For this month, I retained my lead over the Dow and Mom.

	Weekly Return on Investment Stats		
	Dow Jones Industrial Average	Me	Mom
Week 31	6.98%	10.33%	4.50%
Week 32	8.14%	9.14%	5.74%
Week 33	9.30%	13.19%	8.32%
Week 34	10.50%	14.78%	9.85%
Week 35	10.83%	13.89%	9.14%

Overall, for this month I had an unrealized gain of $37,425. Though there were no real loss leaders this month, Energy and Basic Materials lagged behind. Mom had an unrealized gain of $15,968 this month and Utilities lagged for her.

COMPARISON

For October, I was about 3.0 points ahead of the Dow and about 4.5 points ahead of Mom, which was an improvement over last month. We were in a tighter range between top and bottom. In particular, Mom had the most improvement this month.

At this point, my portfolio had 22 items that I invested in based on recommendations from the Pros, which was about 46% (26 items were my picks). On a percentage basis, I came out ahead of the Pros this month as 88.5% of my items increased in value, but only 81.2% of the Pros items increased. Looks like I'd returned to retake the lead from the Pros.

DIVIDENDS FOR OCTOBER

I received 8 payments totaling $449.24, which averaged $56.16 per payment. Mom received 11 payments totaling $360.07, which averaged $32.73 per payment. Mom received more money, but I received more per payment. *I'd sort of rather have her extra $216.* Even though I received fewer payments this month than last, this month's average payment was better by about $9. Mom received almost half as many payments this month but almost doubled her per payment amount. *Excellent!*

LESSONS LEARNED

The theme for this month was patience and understanding. Patience for the processes of the market and learning how that can affect what choices you make. And understanding the how or why you made a particular decision.

○ **Understand your decisions.** Do you like cherry or apple pie better? What if you've never tasted either type of pie and just made a decision for one? Well guess what, if you don't like your choice, it doesn't matter because you're stuck with it, and you can only learn from it. So, do you invest $1000 in a company you know nothing about or in one that you do know something about?

○ **Patience and understanding are not easily acquired.** Because investing can be emotional, your best protection is patience. It's very easy to get caught up in a herd mentality or be scared into making a decision, and once that happens you're likely to end up on the losing end.

I'm not sure if patience is an outcome of understanding or if the opposite is true. I suspect they mirror and support one another. What I'm learning is you need both to prepare and protect yourself.

The following portfolio tables show what the current value (November 1) is compared to the purchase value. Value is presented in both dollar and percentage terms. The last column has the month-to-month (September to October) change as a percentage to show how items fluctuate monthly compared to the ever lengthening time between the start date and current values.

MY PORTFOLIO FOR OCTOBER 2013

Note: '0' in last column reflects ownership of less than a month

Name (Pros in italics)	Purchase $ Value	11-1-13 $ Value	Total Net $ Gain/ Loss	Total Net % Gain/ Loss	Sept to Oct % Change
8x8, Inc.	$744.00	$1,121.00	$377.00	50.7%	7.58%
The AES Corporation	$1,193.00	$1,399.00	$206.00	17.3%	4.56%
Alaska Air Group	$6,273.00	$7,220.00	$947.00	15.1%	11.45%
Alliance Resource Partners LP	$6,725.00	$7,736.00	$1,011.00	15.0%	1.99%
Anika Therapeutics	$2,417.00	$2,963.00	$546.00	22.6%	27.11%
Apple Inc.[3]	$39,354.00	$52,003.00	$6,449.00	14.2%	7.66%
Bank of Nova Scotia	$5,341.00	$6,107.00	$766.00	14.3%	6.56%
BlackRock Inc. [2]	$26,500.00	$30,365.00	$3,865.00	14.6%	0
Coca-Cola Co	$3,870.00	$3,961.00	$91.00	2.4%	6.48%
Consolidated Communications Inc.	$1,637.00	$1,858.00	$221.00	13.5%	5.87%
El Paso Pipeline Partners LP	$4,140.00	$4,005.00	$(135.00)	-3.3%	-4.96%
GasLog Ltd	$1,432.00	$1,501.00	$69.00	4.8%	4.24%
The GEO Group Inc.	$3,448.00	$3,518.00	$70.00	2.0%	7.35%
GlaxoSmithKline PLC ADR [1]	$4,422.00	$5,319.00	$897.00	20.3%	6.15%
Great Northern Iron Ore [2]	$6,944.00	$7,123.00	$179.00	2.6%	4.60%
HCP Inc.	$4,325.00	$4,171.00	$(154.00)	-3.6%	6.81%
Home Loan Servicing Solutions	$2,302.00	$2,348.00	$46.00	2.0%	7.51%

Name (Pros in italics)	Purchase $ Value	11-1-13 $ Value	Total Net $ Gain/ Loss	Total Net % Gain/ Loss	Sept to Oct % Change
Inventure Foods, Inc.	$726.00	$1,120.00	$394.00	54.3%	5.16%
Kinder Morgan Energy Partners LP [1]	$8,672.00	$8,099.00	$(573.00)	-6.6%	1.70%
Kinder Morgan Energy Partners LP [2]	$9,025.00	$8,099.00	$(926.00)	-10.3%	1.70%
Macy's Inc.	$4,067.00	$4,596.00	$529.00	13.0%	4.29%
Merck & Co Inc.	$4,782.00	$4,523.00	$(259.00)	-5.4%	-6.22%
Michael Kors Holdings Ltd	$5,804.00	$7,543.00	$1,739.00	30.0%	-1.20%
Navios Maritime Holdings Inc.	$719.00	$740.00	$21.00	2.9%	-2.37%
NTT DoCoMo Inc.	$1,505.00	$1,587.00	$82.00	5.4%	-1.31%
Oaktree Capital Group, LLC	$5,013.00	$5,590.00	$577.00	11.5%	1.30%
Omnicell, Inc.	$2,318.00	$2,261.00	$(57.00)	-2.5%	-8.05%
Orchids Paper Products Co	$2,724.00	$3,083.00	$359.00	13.2%	11.30%
Pfizer Inc.	$3,043.00	$3,117.00	$74.00	2.4%	7.48%
Protolabs Inc.	$5,505.00	$8,388.00	$2,883.00	52.4%	4.24%
Prudential PLC ADR	$3,349.00	$4,107.00	$758.00	22.6%	7.60%
PVR Partners LP	$2,285.00	$2,596.00	$311.00	13.6%	12.97%
Qihoo 360 Technology Co., Ltd.	$3,440.00	$8,646.00	$5,206.00	151.3%	0.34%
RF Industries, Ltd	$636.00	$862.00	$226.00	35.5%	16.49%
Seaspan Corp	$1,930.00	$2,297.00	$367.00	19.0%	-4.73%
Sonoco Products Co	$3,407.00	$4,066.00	$659.00	19.3%	3.91%
Sunoco Logistics Partners LP	$6,258.00	$6,997.00	$739.00	11.8%	5.44%
Terra Nitrogen Company	$23,461.00	$20,335.00	$(3,126.00)	-13.3%	-1.05%
TJX Companies	$4,498.00	$6,088.00	$1,590.00	35.3%	8.04%
Akre Focus Fund Retail	$1,630.00	$2,006.00	$376.00	23.1%	2.92%

Name (Pros in italics)	Purchase $ Value	11-1-13 $ Value	Total Net $ Gain/ Loss	Total Net % Gain/ Loss	Sept to Oct % Change
Delaware Healthcare I	$1,355.00	$1,766.00	$411.00	30.3%	0.80%
Oakmark Global I	$2,610.00	$3,040.00	$430.00	16.5%	1.98%
Oceanstone Fund	$3,753.00	$4,309.00	$927.00	27.4%	3.88%
Fidelity Select Biotechnology Portfolio [1]	$14,631.00	$17,103.00	$4,898.00	40.1%	-4.30%
Fidelity Select Biotechnology Portfolio [2]	$10,826.94	$12,656.22	$2,439.78	23.9%	-4.30%
Fidelity Select IT Services Portfolio	$2,985.00	$3,486.00	$711.00	25.6%	2.98%
Vanguard Wellington Inv	$3,707.00	$3,845.00	$198.00	5.4%	2.67%
Wells Fargo Advantage Core Builder Series M [2]	$1,098.00	$1,108.00	$10.00	0.9%	0
	$269,352.44	$304,777.22	$37,424.78	13.89%	

MOM'S PORTFOLIO FOR OCTOBER 2013

Name	Purchase $ Value	11-1-13 $ Value	Total Net $ Gain/Loss	Total Net % Gain/ Loss	Sept to Oct % Change
Altria Group	$3,349.00	$3,733.00	$384.00	11.47%	7.55%
AT&T Inc.	$3,601.00	$3,624.00	$23.00	0.64%	6.65%
Buckeye Partners LP	$5,611.00	$6,679.00	$1,068.00	19.03%	1.54%
Caterpillar Inc.	$9,136.00	$8,359.00	$(777.00)	-8.50%	-0.25%
Cleco Corp	$4,418.00	$4,620.00	$202.00	4.57%	2.83%
CMS Energy Corp	$2,645.00	$2,762.00	$117.00	4.42%	5.38%
Compass Securities	$1,574.00	$1,900.00	$326.00	20.71%	6.32%
Deluxe Corp	$3,965.00	$4,687.00	$722.00	18.21%	13.71%
Devon Energy Corp	$5,388.00	$6,366.00	$978.00	18.15%	8.43%
Dominion Res Inc. VA	$5,642.00	$6,409.00	$767.00	13.59%	2.66%
Duke Energy	$6,925.00	$7,251.00	$326.00	4.71%	8.39%

Name	Purchase $ Value	11-1-13 $ Value	Total Net $ Gain/Loss	Total Net % Gain/ Loss	Sept to Oct % Change
Enbridge Energy Partners	$2,763.00	$3,055.00	$292.00	10.57%	0.69%
Enterprise Products	$5,681.00	$6,324.00	$643.00	11.32%	3.84%
Exxon Mobile Corporation	$8,943.00	$8,982.00	$39.00	0.44%	3.36%
Frontier Communications Corp	$419.00	$445.00	$26.00	6.21%	3.73%
General Electric Co	$2,319.00	$2,654.00	$335.00	14.45%	10.35%
Great Plains Energy	$2,199.00	$2,354.00	$155.00	7.05%	5.66%
Hartford Financial Services Group	$2,368.00	$3,365.00	$997.00	42.10%	7.61%
Hudson City Bancorp	$858.00	$896.00	$38.00	4.43%	-1.75%
Integrys Energy Group	$5,610.00	$5,911.00	$301.00	5.37%	5.89%
Intel Corp	$2,103.00	$2,432.00	$329.00	15.64%	5.83%
Medical Property Trust	$1,483.00	$1,315.00	$(168.00)	-11.33%	7.35%
Mondelez International	$2,781.00	$3,359.00	$578.00	20.78%	5.63%
Nat'l Grid Transco	$5,456.00	$6,240.00	$784.00	14.37%	5.05%
Nisource Inc.	$2,793.00	$3,172.00	$379.00	13.57%	3.42%
Occidental Petroleum Corp	$8,265.00	$9,565.00	$1,300.00	15.73%	1.26%
Spyglass Resources Corp	$274.00	$192.00	$(82.00)	-29.93%	22.29%
Pembina Pipeline Corp	$2,821.00	$3,270.00	$449.00	15.92%	-1.09%
Pepco Holdings Inc.	$2,053.00	$1,934.00	$(119.00)	-5.80%	4.82%
Philip Morris International Inc.	$9,144.00	$8,976.00	$(168.00)	-1.84%	2.78%
Piedmont Natural Gas Co	$3,265.00	$3,366.00	$101.00	3.09%	3.06%
Principle Financial Group	$3,155.00	$4,748.00	$1,593.00	50.49%	9.93%
Royal Dutch Shell PLC ADR	$6,578.00	$6,681.00	$103.00	1.57%	1.41%
Scana Corp	$4,906.00	$4,721.00	$(185.00)	-3.77%	2.56%
Southern Co	$4,483.00	$4,102.00	$(381.00)	-8.50%	-0.51%
Spectra Energy Corp	$2,881.00	$3,540.00	$659.00	22.87%	3.60%

Name	Purchase $ Value	11-1-13 $ Value	Total Net $ Gain/Loss	Total Net % Gain/ Loss	Sept to Oct % Change
Teco Energy Inc.	$1,735.00	$1,734.00	$(1.00)	-0.06%	5.03%
US Bancorp	$3,401.00	$3,737.00	$336.00	9.88%	2.38%
Verizon Communications Inc.	$4,672.00	$5,049.00	$377.00	8.07%	7.43%
Wells Fargo & Co	$3,539.00	$4,267.00	$728.00	20.57%	2.60%
DWS Core Equity Fund	$1,983.00	$2,342.00	$359.00	18.10%	4.46%
DWS S&P 500 Index Fund	$2,022.00	$2,344.00	$322.00	15.92%	4.22%
DWS Short Duration Fund	$931.00	$923.00	$(8.00)	-0.86%	0.22%
Fidelity Contrafund	$8,122.00	$9,789.00	$1,667.00	20.52%	4.33%
Wellesley Income Fund	$2,479.00	$2,533.00	$54.00	2.18%	1.85%
	$174,739.00	$190,707.00	$15,968.00	9.14%	

NOVEMBER

GAINING MOMENTUM

The broker said the stock was 'poised to move.'
Silly me, I thought he meant up.

—Randy Thurman

You know you're a novice investor when...

You start using the phrase "kiss my assets."

From:	Ouda Herre
Sent:	Thursday, September 21, 2013 2:29 PM
To:	Mark Slauter <markslauter@novice.investor>
Subject:	My BOLDEST OFFER EVER...

**400 Winners Guaranteed
Over the Next Four Years!
If I Don't Deliver, Your Service is FREE**

Fellow Investor,

I'm sending this note to fewer than 1% of my readers. That's because I can only invite a small, highly qualified group of my most loyal subscribers to take me up on what is quite simply one of the best offers I have EVER made.

One so good, that my publisher has only given me until November 15th to get your RSVP— and then this offer is gone for good. This may sound strange, but this all started with a spreadsheet...

At the end of every month, I spend hours upon hours crunching the numbers, reviewing our results, looking for our next opportunities. But this time around I discovered something fairly shocking."

Another wonderful email. This is great!!!! But I can still lose my shirt right????

November 4, 2013

A minor 25 point up-tick in the market today...but it was enough to pull some of my downers from last week back up. Well...there is the rest of the week to screw things up though.

November 14, 2013

Holy shit…TNH dropped over $11!!! Sell it!!!!!!!!!!! Must be a sell off from post-dividend receipt…dammit…

November 15, 2013

TNH dropped another $11 = 6%!!! Okay, have to sell this again…for another loss. Crap.

November 19, 2013

Couldn't help myself…I bought TNH back at $156. Ever hear the phrase "You know what the definition of insanity is? It's trying the same thing over and over again and expecting a different outcome." Well, I guess a point will be proved in one way or another…

November 25, 2013

Mom broke her hip and went to the hospital today. A not so happy Thanksgiving. (She got through the surgery okay but it was a bumpy ride the first few days as she was having a very hard time swallowing and we weren't sure she was going to make it. Fortunately, both Mom and her portfolio improved…but we'll keep a close eye on both.)

While October was a time for me to learn patience and understanding, November turned into a time for gaining momentum and trying to make sound decisions along the way. As you can see, Terra Nitrogen (TNH) was driving me a bit crazy. I kept thinking that the growth looked good, the dividend was good, earnings were good, and yet, I couldn't determine what was happening with the stock.

Watching the market advance drove my desire to make my portfolio advance with it. But the question of making the right decisions was always in the back of my head, nagging at me. I felt like I was doing the right thing—and I decided to trust my gut.

WATCHING THE MARKET

In trying to do the right thing in November, I scoured the news. One source stated that the recent sell off was minor and could minimize a more frantic unloading of stock later on. What concerned me was the statement that the "…frantic unloading of stocks later on when the market finally does seriously reverse, as it inevitably will at some point." Not sure I agreed that a "serious reverse" was "inevitable." Knowing what the market will do is impossible, because much of it is driven by human emotion. I found it unconscionable for someone to make such a huge assumption in this way. It's arrogant punditry. And as you watch the market and consider differing viewpoints, being aware of such hyperbole can do wonders for your decision-making.

I believed that the market would definitely dip down once the Fed decided to taper off its bond buying. However, I thought that investors could maintain a higher than anticipated value, because it has value and any radical sell off would kill it. Having said this, investors also don't seem to apply what the rest of us would consider a reasonable, logical approach. What would happen if no one sold their equities for a month or two even though the Fed eased back? Prices remain unchanged, right? I suspected part of the problem was connected to those who borrow money to invest with. They'd get screwed if loan rates increased before they paid off their existing debt, possibly creating havoc elsewhere in the economy.

On November 7, the Dow's drop really bit me, and almost every item fell, knocking my return back by about 1.5 points. *Shit!* Then, the very next day, BAM! The market bounced up 167 points. *I swear, if the market was a person, it'd have multiple personalities.*

On November 5, Terra Nitrogen Company, L.P. (TNH) had a seven point drop, which drove me nuts. Understanding the performance of TNH was front and center in my mind. I eventually found a report stating that their third quarter net sales were $128.4

million, compared to third quarter net sales in 2012 of $181 million. I should have taken this as an indicator to sell, but I didn't. As a result, it fell even further later in the month. I missed out and sold for an even greater loss.

I repurchased TNH on the 19th when I thought it bottomed out, and then I came across another article from Investing Daily *after* I made the purchase:

> We have been warning for months that refiners were going to fare poorly, and that turned out to be the case as half of the MLPs that cut distributions were refiners. Fertilizer manufacturers like Rentech Nitrogen Partners (NYSE: RNF) suffered from higher natural gas costs and also found themselves relatively cash poor for the quarter and needing to cut their distributions.

I wondered what role this had on the drop at Terra Nitrogen; it manufactures fertilizer products. My thought at this point was, *I'm probably screwed.*

By November 23, just one day before Thanksgiving and all that Black Friday madness, the market finally closed above the 16000 mark! Despite the momentum, a nagging voice in the back of my head kept wondering how my portfolio would play out once the Fed decided to scale back its bond buying. I was still convinced that the best approach for the Fed would be to scale back incrementally: Start with a drop of $10b per month and see how the market reacted—it may or may not become a frenzied sell off.

Since investors seemed so focused and reactive to what the Fed may or may not do, planning ahead for my own portfolio became difficult. If the Fed did raise interest rates, I anticipated an initial sell off that would result in the market finding a new level. Once that happened, I expected investors would re-enter the market at whatever new level exists. However, it was also entirely possible that investors would overreact and push the markets even lower.

Only time would tell and I would have to wait it out.

CHASING FOR INFORMATION

Throughout November, the market's up-and-down movement kept me glued to my performance and nearly obsessed with checking stock tickers. I knew the importance of finding the right information to provide me with the insight I needed to make sense of the details. So, I was constantly chasing information.

As with other items in my portfolio, I was trying to locate additional information on Alaska Air (ALK). Since purchasing ALK earlier in the year at a higher price, I'd not seen much written on it. At this point, I was up 16%, but I was more than ready to dump this investment several weeks ago due to poor performance. Plus, it had squat for a dividend.

I eventually found an article from Investing Daily that provided some perspective:

> Many investors shy away from the stocks of airline companies—and small wonder. Airlines are notorious for giving headaches to shareholders, employees and passengers alike. Fuel costs are high, labor unions are burdensome and profit margins are thin.
>
> But there's a notable exception: Alaska Air Group (NYSE: ALK), a regional carrier based in Seattle.

The article went on to discuss how ALK was improving its performance, expanding its flight routes, and was one of the top employee and passenger rated airlines.

I also found some information on 8x8 Inc. (EGHT) that stated the company was stable and had been recently named one of America's 100 Best Small Companies. However, the price-earnings ratio was almost 90, which was high, and it would be prudent for future investors to wait for the ratio to come down before investing. *Glad I got in earlier; I was up 38.2% (about $270).*

Early in the month, Twitter was added to the NASDAQ through an initial public offering (IPO), which made some analysts wonder whether or not we were headed for a technology stock bubble similar to what happened in the early 2000s. Twitter was another example of a company that was nowhere near being profitable but promised those big profits would come. What people were not discussing was the difference between now and then. One of the most profitable aspects of online companies these days is the user data they acquire; it's BIG business. Everyone has a digital footprint, and the companies that collect your data can be exceptionally profitable.

Though my sister, Mary, and I considered actually buying shares of Twitter for one of Mom's accounts, as we had also done earlier in the year for shares of Facebook, we decided now was not the time. We felt it was more prudent to wait and let the share value settle down after the IPO. We had to ask ourselves, is this the right thing for Mom?

ANALYZING THE PORTFOLIOS

At this point in my fantasy portfolio, I was seven months into investing. And while I was feeling more confident than ever in my abilities, I was still amazed when a small dip in the market had a big impact on my investments. However, at this point, I wasn't able to identify a direct relationship between all of the movement. At any moment, you have a boatload of factors that seem to hit you at every angle. Some are positive, some are negative, and all are easy to emotionally react to, for better or worse.

I had some substantial jumps in performance this month, specifically Macy's Inc. (M) and Qihoo 360 (QIHU). After Macy's released a good quarterly report on November 13, its performance jumped up more than $4.39—a 9.4% increase that put me to the plus side of almost 25%! Meanwhile, Qihoo 360 also jumped up over 9%. *Oh yeah baby, rolling in the dough now!*

But, about a week later, Qihoo 360's performance shifted downward. After issuing its unaudited third quarter financials, which looked good, its share price dropped almost 9.5%—meaning I lost everything I'd just gained. Digging deeper into the details, I saw that analysts anticipated future growth to slow in 2014. When I looked at Qihoo's financial statements, however, its story showed continued growth and revenue increases. *What gives???* I guess some investors decided it was a good time to take profits. Me? I decided to hold onto to this for now. I think this is a good example of how investors perceive future actions or outcomes, and they'll either buy or sell accordingly. Just because some analysts think growth will slow—opposite of what the company was stating—doesn't necessarily mean it's a valid reason to sell.

From my standpoint, my investment in Qihoo was doing quite well and was continuing to gain momentum resulting in higher share value, and more potential profit for me. Though I wasn't convinced that I should sell, the fact that some analysts were stating concern with Qihoo meant that I should pay more attention to the stock. After all, what's the point of watching your profit slip away?

I had some cash and wasn't sure what to do with it, other than to put it to work. I did acquire a couple of new companies. I was limited on my Basic Materials sector holdings and Arabian was suitable to me. For Fonar, I was still on the hunt for Healthcare sector investments, though this was a little higher than I like for debt and the price/book ratio.

	Arabian American Development Company	Fonar Corporation
Sector	Basic Materials	Healthcare
10-yr EPS	31.39%	63.03%a
10-yr Average for Revenue Growth	19.75%	-0.73%
Dividend Yield	N/A	N/A
Analyst Buy Recommendations	4 of 4	2 of 4

So far, I was feeling more positive about the portfolios and the direction they were headed—up. Allocating some of my cash to acquire a couple of new items also felt like a positive move, somehow it felt more tangible than just having the cash available.

MONTH IN REVIEW

Between November 1 and November 29, 2013, the Dow gained 470 points. Looks like I kept my lead.

Weekly Return on Investment Stats			
	Dow Jones Industrial Average	Me	Mom
Week 36	11.87%	14.55%	8.72%
Week 37	13.29%	16.07%	10.18%
Week 38	14.00%	16.56%	10.19%
Week 39	14.26%	18.41%	9.07%

Overall, for this month I had an unrealized gain of $48,615. Though there were no real loss leaders this month, Energy and Basic Materials continued to lag behind. Mom had an unrealized gain of $15,853 this month and Utilities still lagged for her.

COMPARISON

In November, I was about four points ahead of the Dow and about nine points ahead of Mom. This month was an improvement over last month, though I screwed the pooch on Terra Nitrogen and sold off...again...for another loss...again. This had a direct impact on my bottom line and improved my unrealized gain, but at a heavy cost.

At this point, my portfolio had 24 items that I invested in based on recommendations from the Pros, which was about 48% (26 items were my picks). On a percentage basis, I came out ever so slightly ahead of the Pros this month as 92.3% of my items increased in value, but only 91.7% of the Pros items increased. Looks like I returned to retake the lead from the Pros. I was also further impressed that only four items closed in the red! *Moving on uuppp (cue The Jeffersons theme music)!*

DIVIDENDS FOR NOVEMBER

November was a great month for dividends. I received 19 payments totaling $1,316.09, which averaged $69.27 per payment. Mom received 19 payments totaling $694.91, which averaged $36.57 per payment. We received an equal number of payments, but mine were worth about twice as much. Though my earlier references to momentum target increasing share and portfolio values, there is something to be said for receiving substantial dividend payments. Who wouldn't like to get an extra $1,300 dollars?!

I'd completed my third quarter of investing and felt that I was in fair shape, considering:

o   To date, my losses cost me about $29k.

o   My current value was up $48,615, and I'd received $7,591 in dividends. Mom's was up $15,853 with $5,886 in dividends.

o   I received 112 dividend payments for an average of $67.78 per payment. Mom received 151 payments for an average of $38.98 per payment.

o   I was performing better than the Dow and Mom.

o   I was maintaining my rate of success as compared against the Pros.

LESSONS LEARNED

I think this is the first time that I truly felt forward momentum in my portfolio. Even with the market's vagaries, my portfolio's value was trending upward, and I felt that my decision-making improved…mostly.

o   **Define a strategy to avoid wandering aimlessly.** It's not hard to get distracted by drama created by the media, too much information, or your own emotions. Have a game plan and stick to it.

o   **Wisdom is knowing what you don't know.** I've seen more debates and sayings on what wisdom is or isn't that I could probably write another book. For me, it's important that I recognize my knowledge limits. Investing based on hopes or whims will wipe you out. How well do you think your decisions in life would turn out if you based them all on a lack of knowledge?

While checking the stock ticker every day drove me crazy, I found it gave me a more dynamic perspective than weekly checks. At some point, I expect that I'll scale back on checking every day, but at this point, I continued to do so. I couldn't say for sure that checking the market daily had been the reason for improvements in my portfolio, or contributed to the current upward momentum of my stocks, but I saw it as a necessary action to improve my investing skills—which ultimately was my whole goal.

The following portfolio tables show what the current value (November 29) is compared to the purchase value. Value is presented in both dollar and percentage terms. The last column has the month-to-month (October to November) change as a percentage to show how items fluctuate monthly compared to the ever lengthening time between the start date and current values.

MY PORTFOLIO FOR NOVEMBER 2013

Note: '0' in last column reflects ownership of less than a month.

Name (Pros in italics)	Purchase $ Value	11-29-13 $ Value	Total Net $ Gain/Loss	Total Net % Gain/ Loss	Oct to Nov % Change
8x8, Inc.	$744.00	$1,042.00	$298.00	40.1%	-7.05%
The AES Corporation	$1,193.00	$1,457.00	$264.00	22.1%	4.15%
Alaska Air Group	$6,273.00	$7,774.00	$1,501.00	23.9%	7.67%
Alliance Resource Partners LP	$6,725.00	$7,327.00	$602.00	9.0%	-5.29%
Anika Therapeutics	$2,417.00	$3,435.00	$1,018.00	42.1%	15.93%
Apple Inc.(3)	$39,354.00	$55,607.00	$10,053.00	22.1%	6.93%
Arabian American Development Company	$940.00	$1,032.00	$92.00	9.8%	0
Bank of Nova Scotia	$5,341.00	$6,157.00	$816.00	15.3%	0.82%
BlackRock Inc. (2)	$26,500.00	$30,275.00	$3,775.00	14.2%	-0.30%
Coca-Cola Co	$3,870.00	$4,019.00	$149.00	3.9%	1.46%
Consolidated Communications Inc.	$1,637.00	$1,932.00	$295.00	18.0%	3.98%
El Paso Pipeline Partners LP	$4,140.00	$4,158.00	$18.00	0.4%	3.82%
Fonar Corporation	$1,700.00	$1,930.00	$230.00	13.5%	0

Name (Pros in italics)	Purchase $ Value	11-29-13 $ Value	Total Net $ Gain/Loss	Total Net % Gain/ Loss	Oct to Nov % Change
GasLog Ltd	$1,432.00	$1,593.00	$161.00	11.2%	6.13%
The GEO Group Inc.	$3,448.00	$3,280.00	$(168.00)	-4.9%	-6.77%
GlaxoSmithKline PLC ADR (1)	$4,422.00	$5,292.00	$870.00	19.7%	-0.51%
Great Northern Iron Ore(2)	$6,944.00	$7,368.00	$424.00	6.1%	3.44%
HCP Inc.	$4,325.00	$3,677.00	$(648.00)	-15.0%	-11.84%
Home Loan Servicing Solutions	$2,302.00	$2,327.00	$25.00	1.1%	-0.89%
Inventure Foods, Inc.	$726.00	$1,279.00	$553.00	76.2%	14.20%
Kinder Morgan Energy Partners LP (1)	$8,672.00	$8,197.00	$(475.00)	-5.5%	1.21%
Kinder Morgan Energy Partners LP (2)	$9,025.00	$8,197.00	$(828.00)	-9.2%	1.21%
Macy's Inc.	$4,067.00	$5,326.00	$1,259.00	31.0%	15.88%
Merck & Co Inc.	$4,782.00	$4,983.00	$201.00	4.2%	10.17%
Michael Kors Holdings Ltd	$5,804.00	$8,155.00	$2,351.00	40.5%	8.11%
Navios Maritime Holdings Inc.	$719.00	$774.00	$55.00	7.6%	4.59%
NTT DoCoMo Inc.	$1,505.00	$1,607.00	$102.00	6.8%	1.26%
Oaktree Capital Group, LLC	$5,013.00	$5,572.00	$559.00	11.2%	-0.32%
Omnicell, Inc.	$2,318.00	$2,425.00	$107.00	4.6%	7.25%
Orchids Paper Products Co	$2,724.00	$3,274.00	$550.00	20.2%	6.20%
Pfizer Inc.	$3,043.00	$3,173.00	$130.00	4.3%	1.80%
Protolabs Inc.	$5,505.00	$7,430.00	$1,925.00	35.0%	-11.42%

Name (Pros in italics)	Purchase $ Value	11-29-13 $ Value	Total Net $ Gain/Loss	Total Net % Gain/ Loss	Oct to Nov % Change
Prudential PLC ADR	$3,349.00	$4,274.00	$925.00	27.6%	4.07%
PVR Partners LP	$2,285.00	$2,470.00	$185.00	8.1%	-4.85%
Qihoo 360 Technology Co., Ltd.	$3,440.00	$8,152.00	$4,712.00	137.0%	-5.71%
RF Industries, Ltd	$636.00	$1,378.00	$742.00	116.7%	59.86%
Seaspan Corp	$1,930.00	$2,180.00	$250.00	13.0%	-5.09%
Sonoco Products Co	$3,407.00	$4,006.00	$599.00	17.6%	-1.48%
Sunoco Logistics Partners LP	$6,258.00	$7,078.00	$820.00	13.1%	1.16%
Terra Nitrogen Co. (3)	$15,600.00	$15,625.00	$25.00	0.2%	0
TJX Companies	$4,498.00	$6,288.00	$1,790.00	39.8%	3.29%
Akre Focus Fund Retail	$1,630.00	$2,046.00	$416.00	25.5%	1.99%
Delaware Healthcare I	$1,355.00	$1,820.00	$465.00	34.3%	3.06%
Oakmark Global I	$2,610.00	$3,086.00	$476.00	18.2%	1.51%
Oceanstone Fund	$3,753.00	$4,365.00	$983.00	29.1%	1.30%
Fidelity Select Biotechnology Portfolio (1)	$14,631.00	$17,965.00	$5,760.00	47.2%	5.04%
Fidelity Select Biotechnology Portfolio (2)	$10,826.94	$13,294.10	$3,077.66	30.1%	5.04%
Fidelity Select IT Services Portfolio	$2,985.00	$3,624.00	$849.00	30.6%	3.96%
Vanguard Wellington Inv	$3,707.00	$3,917.00	$270.00	7.4%	1.87%
Wells Fargo Advantage Core Builder Series M (2)	$1,098.00	$1,104.00	$6.00	0.5%	-0.36%
	$264,131.44	$312,746.10	$48,614.66	18.41%	

MOM'S PORTFOLIO FOR NOVEMBER 2013

Name	Purchase $ Value	11-29-13 $ Value	Total Net $ Gain/Loss	Total Net % Gain/ Loss	Oct to Nov % Change
Altria Group	$3,349.00	$3,698.00	$349.00	10.42%	-0.94%
AT&T Inc.	$3,601.00	$3,521.00	$(80.00)	-2.22%	-2.84%
Buckeye Partners LP	$5,611.00	$6,809.00	$1,198.00	21.35%	1.95%
Caterpillar Inc.	$9,136.00	$8,460.00	$(676.00)	-7.40%	1.21%
Cleco Corp	$4,418.00	$4,571.00	$153.00	3.46%	-1.06%
CMS Energy Corp	$2,645.00	$2,654.00	$9.00	0.34%	-3.91%
Compass Securities	$1,574.00	$1,909.00	$335.00	21.28%	0.47%
Deluxe Corp	$3,965.00	$4,969.00	$1,004.00	25.32%	6.02%
Devon Energy Corp	$5,388.00	$6,062.00	$674.00	12.51%	-4.78%
Dominion Res Inc. VA	$5,642.00	$6,491.00	$849.00	15.05%	1.28%
Duke Energy	$6,925.00	$6,996.00	$71.00	1.03%	-3.52%
Enbridge Energy Partners	$2,763.00	$3,009.00	$246.00	8.90%	-1.51%
Enterprise Products	$5,681.00	$6,297.00	$616.00	10.84%	-0.43%
Exxon Mobile Corporation	$8,943.00	$9,348.00	$405.00	4.53%	4.07%
Frontier Communications Corp	$419.00	$468.00	$49.00	11.69%	5.17%
General Electric Co	$2,319.00	$2,666.00	$347.00	14.96%	0.45%
Great Plains Energy	$2,199.00	$2,374.00	$175.00	7.96%	0.85%
Hartford Financial Services Group	$2,368.00	$3,563.00	$1,195.00	50.46%	5.88%
Hudson City Bancorp	$858.00	$934.00	$76.00	8.86%	4.24%
Integrys Energy Group	$5,610.00	$5,374.00	$(236.00)	-4.21%	-9.08%
Intel Corp	$2,103.00	$2,384.00	$281.00	13.36%	-1.97%
Medical Property Trust	$1,483.00	$1,321.00	$(162.00)	-10.92%	0.46%
Mondelez International	$2,781.00	$3,353.00	$572.00	20.57%	-0.18%
Nat'l Grid Transco	$5,456.00	$6,336.00	$880.00	16.13%	1.54%
Nisource Inc.	$2,793.00	$3,162.00	$369.00	13.21%	-0.32%

Name	Purchase $ Value	11-29-13 $ Value	Total Net $ Gain/Loss	Total Net % Gain/ Loss	Oct to Nov % Change
Occidental Petroleum Corp	$8,265.00	$9,496.00	$1,231.00	14.89%	-0.72%
Spyglass Resources Corp	$274.00	$169.00	$(105.00)	-38.32%	-11.98%
Pembina Pipeline Corp	$2,821.00	$3,206.00	$385.00	13.65%	-1.96%
Pepco Holdings Inc.	$2,053.00	$1,908.00	$(145.00)	-7.06%	-1.34%
Philip Morris International Inc.	$9,144.00	$8,554.00	$(590.00)	-6.45%	-4.70%
Piedmont Natural Gas Co	$3,265.00	$3,315.00	$50.00	1.53%	-1.52%
Principle Financial Group	$3,155.00	$5,063.00	$1,908.00	60.48%	6.63%
Royal Dutch Shell PLC ADR	$6,578.00	$6,670.00	$92.00	1.40%	-0.16%
Scana Corp	$4,906.00	$4,717.00	$(189.00)	-3.85%	-0.08%
Southern Co	$4,483.00	$4,063.00	$(420.00)	-9.37%	-0.95%
Spectra Energy Corp	$2,881.00	$3,355.00	$474.00	16.45%	-5.23%
Teco Energy Inc.	$1,735.00	$1,704.00	$(31.00)	-1.79%	-1.73%
US Bancorp	$3,401.00	$3,922.00	$521.00	15.32%	4.95%
Verizon Communications Inc.	$4,672.00	$4,962.00	$290.00	6.21%	-1.72%
Wells Fargo & Co	$3,539.00	$4,402.00	$863.00	24.39%	3.16%
DWS Core Equity Fund	$1,983.00	$2,411.00	$428.00	21.58%	2.95%
DWS S&P 500 Index Fund	$2,022.00	$2,408.00	$386.00	19.09%	2.73%
DWS Short Duration Fund	$931.00	$922.00	$(9.00)	-0.97%	-0.11%
Fidelity Contrafund	$8,122.00	$10,062.00	$1,940.00	23.89%	2.79%
Wellesley Income Fund	$2,479.00	$2,554.00	$75.00	3.03%	0.83%
	$174,739.00	$190,592.00	$15,853.00	9.07%	

DECEMBER

LET IT GROW

Money frees you from doing things you dislike. Since I dislike
doing nearly everything, money is handy.

—Groucho Marx

You know you're a novice investor when...

You think you have the REIT stuff.

From: Flo Caash
Sent: Wednesday, November 14, 2013 1:29 AM
To: Mark Slauter <markslauter@novice.investor>
Subject: 24 Double-Digit Winners 2013

24 Double-Digit Winners in 2013 for an Average 23.6% in Profits...

"TRUST ME WHEN I SAY, INVESTING IN GAME-CHANGING STOCKS WILL CHANGE YOUR LIFE"

It's been one heck of a year. If you missed out on these 2013 profits, don't fret. I'm advising my readers to load up on select stocks NOW for double-digit returns in 2014. This is your second chance!

Bet I get a third chance too...

December 2, 2013

Sounds like Mom has turned around to the positive today. Guess we'll be moving her out of the hospital tomorrow. Unbelievable: an 85-year old with dementia falls and breaks her hip, she has surgery to put pins in, comes out of it okay, and just keeps trucking. This is what healthy living will get you: resiliency.

Fortunately, Mom has insurance and some income to cover the expenses so we only need to focus on her care and recovery. If we had to worry about the money our stress level would be much greater. This is another reminder to me that I have to be better prepared for my own future financial needs.

December 4, 2013

Dang...Terra Nitrogen (TNH) jumped >9% today, and I'm wondering if folks are hedging against a reduction in the Federal bond buying program, since this has a dividend yield of 9.3%. I also just realized that the price reduction I previously mentioned was due to them cutting the dividend in half last month...and I didn't even notice.

December 5, 2013

Dang...TNH dropped almost 7% today wiping out most of the gain from yesterday. Well, with 4 days of consecutive decreases in the market, it pretty much has dropped every item in my portfolio. I can only imagine what mom's will look like when I run the numbers this weekend.

Another kick in the pants this week was my realization I had miscalculated my dividend payments. Not only did I do this all once, but twice before I noticed what happened. So, not only do I have to go back to the beginning and recalculate everything, I have to rewrite several chapters. Dammit!...but it gave my wife something to laugh about...Double Dammit!

My version of "Let it Snow"

Oh, the markets can be so frightful,
But the profits are so delightful,
I really can't let 'em go.
Let 'em grow,
Let 'em grow,
Let 'em grow!

After agonizing through September and October to achieve some level of success in November, I now found myself feeling a truer sense of confidence. While this was primarily due to increased experience and exposure to investing, I think it was also a reflection of having retained many of my original acquisitions, even though not all of them were profitable. I think something relates to length of ownership that supports confidence. *Whoever said size doesn't matter must not have owned a growing portfolio.*

The downside to owning something for a long time is that you can establish an emotional attachment to the item. I have to be wary of not selling something because I'm attached to it—regardless of performance. Once you're in the market, you gain one level of fear towards investing and a different level of fear regarding selling. I'd since realized that containing my fears had contributed to my portfolio's increased value and would ultimately determine how successful I'll be.

WATCHING THE MARKET

Ahhh, December. The time of year when we spends tons of money to show our holiday love. And beyond love, friendship, and good cheer, what better present could I want than to see even better returns on my investments?

During the first week of December, the market was on a downward trend creating a mixed bag of ups and downs in my portfolio. Then, on December 4, my holding El Paso Pipeline (EPB) dropped about $4 when news hit that Morningstar lowered its fair value estimate from $46 to $42 due to "lower-than-expected dividend distribution guidance for 2014." *Ouch!*

EPB had been fluctuating up and down, but I'd generally been on the up side. With this news hovering over me, I felt like I just got screwed. Even if I'd been receiving alerts, I'm not sure I would have sold. Up until this point, the dividend yield was about 6%, and now I was entering an adjustment period to the fair value estimate change—reminding me that, sometimes, all it takes for a stock to move is one action by someone. However, the market response also showed how investors pay attention to what certain companies are saying. I could tell Morningstar was one of those companies.

As the first week closed out, the market made up most of the losses by gaining almost 199 points. *Whew…* No one wants to see their investments go down in value, which inevitably will occur at some point. Naturally, I prefer up rather than down, and after experiencing this type of market behavior for several months, I found that I was no longer getting as nervous as I did when I started.

Once the third week was underway, it appeared that the Fed's monthly bond-buying question was driving trader behavior—again. *Guess this is somewhat like herding cats.* One item that media reported on was "growth leaders" (the sector or industry driving the market's advance), which made me also wonder: Where are the biggest losers? After all, I didn't want to put my money into the losing side.

The investment world is riddled with metrics, and as a novice investor, I wasn't sure of the validity of any of them. However, the metrics are entrenched enough that people seem to pay a sufficient degree of attention to them as a basis for decision-making. I could understand the metrics of earnings per share, return on equity, and price/sales ratio. What I didn't understand is the use of metrics such as the 50-day and 200-day moving averages. What did these really tell me? And why don't we measure a 75-day or 150-day moving average? What would make more sense to me is to tie share price back to calendar quarters: 90-day, 180-day, and 270-day. From my perspective, doing this would feed directly into an annual share price performance. But, I suppose logic isn't always the name of the game once money's involved.

On December 18, the Federal Reserve announced it would begin reducing the monthly bond-buying program from $85 to $75 billion. Obviously, the Bulls were happy with that, since they pushed the market higher by almost 300 points. Even with this big jump, El Paso Pipeline (EPB) and Kinder Morgan Energy Partners (KMP) remained stepchildren in my portfolio and declined further. These two items were in some sort of slump and not a favorite in the investment community. The question was whether this slump was short- or long-term.

Reflecting further on the Fed's decision, I remembered making a statement some weeks back about the Fed tapering by $10 billion, and I personally responded to this idea with the belief that 1) they'd drop the bond-buying by $10 billion, and 2) the market would likely drop back to the 14000 mark. But arriving at this perspective now, I started to believe that investors would hold the line above the 15000 mark—all things being equal. *Glad to see the Fed followed my advice to scale back by $10 billion.* Now we had to wait and see how the investment community reacts.

Regardless of what the Fed was doing, I remained focused on the task at hand: to make my portfolio the best it could be. And I expected for the market to wobble around a bit as investors tried to guess what the Fed would do. Investors can be like journalists—when they find a vacuum in information, they make their own stories to fill the void.

Oh the markets can be so frightful...let 'em blow, let 'em blow, let 'em blow.

CHASING FOR INFORMATION

For my ongoing quest to learn as much as possible, the search for information is more than just looking at stock reports or catching up on the latest market news. It also means finding useful thoughts, ideas, and guidance. In this regard, I read an article from InvestorPlace stating a few guidelines on what new investors should avoid:

o **Trading too often.** Trading costs can add up quickly, considering commissions, fees and taxes. Invest for the long-term by buying stocks that you feel comfortable with holding for years.

○ **Falling for "hot tips."** Resist buying a stock that you haven't thoroughly researched.

○ **Going too deep into one stock.** Diversify your holdings with exposure to different industries, countries and company sizes.

○ **Trading on fear or greed.** Remember, you want to buy stocks on sale and remember to trim your winners now and then to protect your profits.

After reading their tips, I felt relieved that I'd not fallen for the first or third behavior in any manner, sort of. The second? Just a little with the quick trades on Apple and LinkedIn, and a couple others. The fourth one was the hardest to understand, recognize, and use to my advantage. I'd already lost money due to fear and greed. The smart thing was to focus on forcing those emotions into the background, take a deep breath, and step back to think with a clearer head before making a decision.

When you're focused on growing your investments, keeping your eye on the horizon is essential. I landed on the Morningstar article, "Outlook for the Stock Market," and found some guidance worth sharing:

○ Despite the ongoing bull market, stocks continue to look approximately fairly valued.

○ Investors may be tempted to take profits, hoping to buy back in at better prices down the road. However, trying to time the market in this way is enormously challenging.

○ Signs of an improving economy and fears of rising interest rates have caused conservative stocks to fall out of favor, which is a reversal from the first few months of the year.

While this type of guidance wasn't earth shattering or making me feel the need to alter my portfolio, the info was useful in a more general way. I kept reading that we were in an unusual market circumstance, as the bull market had been occurring for several years—meaning seeking out information on my stocks and the larger economic conditions became even more important. In fact, I found that just being aware of the bigger picture allowed me to consider whether or not I might need or want to take an action in the near future. *Knowledge really does beget knowledge.*

And while I was paying attention to the big picture, I was also looking into the details. An opportunity to further evaluate my experiment presented itself when I received an invite to "participate in a great event" for free. Intrigued, I signed on and had access to four investors all promising their stock picks for 2014. However, they did not provide all of their picks for free—as stated in the invite. The unlisted picks required payment. But, since I wanted to see if these folks' suggestions were any good, I decided to track their picks and see what happened. I will caveat this with stating that I was not paying attention to their buy or sell suggestions after this initial starting point, which was comprised of a broad mix across sectors. Acquiring 100 shares of each item totaled about $153,000.

Approximately two weeks after receiving my invite, I received another email that included an article from one of the Pros describing four breakout picks for 2014. Interestingly, three of the four picks in the article were not included in the previous email. I wondered if these three were the same ones I would have had to pay for. Bottom line: By paying attention to these emails, I gained three more picks to look into for free.

Since my fantasy portfolio was about learning more about the investing world, I viewed these emails as an opportunity to evaluate another approach. Though I wouldn't be doing this to compare my portfolio to one based solely on professional recommendations, I could compare results from the Pros portfolio against the DJIA, and that would make me a better investor.

ANALYZING THE PORTFOLIOS

Letting your portfolio grow is the whole point to investing. Increasing your wealth and financial independence allows you to do all of those items on your bucket list: leave some money for the kids, be philanthropic, travel the world, etc. At some point, you'll look at your investments, think back to where you started—maybe remember the things you didn't do or buy—and you'll smile at your success.

In December, I had a few highlights that made my month. For the first time since I started my portfolio, my Merck stock was to the positive by about 3.5%. The increase wasn't much but upward trends are definitely better than being in the negative. Additionally, TJX Companies issued an extra dividend of about $14 while Apple jumped up $21/share on news of a deal with China Mobile. And to round it out, Kinder Morgan, El Paso Pipeline, and Terra Nitrogen improved a little. Yes, I was feeling good.

I did see that Consolidated Communications (CNSL) had a debt load of 916%! I wasn't sure when this happened, but once I realized this detail, I was confident that I surely wouldn't buy it now. If it wasn't for its 8% dividend and my portfolio being up over a 17% increase in value, I would have considered selling. So, I decided to pay closer attention to this one. While debt itself is not a bad thing and can be a useful tool to operate a business, I was wary of very high levels of debt for my investments.

After reviewing my portfolio's key information, I checked for pertinent insights into Mom's portfolio. One example came my way in a Morningstar update about Great Plains Energy (GXP), one of her holdings:

Great Plains began increasing its dividend in 2011 and in the 2013 fourth quarter increased its annual dividend rate by $0.05 per share, or 5.7%. Management is now targeting annual dividend increases of 4%-6% during the next several years. In addition, we estimate that Great Plains' rate base will average about 3.5% annual growth.

I noticed that Morningstar raised their valuation from $23 to $24, and as a result, Mom was now up 9%. When I read that GXP would continue raising their dividend and that the Pros saw the company growing over the next several years, I decided we should hold onto the investment. For now, we'd watch how this one would grow.

I was further pleased when additional good news came my way from Morningstar about one of my holdings, Prudential PLC ADR (PUK). Morningstar analysts increased PUK's fair value estimate from $21 per share to $43 per share—yep, more than doubled! In early November, my PUK holding was up about 22%, and now I was up about 32%. I recalled how earlier in the year, some analysts said PUK was not a buy. *I wonder what they think of their recommendation now. Was I truly smarter than others—or did I just get a little lucky for buying in early? Either way, I'll take it!*

Subscribing to a professional service or working with a broker should provide you with the immediate benefits of access to information, analyses, and insight. In this instance, I received an email report regarding activity of the portfolio manager for two real portfolios managed by Morningstar:

Recent purchases for Morningstar StockInvestor have included consumer defensive firms Coca-Cola (KO) and Philip Morris International (PM), real estate owner HCP (HCP), and utility ITC Holdings (ITC). These firms offer attractive total return prospects with significantly less risk than other areas of the market. In contrast, we find the more economically sensitive technology, industrials, and consumer cyclical sectors to be among the most overvalued.

This particular excerpt contained three pieces of information that were important to me:

○ First, they stated where the manager was investing.

○ Second, three of the four investments were currently or had been in either my or Mom's portfolios.

○ Third, I gained insight into why other sectors were not attractive for investing.

Until recently, Coca-Cola (KO) had been performing well, then the share price began to slowly decrease. Learning that the portfolio manager put new money (compared to me already owning this for months) into KO tempered my perspective on ownership. Due to the decline in share price, I had moved KO into my "potential sale" category. But after reading Morningstar's report, I was slightly less inclined to sell, though I kept a watchful eye on its performance.

Philip Morris (PM)'s performance was important because Mom owned it and the comparable Altria (MO) stock. From my perspective, I'd always thought Altria was the stronger investment, since it had a higher dividend yield and appeared to be performing better. To date, Mom was up about 15% on MO. On the flip side, Mom was down roughly 6% on PM. The fact that PM stock had declined was possibly part of the reason that Morningstar was selecting it as a "buy"—it was undervalued AND in the consumer defensive sector.

Meanwhile, HCP was taking a beating for reasons I didn't fully understand, and my research so far wasn't helping me gain deeper insight. *I needed to get to the bottom of this, if nothing else, for my sanity.* As best I could determine, investors were concerned with

HCP's ability to maintain their occupancy rates, which was understandable—but I couldn't figure out specifically why. I noticed that the five-year growth was projected to be about 6%, which I interpreted to mean that HCP's growth might be too low to invite more investment.

Coincidentally, I received an email from InvestorPlace that provided me with more background on HCP. Though 2012 was a good year, 2013 saw the stock price off 20%. The rationale was that investors backed away due to concerns of rising interest rates; in other words, folks took their profits and got out. What was most telling to me was the fact that while HCP had a strong third quarter, investors remained concerned that HCP's revenue stream was too concentrated on a relatively small number of operators and tenants.

So, the driving force wasn't occupancy rates as much as it was the quantity of tenants. When buying HCP, I was unaware of 2012's activity. Until July, it was on the plus side for me. Now, I was down almost 15% and the dividend payments weren't gonna make up for that.

Once again, the dilemma of deciding to hold and retain for dividend payments versus selling for a 15% loss had me in its grip. But, seeing that the Morningstar portfolio manager had put new money into HCP I was inclined to watch and wait. *The game continues...*

MONTH IN REVIEW

Between November 29 and December 27, 2013, the Dow gained 392 points. I managed to keep my lead, though it was less than last month. Both Mom and the DJIA improved their percentages compared to last month's end, while mine slightly dropped.

	Weekly Return on Investment Stats		
	Dow Jones Industrial Average	Me	Mom
Week 40	13.70%	17.26%	9.33%
Week 41	11.82%	15.51%	7.31%
Week 42	15.12%	17.04%	9.88%
Week 43	16.95%	18.24%	11.12%

Overall, for December, I had an unrealized gain of $48,188. Though I had no real loss leaders this month, Energy was lagging. Mom had an unrealized gain of $19,432 this month and Utilities lagged for her.

COMPARISON

For this month I was about 1.5 points ahead of the market and about 7 points ahead of Mom. This month was a very slight loss over last month for me. Both the value and percentage increase was higher for Mom than for me.

At this point, my portfolio had 24 items that I invested in based on recommendations from the Pros, which was about 48% (26 items were my picks). On a percentage basis, I retained my slight lead over the Pros this month as 88.5% of my items increased in value, but only 83.3% of the Pros items increased.

DIVIDENDS FOR DECEMBER

December's dividends paid well. I received 16 payments totaling $1,137.44, which averaged $71.09 per payment. Mom received 21 payments totaling $1,516.66, which averaged $72.22 per payment—marking the biggest payout for Mom! I noted that her high performance was driven by the funds, particularly Fidelity Contrafund, with a 6.585% yield. One detail that stood out was that many mutual funds only provided an annual payment, typically in December. For me, my funds paid out about $755, while

Mom's paid out about $950 this month. Her Fidelity fund alone was about $660! *Financial security in the making...*

LESSONS LEARNED

So many lessons, and so little time. This month was chock full of lessons learned, enough for me to question if I have an attention deficiency. The most frustrating item this month was screwing up my dividend calculations, just one of those stupid little annoying mistakes...they happen.

○ **Pay attention to changes in dividends.** If a company is projecting they will maintain or increase the amount of money they pay out, it's a good sign that they're confident in their ability to retain or grow profitability. If a company is doing the opposite, then you may have a good indicator to sell.

○ **The market giveth & the market taketh away.** You can make money or lose money; the choice is yours. Don't invest blindly, which I've done.

○ **Sometimes, all the action makes my head hurt.** In part, this relates to information overload—and it also relates to doing more than I needed in order to test myself. However, you'll likely have a similar experience, which I say is related to learning something new; in particular learning about investing. Don't sweat the small stuff. Take a break when you need it.

○ **You can't explain what you don't know.** And sometimes, you just have to be okay with that fact.

One could state that growth or profit is the only objective to investing, and I would almost agree. Seeking profit is not being greedy

(I mean, you enjoy getting a pay raise, right?). Instead, seeking profit is about making the best of your investment strategy to provide you with a more secure financial future. If you invest with an eye toward long-term growth, you are placing yourself in a position to pay future bills with less stress. You need that profit in order to create greater self-sufficiency.

Imagine if every single person was able to create a viable investment portfolio to ensure their future self-sufficiency. If that happened in the U.S., then there'd be a minimal need for the Social Security Administration (SSA). If the SSA disappeared, how much in tax dollars would that save? Imagine.

The following portfolio tables show what the current value (December 27) is compared to the purchase value. Value is presented in both dollar and percentage terms. The last column has the month-to-month (November to December) change as a percentage to show how items fluctuate monthly compared to the ever lengthening time between the start date and current values.

MY PORTFOLIO FOR DECEMBER 2013

Note: '0' in last column reflects ownership of less than a month.

Name (Pros in italics)	Purchase $ Value	12-27-13 $ Value	Total Net $ Gain/Loss	Total Net % Gain/ Loss	Nov to Dec % Change
8x8, Inc.	$744.00	$1,034.00	$290.00	39.0%	-0.77%
The AES Corporation	$1,193.00	$1,445.00	$252.00	21.1%	-0.82%
Alaska Air Group	$6,273.00	$7,201.00	$928.00	14.8%	-7.37%
Alliance Resource Partners LP	$6,725.00	$7,673.00	$948.00	14.1%	4.72%
Anika Therapeutics	$2,417.00	$3,669.00	$1,252.00	51.8%	6.81%
Apple Inc.(3)	$39,354.00	$56,009.00	$10,455.00	23.0%	0.72%
Arabian American Development Company	$940.00	$1,271.00	$331.00	35.2%	23.16%
Bank of Nova Scotia	$5,341.00	$6,165.00	$824.00	15.4%	0.13%
BlackRock Inc. (2)	$26,500.00	$31,638.00	$5,138.00	19.4%	4.50%
Coca-Cola Co	$3,870.00	$4,066.00	$196.00	5.1%	1.17%
Consolidated Communications Inc.	$1,637.00	$1,975.00	$338.00	20.6%	2.23%
El Paso Pipeline Partners LP	$4,140.00	$3,536.00	$(604.00)	-14.6%	-14.96%
Fonar Corporation	$1,700.00	$1,752.00	$52.00	3.1%	-9.22%
GasLog Ltd	$1,432.00	$1,741.00	$309.00	21.6%	9.29%
The GEO Group Inc.	$3,448.00	$3,248.00	$(200.00)	-5.8%	-0.98%
GlaxoSmithKline PLC ADR (1)	$4,422.00	$5,300.00	$878.00	19.9%	0.15%
Great Northern Iron Ore(2)	$6,944.00	$7,058.00	$114.00	1.6%	-4.21%

Name (Pros in italics)	Purchase $ Value	12-27-13 $ Value	Total Net $ Gain/Loss	Total Net % Gain/ Loss	Nov to Dec % Change
HCP Inc.	$4,325.00	$3,650.00	$(675.00)	-15.6%	-0.73%
Home Loan Servicing Solutions	$2,302.00	$2,290.00	$(12.00)	-0.5%	-1.59%
Inventure Foods, Inc.	$726.00	$1,347.00	$621.00	85.5%	5.32%
Kinder Morgan Energy Partners LP (1)	$8,672.00	$8,025.00	$(647.00)	-7.5%	-2.10%
Kinder Morgan Energy Partners LP (2)	$9,025.00	$8,025.00	$(1,000.00)	-11.1%	-2.10%
Macy's Inc.	$4,067.00	$5,270.00	$1,203.00	29.6%	-1.05%
Merck & Co Inc.	$4,782.00	$4,979.00	$197.00	4.1%	-0.08%
Michael Kors Holdings Ltd	$5,804.00	$8,058.00	$2,254.00	38.8%	-1.19%
Navios Maritime Holdings Inc.	$719.00	$1,126.00	$407.00	56.6%	45.48%
NTT DoCoMo Inc.	$1,505.00	$1,639.00	$134.00	8.9%	1.99%
Oaktree Capital Group, LLC	$5,013.00	$5,681.00	$668.00	13.3%	1.96%
Omnicell, Inc.	$2,318.00	$2,545.00	$227.00	9.8%	4.95%
Orchids Paper Products Co	$2,724.00	$3,210.00	$486.00	17.8%	-1.95%
Pfizer Inc.	$3,043.00	$3,064.00	$21.00	0.7%	-3.44%
Protolabs Inc.	$5,505.00	$7,129.00	$1,624.00	29.5%	-4.05%
Prudential PLC ADR	$3,349.00	$4,440.00	$1,091.00	32.6%	3.88%
PVR Partners LP	$2,285.00	$2,685.00	$400.00	17.5%	8.70%
Qihoo 360 Technology Co., Ltd.	$3,440.00	$8,124.00	$4,684.00	136.2%	-0.34%
RF Industries, Ltd	$636.00	$904.00	$268.00	42.1%	-34.40%
Seaspan Corp	$1,930.00	$2,290.00	$360.00	18.7%	5.05%
Sonoco Products Co	$3,407.00	$4,126.00	$719.00	21.1%	3.00%
Sunoco Logistics Partners LP	$6,258.00	$7,403.00	$1,145.00	18.3%	4.59%
Terra Nitrogen Co. (3)	$15,600.00	$14,250.00	$(1,350.00)	-8.7%	-8.80%

Name (Pros in italics)	Purchase $ Value	12-27-13 $ Value	Total Net $ Gain/Loss	Total Net % Gain/ Loss	Nov to Dec % Change
TJX Companies	$4,498.00	$6,338.00	$1,840.00	40.9%	0.80%
Akre Focus Fund Retail	$1,630.00	$2,069.00	$439.00	26.9%	1.12%
Delaware Healthcare I	$1,355.00	$1,806.00	$451.00	33.3%	-0.77%
Oakmark Global I	$2,610.00	$3,002.00	$392.00	15.0%	-2.72%
Oceanstone Fund	$3,753.00	$4,017.00	$635.00	18.8%	-7.97%
Fidelity Select Biotechnology Portfolio (1)	$14,631.00	$18,075.00	$5,870.00	48.1%	0.61%
Fidelity Select Biotechnology Portfolio (2)	$10,826.94	$13,375.50	$3,159.06	30.9%	0.61%
Fidelity Select IT Services Portfolio	$2,985.00	$3,712.00	$937.00	33.8%	2.43%
Vanguard Wellington Inv	$3,707.00	$3,786.00	$139.00	3.8%	-3.34%
Wells Fargo Advantage Core Builder Series M (2)	$1,098.00	$1,098.00	-	0.0%	-0.54%
	$264,131.44	$312,319.50	$48,188.06	18.24%	

Mom's Portfolio for December 2013

Name	Purchase $ Value	12-27-13 $ Value	Total Net $ Gain/Loss	Total Net % Gain/ Loss	Nov to Dec % Change
Altria Group	$3,349.00	$3,831.00	$482.00	14.39%	3.60%
AT&T Inc.	$3,601.00	$3,518.00	$(83.00)	-2.30%	-0.09%
Buckeye Partners LP	$5,611.00	$7,045.00	$1,434.00	25.56%	3.47%
Caterpillar Inc.	$9,136.00	$9,087.00	$(49.00)	-0.54%	7.41%
Cleco Corp	$4,418.00	$4,684.00	$266.00	6.02%	2.47%
CMS Energy Corp	$2,645.00	$2,669.00	$24.00	0.91%	0.57%
Compass Securities	$1,574.00	$1,933.00	$359.00	22.81%	1.26%
Deluxe Corp	$3,965.00	$5,199.00	$1,234.00	31.12%	4.63%
Devon Energy Corp	$5,388.00	$6,169.00	$781.00	14.50%	1.77%
Dominion Res Inc. VA	$5,642.00	$6,441.00	$799.00	14.16%	-0.77%
Duke Energy	$6,925.00	$6,895.00	$(30.00)	-0.43%	-1.44%
Enbridge Energy Partners	$2,763.00	$3,026.00	$263.00	9.52%	0.56%
Enterprise Products	$5,681.00	$6,519.00	$838.00	14.75%	3.53%
Exxon Mobile Corporation	$8,943.00	$10,151.00	$1,208.00	13.51%	8.59%
Frontier Communications Corp	$419.00	$470.00	$51.00	12.17%	0.43%
General Electric Co	$2,319.00	$2,783.00	$464.00	20.01%	4.39%
Great Plains Energy	$2,199.00	$2,419.00	$220.00	10.00%	1.90%
Hartford Financial Services Group	$2,368.00	$3,633.00	$1,265.00	53.42%	1.96%
Hudson City Bancorp	$858.00	$938.00	$80.00	9.32%	0.43%
Integrys Energy Group	$5,610.00	$5,442.00	$(168.00)	-2.99%	1.27%
Intel Corp	$2,103.00	$2,560.00	$457.00	21.73%	7.38%
Medical Properties Trust Inc.	$1,483.00	$1,245.00	$(238.00)	-16.05%	-5.75%
Mondelez International Inc.	$2,781.00	$3,491.00	$710.00	25.53%	4.12%
Nat'l Grid Transco	$5,456.00	$6,499.00	$1,043.00	19.12%	2.57%
Nisource Inc.	$2,793.00	$3,264.00	$471.00	16.86%	3.23%

Name	Purchase $ Value	12-27-13 $ Value	Total Net $ Gain/Loss	Total Net % Gain/ Loss	Nov to Dec % Change
Occidental Petroleum Corp	$8,265.00	$9,485.00	$1,220.00	14.76%	-0.12%
Spyglass Resources Corp	$274.00	$174.00	$(100.00)	-36.50%	2.96%
Pembina Pipeline Corp	$2,821.00	$3,476.00	$655.00	23.22%	8.42%
Pepco	$2,053.00	$1,893.00	$(160.00)	-7.79%	-0.79%
Philip Morris International Inc.	$9,144.00	$8,674.00	$(470.00)	-5.14%	1.40%
Piedmont Natural Gas Co	$3,265.00	$3,288.00	$23.00	0.70%	-0.81%
Principle Financial Group Inc.	$3,155.00	$4,938.00	$1,783.00	56.51%	-2.47%
Royal Dutch Shell PLC ADR	$6,578.00	$7,107.00	$529.00	8.04%	6.55%
Scana Corp	$4,906.00	$4,696.00	$(210.00)	-4.28%	-0.45%
Southern Co	$4,483.00	$4,086.00	$(397.00)	-8.86%	0.57%
Spectra Energy Corp	$2,881.00	$3,492.00	$611.00	21.21%	4.08%
Teco Energy	$1,735.00	$1,714.00	$(21.00)	-1.21%	0.59%
US Bancorp	$3,401.00	$4,037.00	$636.00	18.70%	2.93%
Verizon Communications Inc.	$4,672.00	$4,917.00	$245.00	5.24%	-0.91%
Wells Fargo & Co	$3,539.00	$4,550.00	$1,011.00	28.57%	3.36%
DWS Core Equity Fund	$1,983.00	$2,310.00	$327.00	16.49%	-4.19%
DWS S&P 500 Index Fund	$2,022.00	$2,447.00	$425.00	21.02%	1.62%
DWS Short Duration Fund	$931.00	$919.00	$(12.00)	-1.29%	-0.33%
Fidelity Contrafund	$ 8,122.00	$ 9,574.00	$1,452.00	17.88%	-4.85%
Wellesley Income Fund	$ 2,479.00	$ 2,483.00	$4.00	0.16%	-2.78%
	$174,739.00	$194,171.00	$19,432.00	11.12%	

EMAIL PROS SECTION

This section is to compare the Pros to the market. I can't compare it to Mom or me, because this has a different start date. Also, these details are different than the Pros items in my portfolio, because they are Pro picks for 2014 as relayed by an email invitation. So, I'm treating these picks as a stand-alone evaluation. Remember, the purpose of this analysis is to evaluate the Pros' picks based on a start date of December 16, 20113, to evaluate how well they do compared to the DJIA.

MONTH IN REVIEW

The market closed on December 13, 2013, at 15885 and closed on December 27, 2013, at 16221 — up 593 points.

	Weekly Return on Investment Stats	
	Dow Jones Industrial Average	Pros
Week 1	2.07%	1.24%
Week 2	3.73%	2.18%

Overall, for this month the Pros had an unrealized gain of $3,321 with no real loss leaders.

EMAIL PROS PORTFOLIO FOR DECEMBER 2013

Name	Purchase $ Value	12-27-13 $ Value	Total Net $ Gain/ Loss	Total Net % Gain/ Loss	Nov to Dec % Change
AmerisourceBergen Co.	$6,845.00	$7,021.00	$176.00	2.57%	
Celgene Corp	$16,338.00	$16,893.00	$555.00	3.40%	
Kroger Co	$4,006.00	$3,954.00	$(52.00)	-1.30%	
Magna International Inc.	$7,912.00	$8,080.00	$168.00	2.12%	
Yahoo! Inc.	$3,973.00	$4,049.00	$76.00	1.91%	

Name	Purchase $ Value	12-27-13 $ Value	Total Net $ Gain/ Loss	Total Net % Gain/ Loss	Nov to Dec % Change
Core Laboratories	$19,148.00	$19,083.00	$(65.00)	-0.34%	
FleetCor	$11,860.00	$11,595.00	$(265.00)	-2.23%	
Melco Crown Entertainment Ltd ADR	$3,845.00	$3,893.00	$48.00	1.25%	
Ecolab	$10,210.00	$10,447.00	$237.00	2.32%	
Actavis Plc	$15,966.00	$16,514.00	$548.00	3.43%	
EMC Software	$2,370.00	$2,500.00	$130.00	5.49%	
Quality Systems	$2,089.00	$2,126.00	$37.00	1.77%	
AutoNation	$4,998.00	$5,006.00	$8.00	0.16%	
FutureFuel Corp	$1,527.00	$1,583.00	$56.00	3.67%	
Solera Holdings	$6,940.00	$7,018.00	$78.00	1.12%	
Fortegra Financial Corp	$740.00	$830.00	$90.00	12.16%	
NIC Inc.	$2,270.00	$2,449.00	$179.00	7.89%	
Almost Family Inc.	$3,133.00	$3,290.00	$157.00	5.01%	
Eaton Vance Tax-Managed Global Diversified Equity Income Fund	$988.00	$1,006.00	$18.00	1.82%	
Cheniere Energy Partners	$2,765.00	$2,982.00	$217.00	7.85%	
Apollo Investment	$870.00	$851.00	$(19.00)	-2.18%	
Oaktree Capital Group	$5,519.00	$5,681.00	$162.00	2.94%	
AllianzGlobal NFJ Dividend, Interest and Premium Strategy Fund	$1,804.00	$1,796.00	$(8.00)	-0.44%	
TCP Capital	$1,645.00	$1,698.00	$53.00	3.22%	
Breitburn Energy Partners LP	$1,937.00	$2,028.00	$91.00	4.70%	
Teekay LNG Partners	$3,986.00	$4,258.00	$272.00	6.82%	

Name	Purchase $ Value	12-27-13 $ Value	Total Net $ Gain/ Loss	Total Net % Gain/ Loss	Nov to Dec % Change
Boardwalk Pipeline Partners	$2,514.00	$2,598.00	$84.00	3.34%	
Navios Maritime Partners	$1,789.00	$1,911.00	$122.00	6.82%	
Memorial Production Partners	$2,074.00	$2,215.00	$141.00	6.80%	
Hercules Technology Growth Capital	$1,655.00	$1,657.00	$2.00	0.12%	
AGIC Convertible & Income Fund	$948.00	$973.00	$25.00	2.64%	
	$152,664.00	$155,985.00	$3,321.00	2.18%	

JANUARY

CONVICTION

Don't gamble; take all your savings and buy some good stock and hold it till it goes up, then sell it. If it don't go up, don't buy it.

—Will Rogers

You know you're a novice investor when...

You stay on the top floor of a hotel and decide to sleep or jump later.

From:	Rhea Dempshun
Sent:	Saturday, December 26, 2013 7:47 PM
To:	Mark Slauter <markslauter@novice.investor>
Subject:	Fast Money Windows

Dear Fellow Investor,

I just discovered something really unusual...I call them **Fast Money Windows.** Every year between January 20 and February 3, one stock leaps upward in price. Over the last decade, it's 10-0. All you had to do to make money was buy it in January and sell it in February every year.

The weird thing is, there are 33 other stocks that do the exact same thing—with a 91% to 100% effective rate for 10 years running. They're the only ones in the market that act like this. And when you see why... I think you'll be quite surprised. That's why I created a brand new service to let you know exactly when each window begins and when to get out.

Really? This email is selling me on fast money windows? Not only do animals exist within the investing language (bulls, bears, etc.), but I guess we need to start including architectural definitions as well. We could add doors, ground floor or first floor opportunities, toilet, drain, kitchen sink, etc. Maybe I could start a new mutual fund called EBTKS (Everything But The Kitchen Sink) and build it around dumb-ass phrases. Or, I could just call it DAPX (Dumb-Ass Phrases).

January 3, 2014

RFIL dropped almost 23% from what appears to be a sell off with regard to the release of their unaudited quarterly report, which showed a 9% decline in revenues though revenue is up almost 32% for the year. Net income dropped from $0.17 to $0.03 per share. Maybe this is a buy opportunity? It's still on the plus side from my initial purchase.

January 14, 2014

Another fine example of patience: the Dow dropped 179 points yesterday and gained 116 back today. After all of this, my unrealized gains actually increased and places me more than five points ahead of the market.

January 22, 2014

There's been some talk of a Canadian housing bubble...wonder how much this is affecting Bank of Nova Scotia as it has dropped slightly again. I'm now up more than 178% on Qihoo 360. I hear someone screaming SELL! SELL! SELL!

Having closed out 2013 and started the new year, it was time for the media to look back on 2013 as a whole, review the final quarter, and begin to look at the future. For 2013, the Dow Jones Industrial Average had another banner year ending to the upside about 26%. I didn't do quite as well but ended the year up about 20%. If you'd invested $1000 dollars and had a similar outcome, you'd now have somewhere between $200 and $260 in extra money. Wouldn't it be great if all your money worked that hard for you?

The final quarter of the year brought a shift where investors were focused. I think part of this was based on an expected interest rate hike by the Federal Reserve, and folks taking profits. Recently, the focus had shifted into manufacturing, construction, and consumer cyclical stocks and funds. Media were also reminding us of the need to examine our portfolios and make any necessary adjustments. Take the profit.

In looking to 2014, rebalancing the portfolio may have been a good idea, but given that current market valuations were so high, where was I supposed to go? What should I buy? These are always valid questions to ask yourself, and they're ones I continue to grapple with—where to put the money? Surprisingly, I find that the most difficult action is actually sitting on the money and waiting for an opportunity. I feel like a five-year old kid holding a $100 bill while standing outside of a 10,000-square-foot candy store with locked doors.

As I looked at my portfolio, it contained many items that I would probably not buy at this time, which some professionals suggested as a good reason to sell—providing it was profitable to do so. So many in fact, that selling my profitable ones would have gutted my portfolio and I'd find myself starting over. *But is that a bad thing if I bank solid double-digit gains?* I didn't immediately have an answer to that question, so instead, I used my hard-learned patience, watched the market, and looked for useful information.

WATCHING THE MARKET

So, a new year was here, and I was off to the races. I felt that I'd done well so far, improving my knowledge base, and keeping a check on emotional responses. The first trading day of 2014 was January 2, and it opened with a testy salvo across the bow of my investing boat by dropping 135 points. *Welcome to 2014.*

The first day sell-off affected all sectors, and it appeared that nothing was spared. I started wondering if we were entering a market adjustment of some sort. Little did I know how true this sentiment was. By month's end, the market had dropped about 800 points. Though painful, I was still running a profit.

Overall, the first week was good for me as my unrealized gain jumped from about $48k to almost $55k. Though this growth was good—and definitely made me smile—the market appeared to have some jitters, since 1) company quarterly financials didn't seem to be impressing investors, and 2) the non-farm payroll employment number was nowhere near what analysts expected.

As I've previously mentioned, I'd noticed one component of employment figures that few people discuss: the participation rate. The employment figures you hear on the news focus on either how many new jobs were created (people hired) or on the unemployment figure (6.5%). These two data points only account for working-age people who are either employed or are collecting some type of unemployment benefit. When a person stops collecting unemployment benefits and stops seeking employment, then the Fed considers them not participating and excludes them from the employment datasets.

As of writing this chapter, we were experiencing the highest non-participating employment rate since the 1970s—more than 30%. This statistic means the size of the employment participant pool is smaller, thereby altering the actual number of people counted. Assessing data in this way is like telling your friends you only have six beers because that's what's in the cooler, when in reality you have 12 beers because there's another six-pack in the fridge! So, when unemployment numbers are presented in this way, we should always remain wary about what those numbers really are or aren't telling us.

The market appeared to be in a good place as the month was progressing—up to the week of January 21.

January 23, 2014

The Dow dropped 176 points today, primarily due to an apparent contraction of China's manufacturing output, which may have hurt the financial sector. Also issued today are reports of lower than expected existing home sales and initial weekly jobless claims.

January 24, 2014

The Dow dropped again today…318 points! … with decliners killing advancers by a 6 to 1 ratio. This appears to be driven by the news on the decline of manufacturing output in China, overseas markets declining overnight, and a hesitation surrounding the upcoming Federal Open Market Committee (FMOC) meeting. Add to this that quarterly earnings reports are not as rosy as desired.

With a 580-point loss to the Dow during the third week, investment life was pretty rough. While I was paying close attention, I wasn't nearly as freaked out or spooked this time as I was when this occurred the year before. From experience, I now knew that I had to maintain my investment approach, which was primarily driven by a long-term view. In reality, being aware of what is taking place in the markets and truly knowing how potential actions affect a portfolio or position is difficult. Though I was seeking growth and income, I'd also allocated my portfolio with higher risk investments. As a result, weeks like this one wreaked havoc on my share value; several items had their unrealized gains value crushed with reductions greater than 25%. *Painful, just painful.*

But, on the investment journey, the engine keeps chugging along and doesn't stop unless you pull the breaks. As the train's captain, momentum can be a blessing or a curse.

During the last week of January, the Federal Reserve announced it was tapering back another $10M on its monthly bond buying to only $65B. *Man, our descendants are so screwed!* The announcement disconcerted investors, since they viewed each reduction in bond buying by the Fed as another step closer to raising interest rates. Investors were also concerned with lackluster company quarterly financial reports and downward trends in emerging markets.

Without getting into specifics on the portfolios, this month was a good example of how factors other than a company's performance can alter the investing landscape. Think of it as throwing a stone into still water creating outbound ripples from its point of entry.

If nothing else, investing will absolutely test the conviction of your decisions.

CHASING FOR INFORMATION

While the Federal Reserve continued to spend tens of billions of dollars a month (*I hope folks have set aside enough money to support three to four generations of offspring*) and investors tried to foretell the future, I continued to search for insight that would help me become a better investor.

Every so often when you go chasing information, you'll find a slap-in-the-face item that you absolutely can't avoid paying attention to. And this was the time for me to get slapped. While reviewing my stocks on January 6, I noted that Great Northern Iron Ore (GNI) got crushed by dropping almost 47%. The root of its downward performance stemmed from an article than ran on Sunday, January 5, which stated shares only had a value of $20.89. The current value stated in the article was $67 and anyone owning shares at the current value were guaranteed to lose two-thirds of their investment.

Now, this information was huge for many reasons. One of which was the fact that GNI is a royalty trust set to end in 2015, creating zero share value. Zero. While I was aware of this detail, I had intended to hold on a little longer hoping to maximize its value. *Oh well, I screwed the pooch and overplayed my hand. Dump it and move on!* See how it pays to read? If I had known about the article on Sunday, maybe I would have set my trade for first thing Monday morning—and possibly could have reduced my $3400 loss.

But, as the engine continued chugging, other market details also grabbed my attention. One item that I followed closely was the discussions regarding where the market was headed. With January's sell-off, it almost looked like people just wanted out. While 2013 was a banner year, no one thought the same level of success was going to carry over in to 2014; at least not in the first quarter.

Of particular note to me was a comment I read stating that 2013's performance was driven by improvements to price/earnings (PE) ratios rather than actual growth of companies. As I reflected back on my experiences to date, I concluded there was validity in this sentiment. Between Mom and me, we had many international companies in our portfolios, and for several months now, reports had described the difficulty these companies were having in international economies. For the most part, product sales had remained flat or decreased, though an undercurrent of expectation remained that the international economies would improve. I felt that this was something I would need to pay more attention to.

With regard to the PE ratio, there was a tremendous amount of merger and acquisition activity, along with many companies using cash they had been hoarding for years (post 2008 crash) to buy back outstanding stock shares. In both cases, these actions can result in creating the false appearance of growth, because the share value can increase without the company having become more profitable. And being able to discern the real growth from the perceived growth becomes an essential tool in your investment kit.

As I was making sense of all the market details, I came across a quote that made my stomach churn: "This Fed is focused on finding ways to refill the punch bowl so that the party never stops."

I immediately rolled my eyes and thought, *This guy's a chump.*

Now, let's look back on our economy and reflect on some other notable parties that also weren't going to stop: Michael Milken and junk bonds, the tech bubble of the early 2000s, the savings and loan debacle of the "Keating 5", etc. And that's just since the 1980s. All those parties did stop and negatively impacted the markets as a result. What really disturbed me about the comment was wondering how pervasive this perspective within the financial community might be. Was this really what people think? And to think that people trust this chump with their money! I wondered what types of potentially poor choices this guy was making with other people's money because he views this as a never ending party.

In all, January's performance fit perfectly with a Chinese proverb. "Unless we change direction, we're likely to end up where we're headed."

Analyzing the Portfolios

Throughout January, some professionals were suggesting investors should move into more defensive sectors (Utilities, Consumer goods, Telecommunications, etc.), because they offer more favorable returns and less risk. So, this got me thinking: What does this suggestion mean for our portfolios?

I started checking and couldn't discern if Mom was better off than I was. Her top three holdings by sector were Utilities (31%), Energy (24%), and Financial Services (14%), which accounted for 69% of her portfolio. The top three for me were Consumer Services (17%), Financial Services (14%), and Healthcare (14%), which accounted for 45% of my portfolio. I think I had a better balance in diversification, but I also had a much greater level of risk. *Hmmm, should I be worried?*

At this point, I saw no reason to alter my portfolio in the direction of more utilities, though I did acquire two new financial stocks (banks) with the money I received from selling GNI. Both banks were Over-The-Counter (OTC market) items, and I recognized the associated risk. Though an expectation exists that banks become more profitable when interest rates rise, the two banks I chose were directly tied to China, which did bring with them a red flag of sorts: Some countries were accusing China of currency manipulation, the potential for a Chinese housing bubble, and the country was experiencing slowed economic growth. Nonetheless, I made the acquisitions.

While rebalancing my portfolio, I'd decided that I also wanted to enhance my exposure to international markets, so I acquired

Unilever (UL). I figured that once those markets began to improve, UL could benefit from increasing sales. And since UL was a large and stable company, I felt that this acquisition partially offset some of the increased risk I assumed from purchasing the bank stocks. *Oh, the ongoing balancing act!*

	Unilever PLC ADR	**HSBC Holdings PLC**	**Industrial And Commercial Bank Of China Ltd. ADR**
Sector	Consumer Defensive	Financial Services	Financial Services
10-yr EPS	15.79%	1.15%	22.79%[1]
10-yr Average for Revenue Growth	1.57%	5.04%	16.87%
Dividend Yield	3.46%	4.36%	5.08%
Analyst Buy Recommendations	1 of 4	1 of 4	1 of 4

1. 5-year EPS

A few days after I bought HSBC I read an article explaining that shares fell because the bank may have overstated assets by as much as $92 billion. Just great! As a result, financial institutions were now rating the stock as a sell. I have the OTC shares (HBCYF) of HSBC, which fell almost 2% on the announcement. *Hey, what's $92B among friends....right?*

Amidst all this chatter, China wasn't the only economy analysts were wary about. Canada was seeing its fair share of commentary regarding the potential for a Canadian housing bubble and I noted that Bank of Nova Scotia (BNS) continued trending downward to a level equal to October 2013. One article described the results of a Deutsche Bank report asserting home prices in Canada were 60% above the historical norm, giving them the dubious distinction of having the most overvalued real estate market in the world. Concurrently, Morningstar reduced the BNS fair value estimate from $64 to $61 based on an expectation of a lower return on equity.

Since BNS had a 3.81% dividend yield and I was up 15%, this information was not sufficient enough for me to sell. However, I knew I needed to stay apprised of what was happening with Canada and this stock. Though BNS is an international company, I realized that a negative shift in Canada's economy could cause some major issues for other countries.

Another stock whose fair value estimate was reduced by Morningstar at the end of this month was Apple—from $600 to $570 per share due to a greatly reduced revenue growth projection. I couldn't believe it. Just two weeks ago (January 18) Morningstar had reaffirmed its $600 fair value estimate. What can I say about this? In the third week of January I was up about 20% and now it's up only about 10%. I remembered thinking during the past few weeks it might be a good time to sell this.

Near the end of the month Apple reported that it missed revenue expectations and the aftermarket (overnight trading) share value dropped more than $48. From my perspective, I thought buying at the opening on the next day (January 28) for $501 would be great timing. At the time I remember thinking, *Carl Icahn should have waited so he could have bought the stock cheaper and saved some money.*

Meanwhile, with Apple's performance falling, I was stoked to learn that I was now up 194% on Qihoo 360 (QIHU)! The businessman in me was screaming to sell, though I was fairly sure I couldn't duplicate this success by repurchasing it. But, the cat in me was curious to ride it out and see how far this performance would go.

Yeah….the cat won.

MONTH IN REVIEW

Between December 27 and January 31, 2014, the Dow lost 779

points. Now I was quite far ahead of the Dow and Mom.

	Weekly Return on Investment Stats		
	Dow Jones Industrial Average	Me	Mom
Week 44	16.89%	17.70%	9.99%
Week 45	16.66%	20.12%	10.68%
Week 46	16.81%	21.18%	9.99%
Week 47	12.70%	19.51%	8.22%
Week 48	11.42%	18.07%	8.74%

Overall in January, I had an unrealized gain of $47,625. Ironically, the loss leader this month was Financial Services—after I bought two new ones. Mom had an unrealized gain of $15,271 this month and her Utility stocks were out of favor and lagging.

COMPARISON

For January, I was about 6.5 points ahead of the market and about 9.5 points ahead of Mom. This month was a very slight loss over last month for me. While the Dow and Mom fell by about one third compared to last month, I remained almost unchanged on returns. *Sorry Mom, but that makes me very, very happy.*

At this point, my portfolio had 24 items that I invested in based on recommendations from the Pros, which was about 46% (28 items were my picks). On a percentage basis, I lost my slight lead over the Pros this month as 78.6% of my items increased in value, while 79.2% of the Pros items increased.

DIVIDENDS FOR JANUARY

For January I received 8 payments totaling $462.07, which averaged $57.76 per payment. Mom received 9 payments totaling $334.06, which averaged $37.12 per payment. I made about 38%

more per payment than Mom. *Woo hoo!*

LESSONS LEARNED

After watching my portfolio make steady improvement through November and December I was buoyed by the apparent upward direction for January, up to the point where the market fell back 580 points. Though the total damage for the month was a loss of about 800 points on the DJIA, I was still feeling positive about my performance; my unrealized gains were minimally affected, I was receiving some solid dividends, and—even though many stocks fell back—many of mine were hitting all-time highs on share value.

○ **There are days when doing this is actually enjoyable.** What's more enjoyable than watching your financial position improve? As a novice investor you should be proud of your accomplishments…just don't get cocky.

○ **Try to be aware of macro- and micro-factors.** If China's growth and manufacturing output continued to decline, the consequences could be globally devastating, since they are the second largest economy. As my experience with GNI showed, sometimes all it takes is someone writing an article to crush an investment.

I was still pissed off about my losing trades and would make every effort to learn from them. I couldn't believe I lost another $3400. It is the experiences like GNI or big changes in the market where investing will absolutely test the conviction of your decisions. Though I had some investments that weren't performing well, I felt more comfortable with my position now than previously.

In hindsight, I believe this was due to my creating a level of familiarity with both my portfolio and the stock market in general.

Up to this point, I'd put a sufficient amount of time into this experience and had developed an almost detached perspective to watching the market and managing my portfolio...almost.

The following portfolio tables show what the current value (January 31) is compared to the purchase value. Value is presented in both dollar and percentage terms. The last column has the month-to-month (December to January) change as a percentage to show how items fluctuate monthly compared to the ever lengthening time between the start date and current values.

MY PORTFOLIO FOR JANUARY 2014

Note: '0' in last column reflects ownership of less than a month.

Name (Pros in italics)	Purchase $ Value	1-31-14 $ Value	Total Net $ Gain/ Loss	Total Net % Gain/ Loss	Dec to Jan % Change
8x8, Inc.	$744.00	$1,014.00	$270.00	36.29%	0.50%
The AES Corporation	$1,193.00	$1,406.00	$213.00	17.85%	-0.99%
Alaska Air Group	$6,273.00	$7,907.00	$1,634.00	26.05%	6.11%
Alliance Resource Partners LP	$6,725.00	$8,240.00	$1,515.00	22.53%	7.99%
Anika Therapeutics	$2,417.00	$3,327.00	$910.00	37.65%	-3.14%
Apple Inc.(3)	$39,354.00	$50,060.00	$4,506.00	9.89%	-7.46%
Arabian American Development Company	$940.00	$1,140.00	$200.00	21.28%	-6.17%
Bank of Nova Scotia	$5,341.00	$5,484.00	$143.00	2.68%	-10.83%
BlackRock Inc. (2)	$26,500.00	$30,047.00	$3,547.00	13.38%	-4.36%
Coca-Cola Co	$3,870.00	$3,782.00	$(88.00)	-2.27%	-6.52%
Consolidated Communications	$1,637.00	$1,958.00	$321.00	19.61%	-1.16%
El Paso Pipeline Partners LP	$4,140.00	$3,281.00	$(859.00)	-20.75%	-7.55%
Fonar Corporation	$1,700.00	$1,845.00	$145.00	8.53%	-7.57%
GasLog Ltd	$1,432.00	$2,096.00	$664.00	46.37%	24.17%
The GEO Group Inc.	$3,448.00	$3,348.00	$(100.00)	-2.90%	4.59%
GlaxoSmithKline PLC ADR (1)	$4,422.00	$5,154.00	$732.00	16.55%	-2.39%
HCP Inc.	$4,325.00	$3,915.00	$(410.00)	-9.48%	8.21%
Home Loan Servicing Solutions	$2,302.00	$2,052.00	$(250.00)	-10.86%	-9.80%
HSBC Holdings PLC	$1,104.00	$1,025.00	$(79.00)	-7.16%	0

Name (Pros in italics)	Purchase $ Value	1-31-14 $ Value	Total Net $ Gain/ Loss	Total Net % Gain/ Loss	Dec to Jan % Change
Industrial And Commercial Bank Of China Ltd. ADR	$1,291.00	$1,230.00	$(61.00)	-4.73%	0
Inventure Foods, Inc.	$726.00	$1,253.00	$527.00	72.59%	-6.07%
Kinder Morgan Energy Partners LP (1)	$8,672.00	$7,948.00	$(724.00)	-8.35%	-1.01%
Kinder Morgan Energy Partners LP (2)	$9,025.00	$7,948.00	$(1,077.00)	-11.93%	-1.01%
Macy's Inc.	$4,067.00	$5,320.00	$1,253.00	30.81%	-0.64%
Merck & Co Inc.	$4,782.00	$5,297.00	$515.00	10.77%	6.52%
Michael Kors Holdings Ltd	$5,804.00	$7,993.00	$2,189.00	37.72%	-3.13%
Navios Maritime Holdings Inc.	$719.00	$948.00	$229.00	31.85%	-9.11%
NTT DoCoMo Inc.	$1,505.00	$1,600.00	$95.00	6.31%	-2.20%
Oaktree Capital Group, LLC	$5,013.00	$5,841.00	$828.00	16.52%	1.94%
Omnicell, Inc.	$2,318.00	$2,582.00	$264.00	11.39%	2.34%
Orchids Paper Products Co	$2,724.00	$3,115.00	$391.00	14.35%	-2.96%
Pfizer Inc.	$3,043.00	$3,040.00	$(3.00)	-0.10%	-0.39%
Protolabs Inc.	$5,505.00	$7,936.00	$2,431.00	44.16%	8.68%
Prudential PLC ADR	$3,349.00	$4,036.00	$687.00	20.51%	-8.71%
PVR Partners LP	$2,285.00	$2,804.00	$519.00	22.71%	5.69%
Qihoo 360 Technology Co., Ltd.	$3,440.00	$10,108.00	$6,668.00	193.84%	26.70%
RF Industries, Ltd	$636.00	$662.00	$26.00	4.09%	-3.22%
Seaspan Corp	$1,930.00	$2,225.00	$295.00	15.28%	-1.94%
Sonoco Products Co	$3,407.00	$4,138.00	$731.00	21.46%	0.83%
Sunoco Logistics Partners LP	$6,258.00	$7,858.00	$1,600.00	25.57%	7.35%
Terra Nitrogen Co. (3)	$15,600.00	$15,714.00	$114.00	0.73%	8.77%
TJX Companies	$4,498.00	$5,736.00	$1,238.00	27.52%	-9.81%

Name (Pros in italics)	Purchase $ Value	1-31-14 $ Value	Total Net $ Gain/ Loss	Total Net % Gain/ Loss	Dec to Jan % Change
Unilever PLC ADR	$3,983.00	$3,861.00	$(122.00)	-3.06%	0
Akre Focus Fund Retail	$1,630.00	$2,018.00	$388.00	23.80%	-2.79%
Delaware Healthcare I	$1,355.00	$1,819.00	$464.00	34.24%	1.06%
Oakmark Global I	$2,610.00	$2,923.00	$313.00	11.99%	-2.47%
Oceanstone Fund	$3,753.00	$3,946.00	$564.00	16.68%	-2.74%
Fidelity Select Biotechnology Portfolio (1)	$14,631.00	$20,555.00	$8,350.00	68.41%	13.09%
Fidelity Select Biotechnology Portfolio (2)	$10,826.94	$15,210.70	$4,994.26	48.88%	13.09%
Fidelity Select IT Services Portfolio	$2,985.00	$3,583.00	$808.00	29.12%	-3.45%
Vanguard Wellington Inv	$3,707.00	$3,736.00	$89.00	2.44%	-0.98%
Wells Fargo Advantage Core Builder Series M (2)	$1,098.00	$1,126.00	$28.00	2.55%	2.46%
	$263,565.44	**$311,190.70**	**$47,625.26**	**18.07%**	

MOM'S PORTFOLIO FOR JANUARY 2014

Name	Purchase $ Value	1-31-14 $ Value	Total Net $ Gain/ Loss	Total Net % Gain/ Loss	Dec to Jan % Change
Altria Group	$3,349.00	$3,522.00	$173.00	5.17%	-8.07%
AT&T Inc.	$3,601.00	$3,332.00	$(269.00)	-7.47%	-5.29%
Buckeye Partners LP	$5,611.00	$7,299.00	$1,688.00	30.08%	3.61%
Caterpillar Inc.	$9,136.00	$9,391.00	$255.00	2.79%	3.35%
Cleco Corp	$4,418.00	$4,886.00	$468.00	10.59%	4.31%
CMS Energy Corp	$2,645.00	$2,779.00	$134.00	5.07%	4.12%
Compass Securities	$1,574.00	$1,795.00	$221.00	14.04%	-7.14%
Deluxe Corp	$3,965.00	$4,855.00	$890.00	22.45%	-6.62%
Devon Energy Corp	$5,388.00	$5,922.00	$534.00	9.91%	-4.00%
Dominion Res Inc. VA	$5,642.00	$6,791.00	$1,149.00	20.37%	5.43%
Duke Energy Corporation	$6,925.00	$7,062.00	$137.00	1.98%	2.42%
Enbridge Energy Partners LP	$2,763.00	$2,938.00	$175.00	6.33%	-2.91%
Enterprise Products Partners LP	$5,681.00	$6,638.00	$957.00	16.85%	1.83%
Exxon Mobile Corporation	$8,943.00	$9,216.00	$273.00	3.05%	-9.21%
Frontier Communications Corp	$419.00	$468.00	$49.00	11.69%	-0.43%
General Electric Co	$2,319.00	$2,513.00	$194.00	8.37%	-9.70%
Great Plains Energy Inc.	$2,199.00	$2,468.00	$269.00	12.23%	2.03%
Hartford Financial Services Group	$2,368.00	$3,325.00	$957.00	40.41%	-8.48%
Hudson City Bancorp	$858.00	$904.00	$46.00	5.36%	-3.62%
Integrys Energy Group	$5,610.00	$5,434.00	$(176.00)	-3.14%	-0.15%
Intel Corp	$2,103.00	$2,454.00	$351.00	16.69%	-4.14%
Medical Properties Trust Inc.	$1,483.00	$1,327.00	$(156.00)	-10.52%	6.59%
Mondelez International Inc.	$2,781.00	$3,276.00	$495.00	17.80%	-6.16%

Name	Purchase $ Value	1-31-14 $ Value	Total Net $ Gain/ Loss	Total Net % Gain/ Loss	Dec to Jan % Change
National Grid PLC ADR	$5,456.00	$6,478.00	$1,022.00	18.73%	-0.32%
Nisource Inc.	$2,793.00	$3,437.00	$644.00	23.06%	5.30%
Occidental Petroleum Corp	$8,265.00	$8,757.00	$492.00	5.95%	-7.68%
Spyglass Resources Corp	$274.00	$180.00	$(94.00)	-34.31%	3.45%
Pembina Pipeline Corp	$2,821.00	$3,430.00	$609.00	21.59%	-1.32%
Pepco Holdings Inc.	$2,053.00	$1,943.00	$(110.00)	-5.36%	2.64%
Philip Morris International Inc.	$9,144.00	$7,814.00	$(1,330.00)	-14.55%	-9.91%
Piedmont Natural Gas Co	$3,265.00	$3,302.00	$37.00	1.13%	0.43%
Principle Financial Group Inc.	$3,155.00	$4,357.00	$1,202.00	38.10%	-11.77%
Royal Dutch Shell PLC ADR	$6,578.00	$6,910.00	$332.00	5.05%	-2.77%
Scana Corp	$4,906.00	$4,727.00	$(179.00)	-3.65%	0.66%
Southern Co	$4,483.00	$4,124.00	$(359.00)	-8.01%	0.93%
Spectra Energy Corp	$2,881.00	$3,595.00	$714.00	24.78%	2.95%
Teco Energy Inc.	$1,735.00	$1,638.00	$(97.00)	-5.59%	-4.43%
US Bancorp	$3,401.00	$3,973.00	$572.00	16.82%	-1.59%
Verizon Communications Inc.	$4,672.00	$4,802.00	$130.00	2.78%	-2.34%
Wells Fargo & Co	$3,539.00	$4,534.00	$995.00	28.12%	-0.35%
DWS Core Equity Fund	$1,983.00	$2,250.00	$267.00	13.46%	-2.60%
DWS S&P 500 Index Fund	$2,022.00	$2,371.00	$349.00	17.26%	-3.11%
DWS Short Duration Fund	$931.00	$918.00	$(13.00)	-1.40%	-0.11%
Fidelity Contrafund	$8,122.00	$9,399.00	$1,277.00	15.72%	-1.83%
Wellesley Income Fund	$2,479.00	$2,476.00	$(3.00)	-0.12%	-0.28%
	$174,739.00	$190,010.00	$15,271.00	8.74%	

EMAIL PROS MONTH IN REVIEW

Between December 27 and January 31, 2014, the Dow lost 779 points. The Pros were leading the Dow.

	Weekly Return on Investment Stats	
	Dow Jones Industrial Average	Pros
Week 3	3.68%	1.70%
Week 4	3.47%	3.70%
Week 5	3.61%	2.92%
Week 6	-0.04%	-0.11%
Week 7	-1.17%	-0.55%

Overall, for this month the Pros had an unrealized loss of $838 with the Industrial and Technology sectors as loss leaders.

EMAIL PROS PORTFOLIO FOR JANUARY 2014

Name	Purchase $ Value	1-31-14 $ Value	Total Net $ Gain/ Loss	Total Net % Gain/ Loss	Dec to Jan % Change
AmerisourceBergen Co.	$6,845.00	$6,722.00	$(123.00)	-1.80%	-4.26%
Celgene Corp	$16,338.00	$15,193.00	$(1,145.00)	-7.01%	-10.06%
Kroger Co	$4,006.00	$3,610.00	$(396.00)	-9.89%	-8.70%
Magna International Inc.	$7,912.00	$8,485.00	$573.00	7.24%	5.01%
Yahoo! Inc.	$3,973.00	$3,601.00	$(372.00)	-9.36%	-11.06%
Core Laboratories	$19,148.00	$17,892.00	$(1,256.00)	-6.56%	-6.24%
FleetCor	$11,860.00	$10,632.00	$(1,228.00)	-10.35%	-8.31%
Melco Crown Entertainment Ltd ADR	$3,845.00	$4,099.00	$254.00	6.61%	5.29%
Ecolab	$10,210.00	$10,054.00	$(156.00)	-1.53%	-3.76%
Actavis Plc	$15,966.00	$18,898.00	$2,932.00	18.36%	14.44%
EMC Software	$2,370.00	$2,424.00	$54.00	2.28%	-3.04%
Quality Systems	$2,089.00	$1,841.00	$(248.00)	-11.87%	-13.41%
AutoNation	$4,998.00	$4,939.00	$(59.00)	-1.18%	-1.34%

Name	Purchase $ Value	1-31-14 $ Value	Total Net $ Gain/ Loss	Total Net % Gain/ Loss	Dec to Jan % Change
FutureFuel Corp	$1,527.00	$1,636.00	$109.00	7.14%	3.35%
Solera Holdings	$6,940.00	$6,683.00	$(257.00)	-3.70%	-4.77%
Fortegra Financial Corp	$740.00	$737.00	$(3.00)	-0.41%	-11.20%
NIC Inc.	$2,270.00	$2,174.00	$(96.00)	-4.23%	-11.23%
Almost Family Inc.	$3,133.00	$3,041.00	$(92.00)	-2.94%	-7.57%
Eaton Vance Tax-Managed Global Diversified Equity Income Fund	$988.00	$981.00	$(7.00)	-0.71%	-2.49%
Cheniere Energy Partners	$2,765.00	$2,799.00	$34.00	1.23%	-6.14%
Apollo Investment	$870.00	$844.00	$(26.00)	-2.99%	-0.82%
Oaktree Capital Group	$5,519.00	$5,841.00	$322.00	5.83%	2.82%
AllianzGlobal NFJ Dividend, Interest and Premium Strategy Fund	$1,804.00	$1,786.00	$(18.00)	-1.00%	-0.56%
TCP Capital	$1,645.00	$1,732.00	$87.00	5.29%	2.00%
Breitburn Energy Partners LP	$1,937.00	$2,055.00	$118.00	6.09%	1.33%
Teekay LNG Partners	$3,986.00	$4,047.00	$61.00	1.53%	-4.96%
Boardwalk Pipeline Partners	$2,514.00	$2,462.00	$(52.00)	-2.07%	-5.23%
Navios Maritime Partners	$1,789.00	$1,836.00	$47.00	2.63%	-3.92%
Memorial Production Partners	$2,074.00	$2,193.00	$119.00	5.74%	-0.99%
Hercules Technology Growth Capital	$1,655.00	$1,586.00	$(69.00)	-4.17%	-4.28%
AGIC Convertible & Income Fund	$948.00	$1,003.00	$55.00	5.80%	3.08%
	$152,664.00	$151,826.00	$(838.00)	-0.55%	

February

Dead Cat Bounce

All I ask is the chance to prove that money can't make me happy.
—Spike Milligan

You know you're a novice investor when...

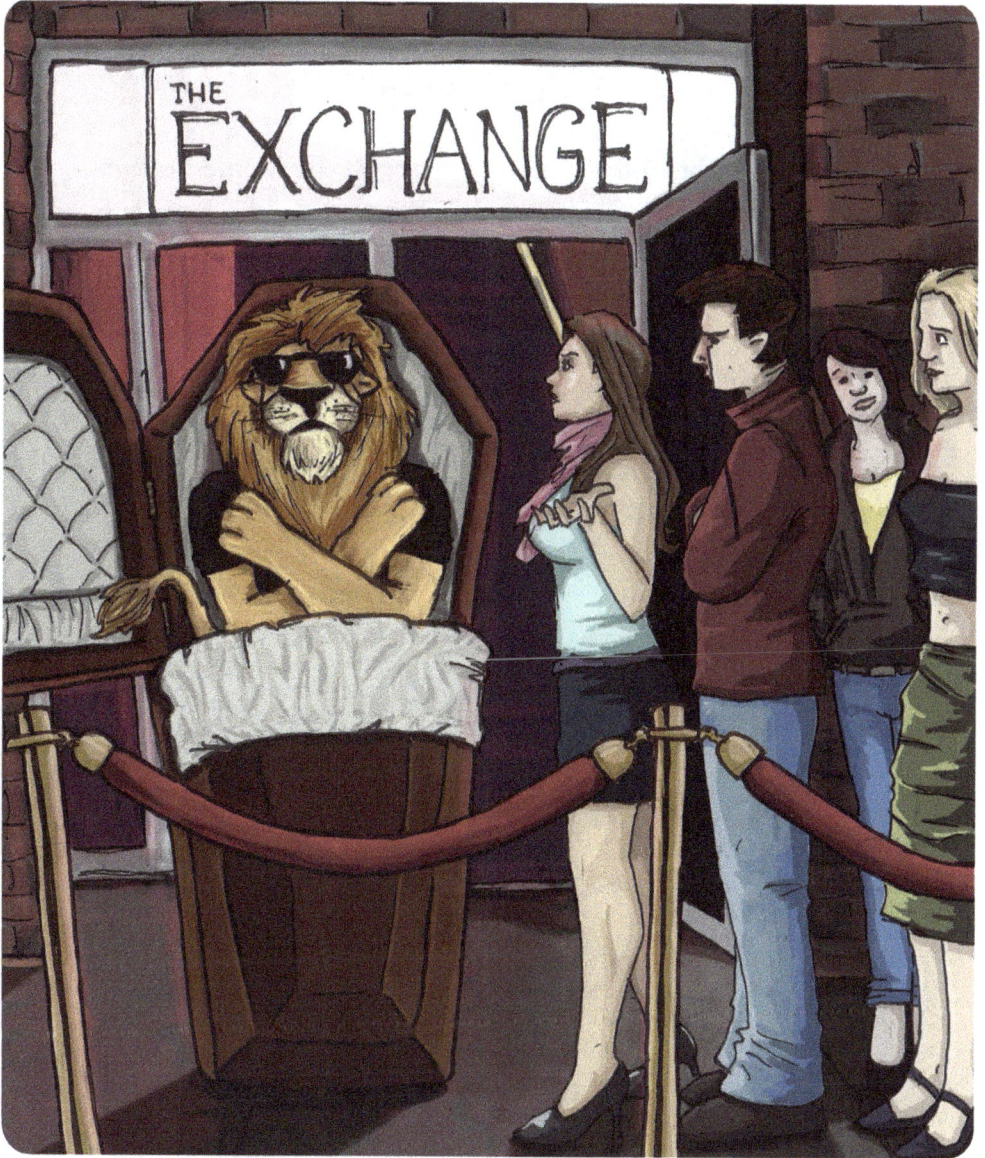

You didn't know dead cats could bounce.

From: Jitney Bach
Sent: Tuesday, January 15, 2014 4:42 PM
To: Mark Slauter <markslauter@novice.investor>
Subject: Canada Risks Intl Incident – Seizes the North Pole

The secret behind why the normally docile Maple Leaf nation has attempted the largest land grab since the Louisiana Purchase...and how you can profit from it.

I just had to include this email. Oh...those Canadians...they're such jokesters, eh?

February 3, 2014

Not the way I wanted to start February. Ouch...the market dropped 326 points today. It's painful to watch profits slip away, but I don't think that selling will be in my long-term interest. This knocks me down to about a 15.5% unrealized gain.

February 4, 2014

The market gained back 72 points today, which translates into my return bouncing up to just over 17%. A bright spot today is Michael Kors Holdings Ltd; a very positive quarterly report and the stock shot up more than 17%. This pushed my stake up to the plus side at almost 50%.

February 7, 2014

Apple bought back $14 billion in shares which pushed the share price up more than $7.

February 20, 2014

Market is up about 93 points and we're back to where we closed on Tuesday. I'm now up 215% on Qihoo 360 and TNH is moving upward enough for me to have gained back my loss on the 2nd purchase...at the moment.

With January behind me, I was able to look ahead with a renewed sense of confidence in my abilities. I'd been investing into my fantasy portfolio for almost a full year, had gained a ton of knowledge, and was now seeing ways to beat the Pros. And then in February, the media used a term that I never expected to see in print: dead cat bounce. In financial slang, "dead cat bounce" means the market experiences a sharp rise in share prices after a sharp decline. The term originated from the old Wall Street saying, "Even a dead cat will bounce once it falls far enough."

WATCHING THE MARKET

As usual, watching the market in February brought me several things to look for: concerns with emerging markets, a drop in U.S. manufacturing, the Fed further reducing its monthly bond buying, and a drop in Eurozone retail sales. One of the big issues for investors was not knowing the position of the new Federal Reserve Chair, Janet Yellen. Would she speed up the reduction of bond buying and institute a rise in interests rate sooner rather than later? Until this question was answered, investors would remain jittery.

While the media and financial community wrapped themselves around the axle regarding Yellen, all the speculations were put to rest on February 11 when she gave her first testimony before Congress stating her support for continuing the bond buying tapering efforts. With her perspective now known, all 10 major sectors finished the day in positive territory. Meanwhile, Congress had decided they wanted to make an issue of the debt ceiling again. *Great. Here we go again.*

As these developments were making headlines, and about mid-way through February, the International Monetary Fund stated it had lowered its global economic outlook for 2014. Included in this announcement were concerns with extended turmoil in emerging markets (Africa, Asia, etc.), and deflation of the euro. The lack of economic recovery in these countries was likely to inhibit activities in countries with improving economies. Concurrently, the Fed also mentioned the possible need to raise interest rates. And just like that, the market dropped about 90 points with the news.

While other factors such as a decline in new private sector jobs, a decline in U.S. manufacturing, and a report stating the lack of confidence by homebuilders played a role in the actions of investors, there was one notable exception to their negative reactions. China's economy had been at the forefront of commentary for months, yet when the media started describing the real potential for a credit bubble in China, investors didn't seem to care. The market moved up 104 points. *Humans are fickle creatures.*

But, I knew we had to remain wary when looking ahead to the markets. With civil unrest in Ukraine and reports that Russia might invade (or at a minimum support rebel troops), market impacts were inevitable. And I had no idea what this would mean for our portfolios. So, I just had to sit, assess, and wait.

CHASING FOR INFORMATION

And so, the dead cat apparently bounced this month. Apart from learning a little Wall Street slang, I thought this was interesting because it's not like this is the only time during my project when the market moved up and down quickly. So, I started questioning if the amount of movement merited the term or if it really stemmed from some writer wanting to just spice up their writing. When media needs to sell, language becomes a manipulative tool. The bottom line was that I needed to ignore the hype, stay focused on my objectives, and determine if the swinging market pendulum was impacting my strategy. If so, I knew I'd need to change my course.

I sift through a lot of articles when looking for information because it makes me a better investor. There are some things I just can't pass up…part of a headline—"Many marijuana stocks have already doubled or tripled in 2014…" It was ironic to me that the current prices were considered as being too 'high'. *Yeah, that's funny. And even more, maybe I should've been looking into the financials of restaurant chains and banks in Colorado. A new meaning of the phrase "funny money"?*

I'll admit, pondering the economic impact that stoners could have on the local food industry was useful and entertaining. Again, it pays to look at the world around you. But, I was chasing a much bigger picture and the information I needed wasn't limited to what the global economy or markets are doing. I had life issues at stake.

Remember, I started my fantasy portfolio in order to establish an informed ability to take care of Mom's investments. With her health dwindling and Dad no longer here to help, her well-being depended on my own abilities to help her. And, through this process, I began to realize I needed to take more control of my *own* future. Experiencing firsthand what it's like to become caretaker of a parent, I realized that I don't want to burden my family—and I have no entitlement to burden future taxpayers. My future care is all on me. What I learn today (or fail to) will either help or hurt me and my family later in life. Everything's connected in one way or another.

And with my future care all on me, I was intrigued when I received an email explaining how I can retire in 10 years. While the advice made sense, I remember thinking, *How the hell could I do this in 10 years?* Their answer?

○ Contribute to your investments regularly.

○ Focus on dividend growth stocks.

○ Buy quality dividend stocks.

○ Create a diversified income portfolio.

○ Reinvest dividends selectively.

Assume for the moment that I could set aside $1000/month for 10 years, giving me $120,000. Also, assume I could at least triple this over 10 years to have a value of $360,000. Healthcare costs alone (elder care is about $36k a year or $84k if you live in California) will chew up a minimum of 10% of the pre-tax value, annually, which means I would have to make at least a 1% return EACH MONTH to preserve my capital. Why should you worry about preserving capital? *Because, it's possible you'll require care for more than 10 years, and then what do you do?*

Ultimately, planning ahead for retirement is all about what lifestyle you want to afford. And what income do you need to support that lifestyle? Of course, wants and needs are typically mutually exclusive—if you're willing to admit it. And a 10-year retirement plan would mean a super aggressive strategy—if you're willing (and able) to take it. The email went on to state that I should own at least 30 stocks with three in each of the 10 sectors. On top of this, I need a 4% dividend and annual share growth of 6%.

Sounds doable? You try it.

Additionally, now that I was heavily immersed in issues associated with elder care and having a strong focus on healthcare in my portfolio, I tended to keep healthcare related information higher on my awareness list. If I'm going to plan for the future, I need to know what future I'm planning for, and it's very likely that I will find myself in need of elder care and end-of-life care just like Mom.

Coincidentally, a few days after receiving the previously mentioned email, I came across another article discussing the top 10 future positions as identified by the U.S. Bureau of Labor Statistics between 2012 and 2022. Surprisingly, four of the top 10 were healthcare related:

Rank	Job Type	% Increase
1	personal care aides	48.8%
2	registered nurses	19.4%
4	home health aides	45.8%
6	nursing assistants	21.1%

Hmmm…think there's anything to this?

These details are why I'm so focused on healthcare investment opportunities. All the aging Baby Boomers are going to impact our economy in more ways than one. I also thought about looking at industries within the Healthcare sector to determine if there were any other investing opportunities. But, since my healthcare holdings were doing well overall, I decided to keep my positions as they were. Sometimes, chasing for information will lead you to realize you're already where you need to be—for now.

ANALYZING THE PORTFOLIOS

Though February did have some ups and downs, the performance was relatively tame compared to last month. I still had a few items that weren't performing well, particularly Kinder Morgan (KMP) and El Paso Pipeline (EPB). But on the other end of the spectrum, my portfolio showed some really good results. I was feeling positive about the direction I was headed.

But by month's end, I'd lost all confidence in KMP and EPB. The holdings I had were causing a three point drag on my unrealized gains and created a $4k loss for me. One of the factors pushing shares down was a rerun of a negative article claiming the company owners were cooking the books, that the company's growth was unsustainable, and it was withholding money from shareholders. But, when I read other reports, none of these factors seemed to be true. However, investors continued to back away from the stock and my concern was that the share value would continue to erode.

After assessing all the movement, I decided to not sell KMP or EPB, though I was seriously evaluating my options. However, I did sell my Bank of Nova Scotia (BNS) stock. The ongoing reports stating concerns with the Canadian housing market and the high amount of debt Canadians were carrying was enough for me to feel uncomfortable with the stock. I took my meager 4.7%/$251 profit and moved on. Sometimes, minimizing your losses means you're not maximizing your gains. But, that's the balancing game you have to play, because more than likely, you have other performers making you squeal with excitement—and that's how I was feeling with my top performers: Qihoo 360 (QIHU), Fidelity Select Biotech (FBIOX), and Inventure Foods (SNAK).

In February, I saw the value of my holdings in QIHU up about 210%, FBIOX up about 82%, and SNAK up about 91%. Those are some major numbers, and I was ready to burst with having such winners. The profits were just dancing across mind, tempting me, *Sell me! Sell me! Make butt-loads of money, money, money!* This is where investing can be tricky: Knowing how and when to take your profits. Along with QIHU and SNAK, I had a few others that were doing quite well, but I had the feeling they were on the edge of a decline. I had a sneaking suspicion that some big institutional investors were experiencing the same big growth and just waiting to sell out for big profits.

I'd already seen an example of my concern unfold when financial legend Warren Buffet sold his stake in GlaxoSmithKline (GSK) in the previous quarter. Now I wondered if this would impact my portfolio at all, and if I should also sell. But, I decided to hold onto GSK, but with a wary eye towards how the stock may be affected in the coming weeks.

Meanwhile, the sale of BNS added to my cash reserve, so

I continued to look for ways to put the money to work. Having cash in reserve was a good thing, but I also didn't want to have my money just sit there and do nothing. I decided to acquire Canadian Natural Resources Ltd (CNQ). It is within the Energy sector and a recommended buy from one of four sources. Plus, it had a 3.46% dividend yield. I also purchased Kindred Biosciences Inc. (KIN) stock, which is a clinical-stage biopharmaceutical company focused on pet issues. KIN had their initial stock offering in December and had already risen 79%. They were also recently selected by esteemed institutional money manager Seth Klarman. *So, even the Pros were paying attention to this one.* After digging into the facts, I realized there was a strong correlation between an improving economy (such as we were in) and an increase in people spending money on their pets. So, I decided to buy this investment at $21.42 per share for a total cost of $2,142.

Usually, I don't chase initial stock offerings, because they appear to skyrocket in the immediate term and then fall off as the initial investors start taking profits. Also, most initial stock offerings are supported by "bookkeepers," which are big finance investment firms that are partially paid by getting stock for their services. However, in this particular instance with KIN, I read about other major investors and mutual funds jumping in as well. So, after considering the investor movements and the fact that people spend billions of dollars on their pets—some probably more than their Homo sapien family members—I determined that KIN was worth the attention, but with high risk. And I knew keeping my pulse on that risk was essential.

With all that said, I did have one major concern: If I was reading and buying into this information, that means other investors were, too. And if we all bought into KIN, the value would ratchet up. Furthermore, that sudden rise could be just the incentive existing stockholders were looking for to sell their shares at a profit. *Ugh, how to play this game of tug of war and not fall into the mud?* As it turned out, KIN quickly moved up almost 24%. I knew my position was risky. *Should I sell for a quick buck? Hmmm…yes.* With the risk-aversion side of my brain spinning, I took my $508. I then waited for the share price decline I anticipated would occur soon, thinking I might be able to buy it back.

Now, I won't say that my quick buy and sell of KIN was smart, but I will say that you need to know your threshold for taking risk. In this instance, I was willing to accept the risk, and by watching the stock closely, I was able to get out with a profit. And this all happened very quickly. If I had not been paying close attention to the markets, I could have easily lost my investment.

Ultimately, risk is integral to investing. Be sure you recognize it and know where you stand.

Month in Review

Between January 31 and February 28, 2014, the Dow gained 623 points. Not only did I retain my lead this month, but I still had a sizable lead. Would it hold?

Weekly Return on Investment Stats			
	Dow Jones Industrial Average	Me	Mom
Week 49	12.09%	19.50%	8.63%
Week 50	14.65%	23.02%	11.36%
Week 51	14.29%	22.83%	11.74%
Week 52	15.84%	23.80%	12.51%

Overall, for this month I had an unrealized gain of $62,339. Ironically, the loss leader this month was Financial Services—after buying two new ones last month. Mom had an unrealized gain of $21,867 this month and her Utilities lagged.

COMPARISON

For February, I was about 8 points ahead of the Dow and about 11 points ahead of Mom. This month was a very good month across the board—the best performance to date. I was very pleased with my results. Wary, but pleased.

At this point, my portfolio had 23 items that I invested in based on recommendations from the Pros, which was about 44% (29 items were my picks). On a percentage basis, I was still slightly behind the Pros this month as 79.3% of my items increased in value, while 82.6% of the Pros items increased.

DIVIDENDS FOR FEBRUARY

February was a strong month for me on dividends. I received 18 payments totaling $1,260.81, which averaged $70.05 per payment. Mom received 21 payments totaling $810.64, which averaged $38.60 per payment. Overall, I had 17% fewer payments than Mom, yet my total dividends were worth 35.7% more. I think I'm getting the handle of this. *Could it be!?*

FINAL YEAR END QUARTERLY OVERVIEW

Having completed my fourth and final quarter of investing, I was in fair shape to close out the year, considering that my losses cost me $32,447 (a whopping 37.9% of my gross profit!). As a result, my net profit was reduced to $53,202, before taxes and fees.

	Me	Mom
No. of Dividend Payments	154	200
Avg. Dividend / Payment	$67.94	$38.46
Dividend Profit	$10,462	$7,692
Profit from Sales	$12,878	N/A
Unrealized Gain	$62,339	$21,867
Potential Gross Profit	$85,679	$29,559

I must admit that this outcome looked impressive to me and I was pleased with the results—except for losing $32k. The fact I lost so much gnawed at the center of my gut. In each area I did better than Mom, exceeding her potential gross profit at a 2.8 to 1 ratio. One of the primary reasons I did so much better on dividends was my intent of acquiring stock with big dividend yield. I was much more purposeful about this than what was going on within Mom's portfolio.

Though chasing dividends mostly paid off for me, there is caution in the result. The trick with high yield dividend stocks is that they sound great, but they can be oh-so dangerous…and the high yield could actually be the warning sign.

Because of my earlier efforts to chase high dividend yields, I'd felt the sting of non-performing stocks. The best two examples were Great Northern Iron Ore (GNI) and Terra Nitrogen (TNH). I lost on GNI because I didn't fully understand their actual financial situation when I bought it. Meanwhile, TNH was a loss due to global economic factors that I was unaware of.

Bottom line? I let the lure of easy money drive some of my decisions so that chasing high dividend yield equated to a bad choice.

LESSONS LEARNED

After a full year of investing, and going through all the ups and downs, ins and outs, and in-betweens, my take-home lesson is: Anything can happen when you invest. I'm not saying that investing is too risky and you shouldn't do it. To the contrary, you should absolutely make an effort to invest! Invest your money, invest your time, and most importantly, invest in your future.

Everyone I know who invests has proven it works. I know plenty of people who say, "I don't know anything about it," or "I know I should but...," or "It seems too risky." Ironically, I don't know anyone who says, "I never should have invested my money."

So, as I closed out the year and assessed the final numbers, I crushed Mom and the DJIA on the rate of return. As great as this sounds, it's not the whole truth. My portfolio consisted of items I selected on my own and items suggested by the professionals that I agreed with. The following key points stood out to me:

	Professional Recommendations	My Selections	Mom's Holdings
Unrealized gains, average	35.94%	18.62%	13.35%
Highest gain	218.66%	81.46%	48.61%
Greatest loss	-27.42%	-17.71%	-32.85% (excluding SGRLF)

Ultimately, the Pros did better than me, but I did better than Mom. Does this bother me? Only in that I feel I should and could do better. Now, with this perspective, I know the Pros give me a level of expertise to shoot for. I also know that I'm better able to take care of Mom's need and my family's needs.

o **Never undervalue the importance of seeking professional opinions.** Essentially, while I've learned a lot and feel confident in the skills I've gained, I couldn't have done this without outside perspectives. Seeking professional advice or input was critical for my success—and the proof for me is in the numbers.

The Diary of a Novice Investor

I don't discount my own efforts, but I readily recognize the shortcomings of my own experience and knowledge. One of the important elements to me in this is that I first had to agree with the professionals before I acquired something—I didn't take their advice at face value alone.

○ **Experimenting with different investment approaches is okay.** And there's no black-and-white answer on which one is right. After investing in my fantasy portfolio, I don't think one investment approach is necessarily better than the other. Mom's portfolio was heavy on Utilities and Energy stocks. Though she didn't experience the same share-value growth or dividend payments that I did, her portfolio experienced far less volatility than mine. So, if you're inclined to reduce your stress or are more risk adverse, taking a more conservative approach may be in your best interest. For doing nothing—as I did with Mom's portfolio—how bad is it to be up more than $29,000? If I was making $7,700 a year in dividends, I wouldn't complain.

On the flip side, my investment approach contained greater risks and greater rewards. But it did come at a price to my bottom line and somewhat to my sanity. To some degree, my inexperience drove these outcomes, but I've learned many lessons along the way. My attitude has changed, my thinking has changed, and I'm not making as many trips to the wine store.

Now, my investment experience is far from over. In fact, I've only started. And I know that at some point, I'll achieve a greater feeling of balance and sanity without chasing the mythical bullet train to wealth. I can't say the seas will always be calm, but I can say that if the water gets choppy, I'll be comfortable trawling the Ocean of Investment in my *dhow*.

The following portfolio tables show what the current value (February 28) is compared to the purchase value. Value is presented in both dollar and percentage terms. The last column has the month-to-month (January to February) change as a percentage to show how items fluctuate monthly compared to the ever lengthening time between the start date and current values.

My Portfolio for February 2014

Note: '0' in last column reflects ownership of less than a month.

Name (Pros in italics)	Purchase $ Value	2-28-14 $ Value	Total Net $ Gain/Loss	Total Net % Gain/ Loss	Jan to Feb % Change
8x8, Inc.	$744.00	$1,058.00	$314.00	42.20%	4.34%
The AES Corporation	$1,193.00	$1,365.00	$172.00	14.42%	-2.92%
Alaska Air Group	$6,273.00	$8,664.00	$2,391.00	38.12%	9.57%
Alliance Resource Partners LP	$6,725.00	$8,616.00	$1,891.00	28.12%	4.56%
Anika Therapeutics	$2,417.00	$3,937.00	$1,520.00	62.89%	18.33%
Apple Inc.(3)	$39,354.00	$52,624.00	$7,070.00	15.52%	5.12%
Arabian American Development Company	$940.00	$1,224.00	$284.00	30.21%	7.37%
BlackRock Inc. (2)	$26,500.00	$30,484.00	$3,984.00	15.03%	1.45%
Canadian Natural Resources Ltd	$3,669.00	$3,662.00	$(7.00)	-0.19%	0.00%
Coca-Cola Co	$3,870.00	$3,820.00	$(50.00)	-1.29%	1.00%
Consolidated Communications	$ 1,637.00	$ 1,906.00	$269.00	16.43%	-2.66%
El Paso Pipeline Partners LP	$4,140.00	$3,005.00	$(1,135.00)	-27.42%	-8.41%
Fonar Corporation	$1,700.00	$2,266.00	$566.00	33.29%	22.82%
GasLog Ltd	$1,432.00	$2,106.00	$674.00	47.07%	0.48%
The Geo Group Inc.	$3,448.00	$3,223.00	$(225.00)	-6.53%	-3.73%

Name (Pros in italics)	Purchase $ Value	2-28-14 $ Value	Total Net $ Gain/Loss	Total Net % Gain/ Loss	Jan to Feb % Change
GlaxoSmithKline PLC ADR (1)	$4,422.00	$5,594.00	$1,172.00	26.50%	8.54%
HCP Inc.	$4,325.00	$3,877.00	$(448.00)	-10.36%	-0.97%
Home Loan *Servicing Solutions*	$2,302.00	$2,052.00	$(250.00)	-10.86%	0.00%
HSBC Holdings PLC	$1,104.00	$1,051.00	$(53.00)	-4.80%	2.54%
Industrial And Commercial Bank Of China Ltd. ADR	$1,291.00	$1,186.00	$(105.00)	-8.13%	-3.58%
Inventure Foods, *Inc.*	$726.00	$1,389.00	$663.00	91.32%	10.85%
Kinder Morgan *Energy Partners* *LP (1)*	$8,672.00	$7,427.00	$(1,245.00)	-14.36%	-6.56%
Kinder Morgan *Energy Partners* *LP (2)*	$9,025.00	$7,427.00	$(1,598.00)	-17.71%	-6.56%
Macy's Inc.	$4,067.00	$5,786.00	$1,719.00	42.27%	8.76%
Merck & Co Inc.	$4,782.00	$5,699.00	$917.00	19.18%	7.59%
Michael Kors *Holdings Ltd*	$5,804.00	$9,803.00	$3,999.00	68.90%	22.64%
Navios Maritime Holdings Inc.	$719.00	$959.00	$240.00	33.38%	1.16%
NTT DoCoMo Inc.	$1,505.00	$1,668.00	$163.00	10.83%	4.25%
Oaktree Capital *Group, LLC*	$5,013.00	$6,168.00	$1,155.00	23.04%	5.60%
Omnicell, Inc.	$2,318.00	$2,878.00	$560.00	24.16%	11.46%
Orchids Paper Products Co	$2,724.00	$3,367.00	$643.00	23.60%	8.09%
Pfizer Inc.	$3,043.00	$3,211.00	$168.00	5.52%	5.63%
Protolabs Inc.	$5,505.00	$7,790.00	$2,285.00	41.51%	-1.84%
Prudential PLC *ADR*	$3,349.00	$4,540.00	$1,191.00	35.56%	12.49%

Name (Pros in italics)	Purchase $ Value	2-28-14 $ Value	Total Net $ Gain/Loss	Total Net % Gain/ Loss	Jan to Feb % Change
PVR Partners LP	$2,285.00	$2,684.00	$399.00	17.46%	-4.28%
Qihoo 360 Technology Co., Ltd.	$3,440.00	$10,962.00	$7,522.00	218.66%	8.45%
RF Industries, Ltd	$636.00	$664.00	$28.00	4.40%	0.30%
Seaspan Corp	$1,930.00	$2,181.00	$251.00	13.01%	-1.98%
Sonoco Products Co	$3,407.00	$4,198.00	$791.00	23.22%	1.45%
Sunoco Logistics Partners LP	$6,258.00	$8,274.00	$2,016.00	32.21%	5.29%
Terra Nitrogen Co. (3)	$15,600.00	$16,516.00	$916.00	5.87%	5.10%
TJX Companies	$4,498.00	$6,146.00	$1,648.00	36.64%	7.15%
Unilever PLC ADR	$3,983.00	$4,103.00	$120.00	3.01%	6.27%
Akre Focus Fund Retail	$1,630.00	$2,684.00	$399.00	17.46%	-4.28%
Delaware Healthcare I	$1,355.00	$10,962.00	$7,522.00	218.66%	8.45%
Oakmark Global I	$2,610.00	$664.00	$28.00	4.40%	0.30%
Oceanstone Fund	$3,753.00	$2,181.00	$251.00	13.01%	-1.98%
Fidelity Select Biotechnology Portfolio (1)	$14,631.00	$4,198.00	$791.00	23.22%	1.45%
Fidelity Select Biotechnology Portfolio (2)	$10,826.94	$8,274.00	$2,016.00	32.21%	5.29%
Fidelity Select IT Services Portfolio	$2,985.00	$16,516.00	$916.00	5.87%	5.10%
Vanguard Wellington Inv	$3,707.00	$6,146.00	$1,648.00	36.64%	7.15%
Wells Fargo Advantage Core Builder Series M (2)	$1,098.00	$4,103.00	$120.00	3.01%	6.27%
	$261,893.44	$324,232.52	$62,339.08	23.80%	

MOM'S PORTFOLIO FOR FEBRUARY 2014

Name	Purchase $ Value	2-28-14 $ Value	Total Net $ Gain/ Loss	Total Net % Gain/ Loss	Jan to Feb % Change
Altria Group	$3,349.00	$3,626.00	$277.00	8.27%	2.95%
AT&T Inc.	$3,601.00	$3,193.00	$(408.00)	-11.33%	-4.17%
Buckeye Partners LP	$5,611.00	$7,323.00	$1,712.00	30.51%	0.33%
Caterpillar Inc.	$9,136.00	$9,697.00	$561.00	6.14%	3.26%
Cleco Corp	$4,418.00	$4,943.00	$525.00	11.88%	1.17%
CMS Energy Corp	$2,645.00	$2,843.00	$198.00	7.49%	2.30%
Compass Securities	$1,574.00	$1,874.00	$300.00	19.06%	4.40%
Deluxe Corp	$3,965.00	$5,048.00	$1,083.00	27.31%	3.98%
Devon Energy Corp	$5,388.00	$6,442.00	$1,054.00	19.56%	8.78%
Dominion Res Inc. VA	$5,642.00	$6,940.00	$1,298.00	23.01%	2.19%
Duke Energy Corporation	$6,925.00	$7,088.00	$163.00	2.35%	0.37%
Enbridge Energy Partners LP	$2,763.00	$2,752.00	$(11.00)	-0.40%	-6.33%
Enterprise Products Partners LP	$5,681.00	$6,711.00	$1,030.00	18.13%	1.10%
Exxon Mobil Corporation	$8,943.00	$9,627.00	$684.00	7.65%	4.46%
Frontier Communications Corp	$419.00	$488.00	$69.00	16.47%	4.27%
General Electric Co	$2,319.00	$2,547.00	$228.00	9.83%	1.35%
Great Plains Energy Inc.	$2,199.00	$2,627.00	$428.00	19.46%	6.44%
Hartford Financial Services Group	$2,368.00	$3,519.00	$1,151.00	48.61%	5.83%
Hudson City Bancorp	$858.00	$950.00	$92.00	10.72%	5.09%
Integrys Energy Group	$5,610.00	$5,727.00	$117.00	2.09%	5.39%
Intel Corp	$2,103.00	$2,476.00	$373.00	17.74%	0.90%
Medical Property Trust Inc.	$1,483.00	$1,319.00	$(164.00)	-11.06%	-0.60%
Mondelez International Inc.	$2,781.00	$3,403.00	$622.00	22.37%	3.88%

Name	Purchase $ Value	2-28-14 $ Value	Total Net $ Gain/ Loss	Total Net % Gain/ Loss	Jan to Feb % Change
National Grid PLC ADR	$5,456.00	$6,980.00	$1,524.00	27.93%	7.75%
Nisource Inc.	$2,793.00	$3,482.00	$689.00	24.67%	1.31%
Occidental Petroleum Corp	$8,265.00	$9,652.00	$1,387.00	16.78%	10.22%
Spyglass Resources Corp	$274.00	$184.00	$(90.00)	-32.85%	2.22%
Pembina Pipeline Corp	$2,821.00	$3,606.00	$785.00	27.83%	5.13%
Pepco Holdings Inc.	$2,053.00	$2,039.00	$(14.00)	-0.68%	4.94%
Philip Morris International Inc.	$9,144.00	$8,091.00	$(1,053.00)	-11.52%	3.54%
Piedmont Natural Gas Co	$3,265.00	$3,382.00	$117.00	3.58%	2.42%
Principle Financial Group Inc.	$3,155.00	$4,535.00	$1,380.00	43.74%	4.09%
Royal Dutch Shell PLC ADR	$6,578.00	$7,287.00	$709.00	10.78%	5.46%
Scana Corp	$4,906.00	$4,950.00	$44.00	0.90%	4.72%
Southern Co	$4,483.00	$4,235.00	$(248.00)	-5.53%	2.69%
Spectra Energy Corp	$2,881.00	$3,728.00	$847.00	29.40%	3.70%
Teco Energy Inc.	$1,735.00	$1,678.00	$(57.00)	-3.29%	2.44%
US Bancorp	$3,401.00	$4,114.00	$713.00	20.96%	3.55%
Verizon Communications Inc.	$4,672.00	$4,758.00	$8.00	1.84%	-0.92%
Wells Fargo & Co	$3,539.00	$4,642.00	$1,103.00	31.17%	2.38%
DWS Core Equity Fund	$1,983.00	$2,356.00	$373.00	18.81%	4.71%
DWS S&P 500 Index Fund	$2,022.00	$2,478.00	$456.00	22.55%	4.51%
DWS Short Duration Fund	$931.00	$919.00	$(12.00)	-1.29%	0.11%
Fidelity Contrafund	$8,122.00	$9,820.00	$1,698.00	20.91%	4.48%
Wellesley Income Fund	$2,479.00	$2,527.00	$48.00	1.94%	2.06%
	$174,739.00	$196,606.00	$21,867.00	12.51%	

EMAIL PROS SECTION

Between January 31 and February 28, 2014, the Dow gained 623 points. The Pros had expanded their lead over the Dow.

	Weekly Return on Investment Stats	
	Dow Jones Industrial Average	Pros
Week 8	-0.57%	0.00%
Week 9	1.69%	1.86%
Week 10	1.37%	3.46%
Week 11	2.75%	5.33%

Overall, in February, the Pros had an unrealized gain of $8,137 with the industrial and technology sectors as loss leaders.

EMAIL PROS PORTFOLIO FOR FEBRUARY 2014

Name	Purchase $ Value	2-28-14 $ Value	Total Net $ Gain/ Loss	Total Net % Gain/ Loss	Jan to Feb % Change
AmerisourceBergen Co.	$6,845.00	$6,785.00	$(60.00)	-0.88%	0.94%
Celgene Corp	$16,338.00	$16,075.00	$(263.00)	-1.61%	5.81%
Kroger Co	$4,006.00	$4,194.00	$188.00	4.69%	16.18%
Magna International Inc.	$7,912.00	$8,912.00	$1,000.00	12.64%	5.03%
Yahoo! Inc.	$3,973.00	$3,867.00	$(106.00)	-2.67%	7.39%
Core Laboratories	$19,148.00	$18,805.00	$(343.00)	-1.79%	5.10%
FleetCor	$11,860.00	$12,993.00	$1,133.00	9.55%	22.21%
Melco Crown Entertainment Ltd ADR	$3,845.00	$4,292.00	$447.00	11.63%	4.71%
Ecolab	$10,210.00	$10,775.00	$565.00	5.53%	7.17%
Actavis Plc	$15,966.00	$22,082.00	$6,116.00	38.31%	16.85%
EMC Software	$2,370.00	$2,637.00	$267.00	11.27%	8.79%
Quality Systems	$2,089.00	$1,746.00	$(343.00)	-16.42%	-5.16%
AutoNation	$4,998.00	$5,264.00	$266.00	5.32%	6.58%

Name	Purchase $ Value	2-28-14 $ Value	Total Net $ Gain/ Loss	Total Net % Gain/ Loss	Jan to Feb % Change
FutureFuel Corp	$1,527.00	$1,735.00	$208.00	13.62%	6.05%
Solera Holdings	$6,940.00	$6,842.00	$(98.00)	-1.41%	2.38%
Fortegra Financial Corp	$740.00	$699.00	$(41.00)	-5.54%	-5.16%
NIC Inc.	$2,270.00	$1,944.00	$(326.00)	-14.36%	-10.58%
Almost Family Inc.	$3,133.00	$2,742.00	$(391.00)	-12.48%	-9.83%
Eaton Vance Tax-Managed Global Diversified Equity Income Fund	$988.00	$1,023.00	$35.00	3.54%	4.28%
Cheniere Energy Partners	$2,765.00	$2,844.00	$79.00	2.86%	1.61%
Apollo Investment	$870.00	$856.00	$(14.00)	-1.61%	1.42%
Oaktree Capital Group	$5,519.00	$6,168.00	$649.00	11.76%	5.60%
AllianzGlobal NFJ Dividend, Interest and Premium Strategy Fund	$1,804.00	$1,818.00	$14.00	0.78%	1.79%
TCP Capital	$1,645.00	$1,768.00	$123.00	7.48%	2.08%
Breitburn Energy Partners	$1,937.00	$1,999.00	$62.00	3.20%	-2.73%
Teekay LNG Partners	$3,986.00	$4,167.00	$181.00	4.54%	2.97%
Boardwalk Pipeline Partners	$2,514.00	$1,231.00	$(1,283.00)	-51.03%	-50.00%
Navios Maritime Partners	$1,789.00	$1,710.00	$(79.00)	-4.42%	-6.86%
Memorial Production Partners	$2,074.00	$2,234.00	$160.00	7.71%	1.87%
Hercules Technology Growth Capital	$1,655.00	$1,574.00	$(81.00)	-4.89%	-0.76%
AGIC Convertible & Income Fund	$948.00	$1,020.00	$72.00	7.59%	1.69%
	$152,664.00	$160,801.00	$8,137.00	5.33%	

CLOSING WORDS

If you're given a choice between money and sex appeal, take the money. As you get older, the money will become your sex appeal.
—Katherine Hepburn

You know you're a novice investor when...

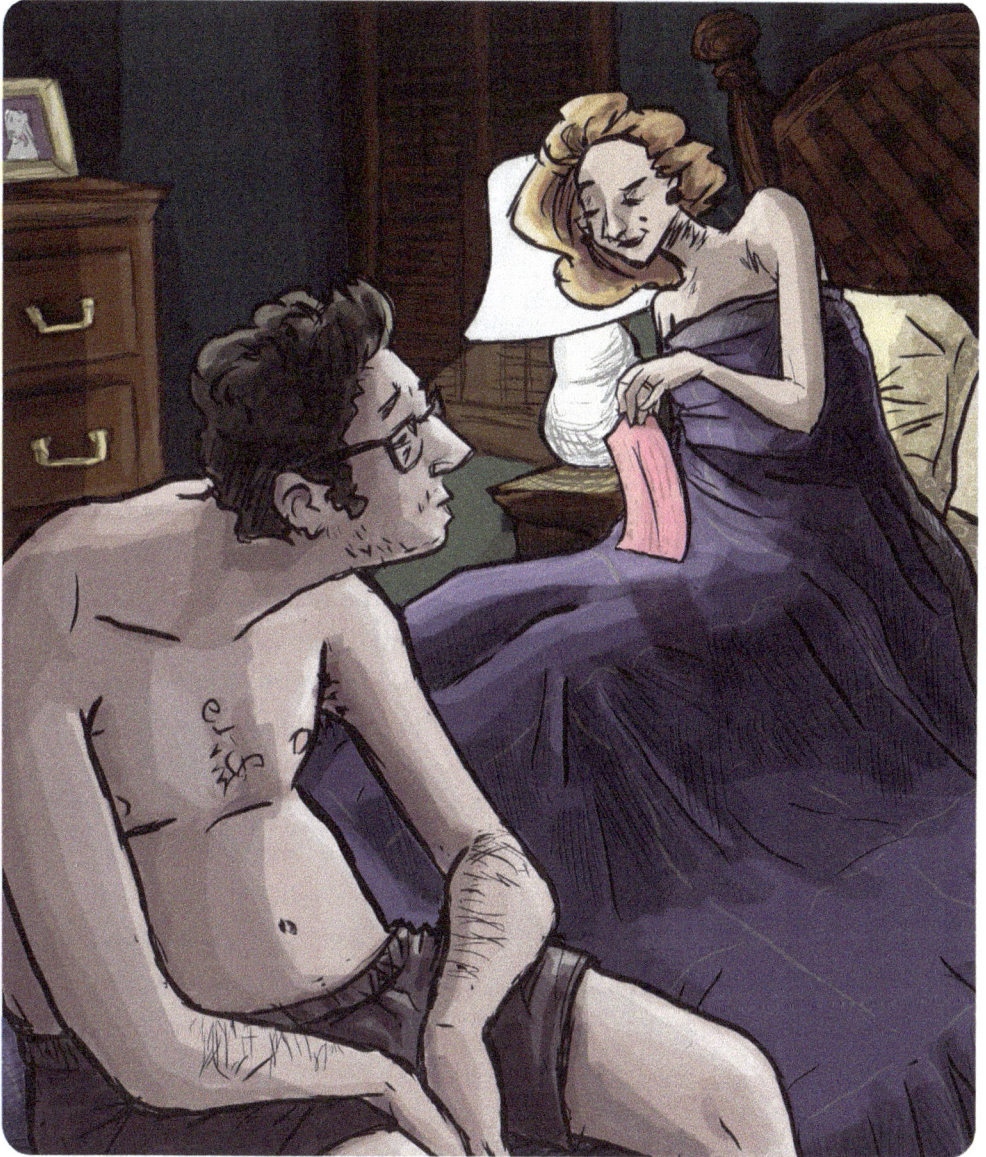

You thought only your spouse could penalize you for early withdrawal.

Wow, here I am. One year through my fantasy portfolio experience. And what a ride it was. Though my wife continues to shake her head at my endeavor (I'm way, way behind on the to-do list), we've gained a mutual desire to improve our financial security. We've set aside some money and established a new account that includes a mix of our own selections and a few from an advisor, and we're already up about 15%. No complaints on this score.

Meanwhile, Mom continues to exist (I can't really say she's "surviving.") within the hell of Alzheimer's, without any indication she's recognizing life revolving around her. While difficult to watch, my sister and I are okay with Mom not knowing who we are. The most important things are making Mom as comfortable as possible and managing her money wisely.

When Mom broke her hip just after Thanksgiving in 2013 we were quite concerned. Though I have no doubt that she could feel the pain on some level, I have no way of knowing if she actually recognized the pain for what it was. While this inability to communicate is daunting, what really scared us was her inability to swallow during the first few days after surgery. Her living will clearly states that she doesn't want her life extended by depending on machines. Having to consider this as a possible outcome was a horrible conversation to have with my sister.

Fortunately, Mom recovered her ability to swallow, and we moved her into another place for a few weeks of rehabilitation. However, as a result of everything, Mom needed to use a walker and eventually a wheelchair. But, because you can't keep her down for long, Mom resumed her habit of walking and would not use either the walker or wheelchair. While I applaud Mom's internal desire to return to her old habit of walking around, it was dangerous to her health, and retraining her to rely on a wheelchair required huge effort on my sister's part. She may not be fully aware of what's going on, but she definitely didn't lose her opinions.

Ultimately, the decisions you make about your own financial

security aren't just about you. Sure, everyone wants to have the financial means to take care of themselves when they retire or are unable to work; but financial security's about preparing for unforeseen circumstances. There is no guarantee in life that someone else will take care of you. It requires being real with yourself and asking the hard questions. Frankly, do you want to end up in a situation where you have no one to take care of you and no money to support you? I can't think of a single person who'd sanely answer "yes."

Really, you just never know what life will bring you. Just as the market can rise and fall at the drop of a random hat, so too can life. I know retired people who've had to assume raising their grandchildren and didn't expect to. I also know people who've had to take their parents into their household and become the primary caregiver while raising their own children. That is a tremendous responsibility. Rather than being a singular issue for yourself, your financial security becomes a family affair.

And this insight was made clearer through managing my fantasy portfolio. So, now the end is here...sort of. Through this effort, I've taken a path and landed at a place that I didn't intend or foresee, at least in part. I did set out to re-enter the world of investing—and I've done that. But, I recognize that I still have much to learn and many pathways to get there. As a result, I intend to carry my experiment forward. I'm working on Volume II of my efforts, because I realized that one year of experience and learning is not necessarily sufficient to relay or capture a longer term approach to investing. And one of the mantras of investing is to invest with a long-term viewpoint.

Before you invest in the markets, I highly recommend you create your own fantasy portfolio. Use play money and keep your selections to a manageable few, maybe one selection for each of the 10 sectors. But also work in a few selections from the Pros—and compare your performance against theirs. Also, choose items that are different from the Pros. And don't overlook bringing two or three mutual funds into the mix, since they can temper the vagaries of individual equities on a portfolio. And most importantly, always do your happy dance when you're doing well, just don't trip up.

But, if I've emerged with any big takeaway lesson to share with you, it's this: Keep a tight leash on your emotions, particularly fear and greed. I'm not sure which emotion is worse, but I am sure that a lack of knowledge and understanding drive both. I'm reminded of Charles Dickens' *A Christmas Carol* where Scrooge talks with the Spirit of Christmas Present, and at the end of their time together, Scrooge notes something peaking from beneath the Spirit's robes:

Scrooge: Spirit. Are they yours?

Spirit: They are Man's and they cling to me, appealing from their fathers. This boy is Ignorance. This girl is Want. Beware them both, and all of their degree, but most of all beware this boy, for on his brow I see that written which is Doom, unless the writing be erased. Deny it. Slander those who tell it ye. Admit it for your factious purposes, and make it worse. And abide the end.

Greed and Fear. Ignorance and Want. Either pair spells trouble. And, I admit that I've still not completely conquered these emotions. I see a 15% dividend and salivate. I see a 10% decline and freak out...well not really...sort of. In my fantasy portfolio, fear and greed cost me $32,000. Anger is a much stronger emotion and eventually wins out. So I lost money, got pissed off, and acquired knowledge and understanding.

Some people may view the market as a form of legalized gambling, but I say if it is, then it's in the investors favor. It does no good for a company to perform poorly, since if they do, investors will stop investing in the company. And when that happens, the company loses access to capital that allows it to become more profitable.

Companies need the markets, and our economy needs these companies. And yes, the market is unforgiving. If you make a bad decision there's no do-over. Lost money is lost money. Even thinking that you can get your money back in a theoretical sense is like believing sleeping an extra hour today will get you back the hour you lost yesterday. It just isn't possible. So, when investing, understand and embrace that you live and you learn—and hopefully, become a better decision-maker as a result.

All in all, I made some good and bad decisions. The bad ones cost me over $32,000. My losses on sales were 2.6 times greater than my gains on sales. So, how the hell do you get $20,000 back? Frankly, you don't. Lost money is lost money even when it's fantasy money.

Since each stock and fund sale or acquisition has a fee, I've tried to represent those costs below. Capital gains are taxable income from an IRS perspective and deductible capital losses are limited to $3,000 per year. Remember, ALWAYS consult with a tax advisor.

This table shows the initial total acquisition cost for each portfolio, which is the baseline value. Since I was actively trading only mine, the available cash line item is not applicable to Mom's portfolio. Both of us were successful in making the portfolios more valuable.

	Me	Mom
Initial Acquisition Baseline Value	$287,736.00	$174,739.00
Current Portfolio Baseline Value	$261,893.44	$174,739.00
Available Cash	$25,842.56	N/A
Current Portfolio Value	$324,232.52	$196,606.00
Percentage Value Increase	23.80%	12.51%

So here's what it looks like for me and Mom for the year.

	Me	Mom
Capital losses	$(32,447.00)	$(0.00)
Transaction Fees @ $10 each	$(740.00)	$(0.00)
Estimated Mutual Fund Fees	$(5,541.69)	$(1,290.28)
Tax on Sales & Dividends @ 15%	$(3,501.02)	$(1,153.87)
Sub-total Expenses	$(42,229.71)	$(2,444.15)
Capital Gains (sales)	$12,878.00	$0.00
Dividends	$10,462.15	$7,692.44
Tax Deductible Capital Loss	$3,000.00	$0.00
Sub-total Gross Profit	$26,340.15	$7,692.44
Total Net Profit (gross profit minus expenses)	($15,889.56)	$5,248.29
Unrealized Gain/(Loss) (current portfolio value)	$62,339.00	$21,867.00
Potential Profit	$46,449.44	$19,422.85

With regard to actual net profits, Mom did better than me. However, if I sold everything right now then I would have more than twice her profit. Simply stated, Mom and I made about $66,000 by allowing our money to work for us rather than working for our money.

That's the power of investing. Learning to view money as a tool that'll work for you is the most important understanding you should develop. While you can't control the markets, you can control your decisions. And owning your decisions so they help you create financial security for yourself and your family into the future is one of the greatest feats you can do.

So go forth and become a Fantasy Portfolio investor. And always remember: Where the ride takes you isn't what matters; it's what you learn from the journey that'll be with you the rest of your life.

GLOSSARY

Form 13F. Reports Filed by Institutional Investment Managers (as stated on the Securities & Exchange Commission website):

An institutional investment manager that uses the U.S. mail (or other means or instrumentality of interstate commerce) in the course of its business, and exercises investment discretion over $100 million or more in Section 13(f) securities must report its holdings on Form 13F with the Securities and Exchange Commission (SEC).

In general, an institutional investment manager is: (1) an entity that invests in, or buys and sells, securities for its own account; or (2) a natural person or an entity that exercises investment discretion over the account of any other natural person or entity. Institutional investment managers can include investment advisers, banks, insurance companies, broker-dealers, pension funds, and corporations.

Asset Allocation. The process of dividing investments among different kinds of asset categories, such as stocks, bonds, real estate and cash, to optimize the risk/reward trade-off based on an individual's or institution's specific situation and goals. A key concept in financial planning and money management.

Blue Chip Stocks. Shares of strong, well-established companies that have demonstrated their ability to pay dividends in both good and bad markets

Commodities. Raw goods used to make something else. You can physically acquire commodities such as wheat, corn or oil. These tend to be high risk investments.

Dividend. A dollar amount associated with a share (one share equals one unit of ownership in the company —yes, you actually own a piece of the company when you buy shares of stock) of company stock that is paid out to shareholders as a distribution of a portion of the company's earnings.

EBITDA. Short for Earnings Before Interest, Taxes, Depreciation, and Amortization. EBITDA is often used instead of net income by companies with heavy depreciation charges on their income statements. Investors should always look at EBITDA with caution, because it's not officially sanctioned by the nation's accounting rules, and there's no standard way of figuring it. Still, it can be a useful number to know in conjunction with—but not in place of—reported net income.

Earnings Per Share (EPS). How much profit a company has made per share within a given period.

Index Fund. Tracks a particular index in an attempt to match its returns. For example, if the S&P 500 has a current return of 5%, then an index fund that is tracking the S&P 500 is trying to match or outperform the index itself.

Institute for Supply Management (ISM). ISM's mission is to lead the supply management profession through its standards of excellence, research, promotional activities, and education.

Large-Cap Stocks. Value of more than $10 billion.

Long-Term Capital Gain. A gain from a qualifying investment owned for longer than 12 months and then sold. The amount of an asset sale that counts toward a capital gain or loss is the difference between the sale value and the purchase value. Long-term capital gains are assigned a lower tax rate than short-term capital gains in the United States.

Market Capitalization. The total equity market value of the company, expressed in millions of dollars. It equals shares outstanding times the stock price.

Mid-Cap Stock. Value between $2 and $10 billion.

Mutual Fund. Money is pooled with that of other investors, and then it is managed by a group of professionals who try to earn a return by selecting stocks for the pool.

Over-The-Counter Market. The term refers to transactions made over-the-counter in unlisted securities, or for a transaction involving securities not completed on a recognized stock exchange.

Return on Investment (ROI). Return is the amount of money your investment made for you and is usually shown as a percentage of the amount you invested.

Sector. A company's general area of business: Basic Materials, Communication Services, Consumer Cyclical, Consumer Defensive, Energy, Financial Services, Healthcare, Industrials, Real Estate, Technology and Utilities. Because sectors can differ greatly in their characteristics, comparing a stock with its sector rather than the market as a whole is generally a better way of putting it in the proper context.

Short-Term Capital Gain. A capital gain realized by the sale or exchange of a capital asset that has been held for exactly one year or less. Short-term gains are taxed at the taxpayer's top marginal tax rate.

Small-Cap Stock. value between $300 million to $2 billion.

Unrealized Capital Gain. An unrealized gain is a profitable position that has yet to be cashed in, such as a winning stock position that remains open. A gain becomes realized once the position is closed for a profit.

Unrealized Capital Loss. An unrealized loss, on the other hand, occurs when an investor is holding onto a losing investment, such as a stock that has dropped in value since the position was opened. A loss becomes realized once the position is closed for a loss.

Yield. This is the annual dividend per share divided by the current stock price and displayed as a percentage.

www.ingramcontent.com/pod-product-compliance
Lightning Source LLC
Chambersburg PA
CBHW052120230326
41598CB00080B/3914